MEDICAL COST CRISIS!

A Solution Before
It's Too Late

**A Plan for Quality
Medical Care for Everyone
that Preserves Your Choice!**

DONALD G. LINDSAY, M.D.

TONAL CO. PRESS

MEDICAL COST CRISIS—A SOLUTION BEFORE IT'S TOO LATE
BY DONALD G. LINDSAY M.D.

Published by:　　　TONAL CO. PRESS
Post Office Box 3233
Ventura, Ca 93003

Printed in the United States of America

PUBLISHER'S CATALOGING-IN-PUBLICATION DATA
Lindsay, Donald G., 1922
Medical Cost Crisis: A Solution Before It's Too Late
Donald G. Lindsay—First Ed.
p. cm
Includes bibliographical references and index.
1. Medical care—United States. 2. Insurance, Health—
United States 3. Medical economics—United States. I. Title.

RA 395.A3L44 1993　　　　　369.3'82'00973
　　　　　　　　　　　　　　QBI93-1265

ISBN 0-9638348-3-5　$15.95

Library of Congress Catalog Card Number: 93-95004

■ CONTENTS

1 An Overview 1

2 Cherish Your Choice 21

3 Medical Insurance 30

4 Risk 68

5 Doctors and Lawyers 82

6 The Problems 118

7 Developing a Solution to the Medical Cost Crisis 126

8 The Safety Net Hospital-Clinics: An Overview 136

9 Triage and Delegation 154

10 The Safety Net Hospital-Clinics 173

11 More About the Safety Net Hospital-Clinic 210

12 Physicians and Their Patients 226

Conclusion 255

Afterword 257

Suggested Readings 273

Index 285

Warning and Disclaimer

■ ABOUT THE AUTHOR

Donald G. Lindsay was born into poverty in 1922 in a small Indiana town. He went on to obtain his M.D. from the University of Illinois in 1947. After a one-year residency in General Practice, he served as a general practitioner in a small California town for three years. From there he was called to duty in the Korean war where he was given a year of specialty training in psychiatry. Subsequently, Dr. Lindsay served as an Army psychiatrist for the duration of the war.

In 1974 he completed a two-year postdoctoral fellowship in Endocrinology at Harbor Hospital-UCLA.

He is speciality Board Certified in Dermatology, and in Dermal Pathology. He has taught Dermatological Surgery as a part-time volunteer instructor at the University of Southern California for over twenty-five years. He practiced Dermatology part time until his retirement in 1991.

As a practicing physician and as a patient himself, he became increasingly concerned with the direction medical practice was taking. Therefore, he retired from practice to devote full time to develop a solution to the medical care situation in this country and to write this book.

Dr. Lindsay has many interests and is very active in life-span regulation in marine life forms and genetic control of life-span in simple life forms incorporating computerized decision support systems. He is Founder and President of The Foundation for Research in Aging and currently resides with his wife Donann in Ventura, California.

■ ACKNOWLEDGMENTS

Many gracious and wonderful people helped make this book possible. I nearly added a psychiatrist to the list—perhaps I should have.

Special thanks goes to Judge Robert R. Willard. He edited the manuscript in its early four hundred page form twice, every word. His painful comments in nearly every margin were a labor of love indeed; so was his forward.

Much thanks also goes to my daughter Ms. Diane Lindsay of "Slightly Tortured Music" who did the final content and copy editing—with an iron hand. She literally rescued the project from failure. Some chapters we rewrote four times. If you have a daughter who has worked as a professional editor, and if you want a very humbling and educational experience, I suggest you try her. My daughter's unerring eye for my copy errors, and her unfailing giant red X for my self-pity, even a trace of it, no doubt made this book possible.

Many other people helped in various ways, including Dr. Stanley Kaplan, Mrs. Michelle Chekov, Mr. Don Sisler, Mr. Dan Poynter, Mindy Bingam. My sincere thanks to them all.

Very special thanks goes to Mr. Paul Glenn of the Glenn Medical Foundation, to Mr. Mark Collins and Ms. Nancy Lessner for their enormous help in making this project possible.

My wife Donann not only tolerated these long years at the computer, my moments of hysteria and nights of insomnia, she too lent a sharp eye to the copy editing.

Design and Production:

Chris Nolt of Cirrus Design did the book design, typesetting, and layout.

Ms. Carolyn Porter of One On One did the cover design and general production, together with Mr. Alan Gadney who supervised the printing, promotion and marketing.

■ *FOREWORD*

For the past thirty years Donald Lindsay has never ceased to amaze me. His talents are varied and substantial. I have known him as a general medical practitioner, psychotherapist, dermatologist, endocrinologist, and medical teacher. In addition to his medical competence, he is talented and knowledgeable as a musician, mathematician and computer whiz. Above all, he is interested in people and their health.

This book is a product of personal experience, original thinking, and abundant energy. He presents innovative ideas on the problem of providing efficient health care at affordable costs. I am confident that many of his suggestions ultimately will be adopted, to the great benefit of those in need of health care and of health care providers.

Robert R. Willard
Retired Superior Court Judge

To cure sometimes
To help often
To comfort always

THE BLIND MEN AND THE ELEPHANT

A Hindoo Fable

It was six men of Indostan
    To learning much inclined,
Who went to see the Elephant
    (Though all of them were blind),
That each by observation
    Might satisfy his mind.

The *first* approached the Elephant,
    And happening to fall
Against his broad and sturdy side,
    At once began to bawl:
"God bless me! but the Elephant
    Is very like a wall!"

The Second, feelin of the tusk,
    cried, "Ho! what have we here
So very round and smooth and sharp?
    To me 'tis mighty clear
This wonder of an Elephant
    Is very like a spear!"

The *third* approached the animal,
    and happening to take
The squirming trunk within his hands,
    Thus boldly up and spake:
"I see,"quoth he, "the Elephant
    Is very like a snake!"

The *forth* reached out an egar hand,
    And felt about the knee.

"What most this wonderous beast is like
    Is mighty plain, "quoth he;
'Tis clear enough the Elephant
    Is very like a tree!"

The *fifth* who chanced to touch the ear,
    Said: "E'en the blindest man
Can tell what this resembles most;
    Deny the fact who can,
This marvel of an Elephant
    Is very like a fan!"

The *sixth* no sooner had begun
    about the beast to grope,
Than, seizing on the swinging tail
    That fell within his scope,
"I see," quoth he, "the Elephant
    Is very like a rope!"

And so these men of Indostan
    Disputed loud and long
Each in his own opinion
    Exceeding stiff and strong,
Though each was partly in the right,
    And all were in the wrong!

MORAL

So oft in our polemic wars,
    The disputants, I ween,
Rail on in utter ignorance
    of what each other mean,
And prate about an Elephant
    Not one of them has seen!

John Godfrey Saxe (1816-1887)

CHAPTER ONE

An Overview

There is no medical care crisis. There is a medical cost crisis. This is a book about our medical cost crisis. It is about patient freedom and patient power. It should be of vital interest to everyone likely to become a patient.

The book is divided into three parts: 1. Some problems causing the crisis, 2. a solution, and 3. a physician's perspective—a bit of what it is like to be a doctor.

This is a book about the quality as well as the cost of our medical care. The book emphasizes ways to maintain, even improve that quality while holding the line on costs.

The book is written for those of all walks of life. It tries to contrast what central governing bodies and some other laypeople think is happening, with what actually is happening on site.

Our nation's medicine is at it's finest hour technically, yet finds itself in chaos in the social and political arena. People throughout the world who can afford it, come to this country for medical care. Our medical journals are prized the world over. Scientifically sophisticated medical care is expensive. Physicians have allowed themselves to be blamed for this. They have allowed themselves to be blamed for this and a host of other things, for example the inability to achieve zero risk.

Many solutions have been offered for our medical care cost crisis. Most involve constructing the illusion that someone else can be made to pay. But competition, not coercion will lower medical costs. And this very illusion of free care, which eventuates into the public perception the system is costless becomes a major problem, one even now undermining functioning socialized systems such as those in Canada* and Britain.†

Solutions are put forth by people with no experience whatever in actual medical care. Such people are given credence on the basis of power, some other training, experience, or media exposure. The solutions arrived at, while often plausible, frequently have so little relevance, foresight, or helpfulness. Some are even dangerous.

Many of the authors of these plans would cringe if they personally were subjected to the schemes they offer for others. Most reflect a naivete, an experience far removed from actual events. Political solutions are common. Political solutions will not solve medical problems.

Especially in the medical field, people cannot understand well what they have not lived. Misconceptions are inevitable. This book hopes to correct as many of these as it can, in an honest effort to protect patients and resist any decline in the advance of medical science.

The reader should have some idea of the contemporary medical situation as a prerequisite to understanding the

---

* Adam,J.M. "The Lessons Of The Canadian System", *Dermatology World,* July (1993): p.8.

† Cavenagh, A.J.M. "THE RISE AND FALL OF SOCIALIZED MEDICINE IN BRITAIN": 1948-1991 *The Pharos of Alpha Omega Alpha Honor Medical Society* (Spring 1993: 2-4.)

proposed solutions. This information seeps in through out the book, and a final section is devoted to this world of medicine.

Our medical care is extremely complicated and complex. It is at real risk of being damaged by oversimplified, opportunistic solutions, to the detriment of us all. On the one hand we expect unrealistic omnipotence from our physicians. On the other, we treat them as if they were incompetent, or too greedy to formulate and deliver our medical care. Why? Nearly fifty years of third party interference must share the blame.

By third parties, I mean laymen who would control the medical care delivery process, people who blatantly or unwittingly would drive a wedge between patient and physician. By patients I mean all of us. Sooner or later we will all become patients. Physicians as a group are probably less greedy than most. Yet physicians are to blame too, because they have allowed themselves to be used, then some reacted by becoming cynical and greedy. Also physicians are easy to overpower and to dominate by those with adversarial skills. Physician's training did not prepare them for this. They are intensely concerned with other areas. We would not want them any other way. Nevertheless physicians have not been the best advocates for patients rights. Now, more than ever mature responsible patient behavior is needed.

Medical care is not a product, or even a service. It is a fight against disease and death that not infrequently requires more than the most knowledgeable professional has to offer. It is essential that the utmost degree of freedom and trust exist directly between patient and physician.

Most illness does not require expensive care; but skilful reassurance, and kind but always very knowledgeable evaluation. Of course you can get cheaper medical care.

Sure, we can train more general practitioners, or nurses, or others so that medicine can be practiced more economically. Of course the number of mistakes are increased thereby, unless at the point of diagnosis, at the point of delegation, the maximum training is applied. The very reason the expert must be highly trained is to know when and how to use or not to use the expert procedures.

Physicians deserve more than the term "providers." The implications tell much. Physicians are not workers that government, attorneys, or business leaders can control, except at their own peril. The danger here is not from physician malice at all. The reality is that some seemingly innocuous constraint or threat may well, in some unforeseen way, cost a life, or shorten a life span. Junk science may fool a jury; but it will not fool the Grim Reaper.

Our medical care, our medical training, demands the epitome of intelligence, skill, dedication, character, and strength of will from its medical students, and hence from its physicians. Medicine is both an art and a science, and so requires students with attributes suited for both aspects. To reduce these demands, to lower this quality, will not produce economy.

The intrusion of government into medical care in the ways now advocated will lead to further decline. Central planning will not produce better medical care. It will not even accomplish more accessible medical care. Central planning will not work in any case, because no one group of contemporaries has the requisite foresight. Alternative options must be kept available. A free market will do better, simply because it employs the ancient biological verity of survival of the fittest-and removal of the others.

There are abuses on both sides. Which is the greater chicanery? Is it that of the physician who performs a procedure in half and hour, tells the patient not to worry about the bill, and by creative insurance billing gains a large fee; or that of the politician who buys votes—hence power and money—by telling the patient not to worry, their medical needs will be taken care of by government. Government cannot provide this. Government can audit. It can tax. It can punish. It is very poor at enterprise. Neither legal training, campaign experience nor parliamentary skills furnish the requisite expertise for medical practice innovation.

Consider the almost unassailable statement that everyone is entitled to medical care as a right. But entitled to what kind and how much? Of course everyone should have a broken arm fixed, perhaps even their rotten teeth should be attended to. What about those hundred dollar prescriptions so common today? Can we serve these as an entitlement?

Next, consider the faddish belief we have too many specialists who increase the cost of medical care by doing too many expensive procedures. Once again we are mixing cost (an aspect of our economic system) with the sophistication and research capability of our medical knowledge base. We cannot have too many too educated people, whether among our physicians or our congressmen.

Consider this: Your grandfather died of cancer of the stomach. You were there. It was awful. Your uncle died of cancer of the stomach. You are now approaching your grandfather's age, you are having constant stomach troubles. You have been treated, off and on, for a gastric ulcer for years. You are now taking a new medicine that costs three dollars a pill. So long as you take these, your stomach seems better; but your stomach reminds you when your next dose is due.

Often stomach cancer is incurable before it is discovered, the first sign being a metastatic lesion, usually a fatal sign. Would you prefer to consult a gastroenterologist and have a gastroscopic examination at a cost of say seven hundred dollars, or would you prefer to conserve health care costs and stay on the medication? Which would be the cheapest: (a) Early diagnosis and perhaps cure; (b) continuing indefinitely to take three dollar pills; or (c) the chance of later treatment for an overlooked cancer? Some will say another alternative is not being able to afford to see a physician. Another common one is simply neglecting to see a physician.

The gastroscope is a marvelous flexible tube able to see around corners, fitted with lenses, a tiny camera, and tiny jaws for taking a piece, a biopsy, of any suspicious areas. For the sake of this example let's say you had the procedure done, and all they found was a chronic irritation of your stomach wall. A biopsy showed a heavy growth of a bacteria recently thought to be the cause of your kind of stomach irritation. Whether certain antibiotics will cure this or not is still being experimentally evaluated.

Was this an unnecessary procedure? Should everyone be entitled to this? I think they should, and I detail in this book how this could be done relatively inexpensively.

Consider another example.

Colon cancer is a common cause of death. It often goes unnoticed until too late. Two of your relatives have been found to have intestinal polyps (little finger-like protrusions inward from your gut lining). Intestinal polyps are known precursors of one kind of colon cancer. You are middle aged. You have no symptoms. Should you have a proctoscopic exam (another of those marvelous tubes up your rear) to see if you have intestinal polyps? You had this examination. They found no polyps. Was this an unnecessary procedure? Was the physician who recommended the procedure one of those specialists making too much money from special procedures? Would you rather the examination had been positive?

Now there is another side of this coin. Take Mr. Jones, he is a hypochondriac (Hypochondriacs keep imagining, fearing, they are sick). He feels he needs all these special procedures. Dr. Smith, his primary care family physician, has a difficult time with Mr. Jones, for Dr. Smith must steer Mr. Jones away from demanding unnecessary procedures. Were Mr. Jones to walk into a specialists office and recite suspicious symptoms, he might indeed be given an unnecessary and expensive procedure. Were Mr. Jones to walk into the office of another primary care general physician, one not familiar with him, that physician might well refer him for one of those expensive procedures. The point then is not whether a specialist or a primary physician sees Mr. Jones. The point is continuity of care, familiarity with a patient over time. And if Mr. Jones' hypochondria is primarily localized to his gastrointestinal tract, a specialist in gastroenterology might well give equal or better continuity of care. Hypochondriacs die too, just like all the rest of us.

What is primary care? A primary care physician to some people means any physician consulted directly (primarily) for care. About 24% of patients in 1991 directly consulted a specialist. Many of these specialists are now calling themselves primary care physicians with justification. In 1991, 6.7% of patients were referred from one physician to another. Trends are changing. Patients know it. Physicians know it. It is time the controllers and the medical insurance people caught-on.

To other people the term primary care physician means a general physician. Another term for a general physician is family physician. These terms may be applied to a physician who has completed a year of internship, or to one who has completed three years of residency (physicians in specialty training are called residents) in the common general areas of medical care.

There are also primary care physicians as much after money as are some specialists. To many specialists, or too few primary care physicians may not be the problem at all. Once again, economic factors are not to be confused with medical skills. The causes of the economic problems are complex, perhaps one is inherent in the present insured fee for service independent private practice. There are physicians and patients who would prefer to keep this system, because it has advantages as well as faults.

That does not mean we cannot institute another system too, and keep competitive alternatives. This is not wasteful. More options over time will teach us more, and lower costs. Options empower patients.

Specialists can be thought of as primary care physicians in their specialty. They see the common things within their specialty more often than the general physician. Medicine is becoming increasingly more technical. We need not fewer, we need more specialists—but specialists who are acting more like primary care physicians in their area, who were well grounded in general medicine in their internship and in their residency training, whose practice life and whose expectations are structured to remove the need to do unnecessary expensive procedures.

Remove the economic, insurance, legal or whatever the need for preforming unnecessary procedures, and in a specialist one has a physician *best able* to judge when these expensive procedures are not necessary. Many specialist physicians do this well already.

But lets overview something else. Consider two kinds of physicians: Those for whom a high medical practice income is important, yet who practice high quality ethical medicine, and those for whom other values are more important. The latter group will work happily for less money. We shall make use of this trait. Neither is necessarily bad, incompetent, undesirable, etc. They are simply different. The former type may be far more willing to go out of their way for you.

For the latter type, some non-monetary "other values" might be: an aversion to rushing, an aversion to irregular hours, a strong need for bother-free financial security even at a lower income level, satisfaction from study, teaching and innovation, or perhaps simply having other sources of income. Most professions in a rough way can be separated into two such groups.

In medicine there is a third type of physician. This is the young physician in training. After a year of internship, a young physician can be licensed to practice, yet many will spend about five years in further training at fairly low pay, often at considerable hardship. This hardship is increased by the financial drain from the previous eight years of formal university training. These residents, as they are called, are rapidly becoming very well trained.

We are developing a preview of the solution detailed later in this book. That solution is to first keep the options, the types of medical practice we have, and radically change the insurance and the legal interference. Both of these are part of the problem. Then, underlying all this, provide a Safety Net Hospital-Clinic (SNHC) system that is free to all. Allow me to repeat: *free to all*, millionaires and paupers alike. You would be amazed at what poor medical care many millionaires get, no joke. There are many reasons for this. They do not know, any more than you do, who is the most competent physician for their needs. *It is difficult to buy better medical care. You can only buy more expensive medical care. That is not to say more expensive medical care is never better medical care.*

The Safety Net Hospital-Clinic system will be financed by a highly visible surtax, (the same percentage for everyone), of each individual's annual income tax **payment.** For example, if last year the percentage were 10%, and if you paid the government five thousand dollars in income tax that year, then you would owe a surtax of ten percent of that five thousand, or five hundred dollars. Each year the percentage paid equally by all would be subject to change depending on the needs of the system for the previous year and the projected need for the coming year. The details, including cost control, come later in the chapters about the solution. These include methods to control overuse.

Two important aspects need reemphasis here. First this surtax should be highly visible, and all should pay, to help dispel this notion of free medical care (even though in a way it really is free, for you will not be charged for care no matter who you are; but there will be gentle safeguards to see that you do not abuse this marvelous privilege). Second, we citizens must keep the government out of the whole thing, except have the federal government do one thing it has demonstrated it can do well. That is collect taxes.

This surtax money must be carefully kept out of the grasp of the federal government, and should be allocated directly to each state. The money for each state should be kept away from the state government as well, and go directly to each Safety Net Hospital-Clinic in a manner to be described. States would be given considerable discretion as to when and how, or if, each instituted the system.

How these Safety Net Hospital-Clinics should be originated and then operated by salaried physicians is necessarily complex, and even the many pages of details that follow in the chapters about the solution are necessarily abbreviated. May they serve as a beginning for others to build upon.

These Safety Net Hospital-Clinics would first of all be clean, well-equipped and run as top academic teaching hospital-clinics. They would be staffed as are our medical school teaching hospitals now; by a small cadre of knowledgeable, hard-working clinical professor types with much of the work being done at greatly reduced cost by competent residents and interns, working under close supervision, and by a voluntary clinical teaching staff. There exists much precedent for this.

By using residents in specialty training in the SNHC, the expense of that long five year period of training is reduced, its utility expanded and everybody wins. Excellent, ever improving medical care is given to those who come for it, in surroundings of highest idealism and technical acumen. Couple this with an inbuilt lack of need to make a financial windfall, whether by physicians, insurance executives or attorneys, and you have what is advocated in brief as a solution to our medical cost crisis. And don't forget the patient retains the freedom to move among other options as well.

A new form of initial TRIAGE would allow the sick patient more quality time with their physician. Patients, so often do not know who they should see, or how serious is their problem. Triage as used here means the process by which each new SNHC patient is seen briefly and told by a physician expert who to see for their problem.

So each new patient coming to the SNHC would be told by an expert physician, who would be the best to see for that condition. At the Safety Net Hospital-Clinic, that expert knows equally well who your primary care physician is, and sends you there most of the time, for this would be in the best interest of all concerned. Remember, if you have a chronic illness your primary care physician might be the specialist in your condition. You could request a referral out of the SNHC system. The physician of your choice might well be one of the volunteer clinical professors teaching part time at that SNHC.

This Safety Net Hospital-Clinic solution would accomplish many things. It would in a simple manner guarantee medical care for all with a minimum of loss of freedom. It would be your system also in the sense it would give each patient power. It would empower you even though you had decided never to use it, because you could use it with confidence if you needed it; and your private physician would be well aware of that.

If you did not want to use the facility, and preferred your private physician, you could always go to the Safety Net Hospital-Clinic for an honest second opinion. Do you suspect your private physician is advocating an unnecessary surgery? Go to the Safety Net Hospital-Clinic and get a free second opinion.

Do you firmly believe in socialized medicine? Fine— you have it. Do you firmly dislike the idea of bringing everyone to the same level of care that socialization implies? Fine—the familiar old medical care system is still there as an option. Indeed the best medical care is there for you in either case. It is simply delivered in two different ways.

We must exercise objective care lest our vast plans for reforming our medical care system do not come from half-vast concepts, and then result in unintended consequences.

Sometimes in an effort to solve problems we create more problems. Take for example Medicaid and Medicare. In part, because of the lack of foresight and understanding inherent in such complex situations, abuses arose. Each side reacted to the other; a polarization and an aura of confrontation developed, not at all the envisioned solution.

As detailed in the section on insurance, physicians began to devote a greater portion of their energy to confronting what could only be called insurance and government abuses of physician prerogative. And government began arbitrarily to lower previously agreed upon payments. It began to audit and otherwise use its tested IRS terror tactics against what it considered physician abuses of its insurance system. Both were partially correct (and as always there were those fraudulent bad apples); but the end result was wrong.

For what it is worth, today, physician morale is lower than any time in my forty four years in medicine. Furthermore the rift between patients and physicians was never wider in my experience.

Once again, government finds itself micro-managing people's private lives; enforcing, and extracting more money from its productive citizens, tacitly fomenting discontent and distrust among people of differing productive capacity. Patients must actively oppose this, for their best interests will surely be lost somewhere in the shuffle—and for what?

Remember government had set out to help the patient. Now the patient must pay ever increasing amounts, carry ever costlier supplemental insurance, and now government is once again going to fix the problem by forcing more of the same on patients and their physicians; worse, it has set itself the task of doing this hurriedly.

Realize that the best medical care delivery system has yet to be found. It is unlikely that any government will find it.

There are many problems. Large amounts of capital are required to provide the medical care we have come to expect—capital in the conventional sense of money, and capital in the form of long periods of intense education. Why else do doctor and especially hospital bills cost so much?

Medical care is expensive because it is valuable. Some of the reasons follow:

- An ancient, abiding dedication to providing charity care
- Rapid, costly, but wonderful scientific advances
- Demanding sophisticated practices
- Third party interference
- High physician incomes
- High ancillary personnel incomes
- Long, costly training required for many ancillary people
- Exacting, demanding responsible dedication required
- Expensive infrastructure required
- Constantly increasing use and demands on the system
- Lack of accountability in many present situations and profligate attitudes
- Costly, inept, meddling government regulations (paperwork)
- The contingent fee malpractice crisis

- Societal and cultural changes, including:
  Rapidly increasing use by immigrants and aliens
- Medical insurance, its costly effects &
  infrastructure

To work on a problem adequately, it must be defined and exposed. With the medical cost crisis this is difficult. What is happening in medicine is the result of complex and far-reaching events occurring in our society. An example is the attempt, in the case of medical care, to mix humanitarianism, socialism, and commercialism. A major problem is the conflicting expectations of the parties involved, and the failure of any group to see the problem as a whole.

Patients refer to "my doctor." Doctors refer to "my patient." Curiously, for many patients and doctors, that bond feels prostituted by the interposition of money. It is difficult for many sick patients to pay a physician. It is like heaping misfortune on misfortune; and they charge so much. Most physicians are embarrassed to ask a patient directly for money. They have an employee do it. More curious still, this very feeling has been sensed by politicians and truly exploited. Have someone else pay the medical bill.

In their pursuit of science, physicians have unwittingly fulfilled a salesman's dream. Their product is now considered essential. It is considered so essential, in fact, that it has attracted those who prey on financial success. It has also attracted some who would control, for they are convinced they know best. The latter have invented and imposed the politics of dependence and deception.

It has become accepted that it should appear to the patient they are not paying for the cost of their medical care. The physicians have come to act as if they were not extracting money from the patient; but from a third party. We do not say there are many who cannot afford medical care. We say instead, there are many who do not have medical insurance. The uninsured and underinsured are the subject of many pronouncements.

"Patients should not have to pay for medical care, the insurance companies should." Or, "Patients should not be required to pay for their medical care, their employers should." The issue of denial and also practices of shifting and hiding costs is central to the problem of medical costs and quality care. These deceptions are indeed expensive and unnecessary.

It is crucial that patients and physicians begin to work together. How to achieve this dream of patient and physician happily left alone to work through their own problems appears throughout this book.

The Litigation Crisis

The tort law contingency fee crisis is much more than a "malpractice" litigation crisis. It is more than an industrial compensation insurance crisis. Many of our legal profession are our greatest asset. Unfortunately, some attorneys are abusing the coercive advantage given them. It is an example of raw power gone wild. The power of precedence, persuasion, and polemics against the power of science is as ancient as Galileo. Expert testimony within an adversarial situation usually does little more than upgrade the sophistication of the polemics. What will stop these excesses?

Life is fragile and risk is everywhere. So is uncertainty. Risk is the shadow of medical care. There are those who would capitalize on this fact. Responsibility and account-ability are essential. Of even greater importance is prevention, removal or retraining of incompetents before problems occur. The medical profession is dodging defamation of character lawsuits from some disgruntled physicians to reduce the risk of medical care. They are doing this through advances in risk assessment, and through revived efforts in outcomes research. These endeavors, discussed further on, go beyond that specious term the courts call negligence, which in the opinion of some has come to have no boundaries, hence no meaning.

A profession should govern, should control itself, for only it is privy to that body of knowledge. This is as essential for the medical profession and the legal profession as for any other. The legal profession is incapable of adjudicating the increasingly esoteric scientific aspects of the medical profession. It has no business meddling there. The medical profession has no interest in controlling the legal profession.

But there are those who have sold a large segment of the public the notion that every untoward event that in some way could be labeled negligence, was malicious or preventable, and must be financially compensated. Again, it is curious indeed that money, should be the cure. The search is on for the deep pocket.

Contingency fees are of no use to anyone if the transgressor is poor and a large monetary settlement not probable (refer to family law); nor do contingency fees help the person who is aggrieved, unless that grief can be relieved by money. Indeed that person is not uncommonly used as a basis for a financial windfall by a venture capitalist of the courtroom. While there are certainly idealistic attorneys who would take a case solely to redress an injustice, usually any plaintiff's case, almost regardless of merit, will be taken if there is a good chance of winning a large sum.

The deep pocket is usually capable of passing the cost along, and back to the consumer. The myth that physician errors and omissions ("malpractice") can be redressed by exchange of money (which is usually covered by insurance) is often incorrect. The myth that physician money loss improves physician competence is wrong. Patients pay for malpractice insurance. These lawsuits for money are a windfall for a few; a deception for most. The hidden cost is enormous, physician cynicism and fear being a substantial cost.

This is no cover-up. Of course their are legitimate cases, and their are victims of all manner of errors and omissions. This vital issue is sadly not the point. *Malpractice litigation never has and never can achieve the degree of physician accountability patients deserve.* In spite of some outstanding exceptions, malpractice litigation is about money and its persistence is about power. This is a travesty that should be reformed. Many of us know that. There are numerous excellent ideas for reform, but who has the power to change the system?

We should terminate the common law concept of monetary liability for medical negligence!

Although malpractice insurance costs are passed directly to the patient, physician disgust at the unreasonableness and domination implicit in these lawsuits is what is so costly. It is much like a rape victim must feel. The cost of malpractice litigation and especially the threat of such litigation increases medical costs about 30%. There is no good source for this figure. The cost is so difficult to assess because the effects are so far reaching, some subtle.

The job of governing justly, and the just settlement of medical disputes increasingly involves esoteric knowledge, a high degree of skill, and the appreciation of the boundaries of medical skill in complex tense situations. The composite of such endeavors has grown beyond the capacity of our system of jurisprudence in some areas. Many attorneys, judges and lawmakers refuse to face this reality, and to provide for it realistically. Egregious injustice has been done by some who have taken advantage of such situations for their own enrichment.

As the culture accumulates complexity and specialization, achieving accountability becomes ever more difficult. Perversions of accountability will in time reveal themselves. Systems that allow or abet such perversions are unsound and will ultimately become unable to compete, or their excesses will force radical change and redress. This is happening here, now.

To Conclude

Three very important things must be preserved in any solution for the medical cost crisis. These are **consumer choice, physician choice, and competitive alternatives.** In a word, freedom. Freedom is the key, reality is the lock. Bleeding hearts belong in the operating room.

We are tampering then, with powerful forces, the extent of which we do not completely understand. We are attempting to socialize part of a thriving capitalistic industry in a somewhat capitalistic country, where individual freedom and ownership is highly valued. We are tampering with the drive and incentive of our physicians, and perhaps our medical students of the future.

There follows an attempt to tiptoe through this morass and create a satisfactory solution, by someone who early in life fell in love with the wonder of being a physician.

■ CHAPTER TWO

Cherish Your Choice

I am a physician who is no longer practicing. For many years, as a part-time voluntary clinical professor, I taught medical students and young specialists in training. I have discontinued this. I can no longer afford to take the risk my life savings will be wiped out by some lawsuit or fine. I no longer have the stomach for what medical practice has become.

The idealism and the personal human interchange that made medical practice so rewarding have been replaced by a constant wariness. Doctor-patient relationships have become enveloped with a shell of third party interference. High overhead forces ever higher fees. Medical practice has become a maze of regulations, with threats of fines and punishments. Always there is insurance.

More and more, physicians must be ever-vigilant about what they say for fear of committing harassment or discrimination. The practice of medicine, always fraught with risk is now fraught with blame and fear of defamation or punishment. Patients do have unexplained illnesses, idiosyncratic or allergic reactions. Where once these were challenges, now they are real personal threats, even cause for panic. I found myself concerned as much about my safety as my patient's. My patients were buying insurance to protect themselves from me, and I was buying insurance to protect myself from them. How did this come about?

Where once an office medical chart was a confidential diary and personal memory jogger, a physician now must be ever careful to take notes that could appear in a courtroom. This abbreviates quality time spent with the patient. I had become a tense harried scribe in need of a court reporter. I had become afraid of my patients and my employees. For years I was not fully aware of this. Then one day it hit me.

I simply can no longer afford to practice medicine. It is no longer rewarding anyway. But what about my patients? Who would take care of them? I miss them.

I was told I was a good doctor. I had a loyal and trusting following for the most part. I was considered sensitive and compassionate. That is why I quit. To me the practice of medicine no longer has a place for such a person. What kind of physician will take my place? One of these survivors expressed it as follows: "I do not want problems. Take your problems elsewhere. I want procedures I can do, trouble-free, lucrative procedures." Have we lost sight of what is happening to people who become patients? That is the bottom line. There is so much more to this than money.

An Example from Real Life

Here is a story by a patient who had been active in the present government effort to reconstruct our medical care system. In one of these meetings, suddenly and unexpectedly he became a patient. He asked that I put you in his shoes.

You are appointed to a high-level post concerned with health care reform. You advocate discouraging fee-for-service medicine in favor of prepaid health plans, and the end of second opinions, since second opinions increase costs and utilization without improving care. Terms like utilization review and global budgeting are bandied about (global budgeting is political talk for medical price control— Medicare has been at this for years. Refer to the chapter on insurance).

You have been involved with the group discussing Health Plan Purchasing Cooperatives. Another group discusses the access of people with low incomes to medical care. Your group debates insurance coverage changes, that dictate no federally qualified health care provider can exclude high-risk, chronically ill, or seriously ill persons. (Someone must bear the cost of risk).

Your group is an advocate of a National Health Board that would define a standard health plan benefit, standardize outcome reporting, set quality standards, etc.

The words "a sick patient," even "illness," seem not to be in you or your colleague's lexicon. The reference is always to the insured or the uninsured. It is as if the insured were assured of health and the uninsured were doomed. Terms (hence concepts) like "patient" are rarely, if ever, used. The groups involved in these high-level discussions are above that. Or is it they do not know how to deal with this pragmatic level, so they avoid it?

In your view, the patient is, at best, a unit to process, and this process is to be done at the least possible government expense that will keep the masses quiet and the statistics politically palatable. The possibility is overlooked that getting those thirty million uninsured patients insured may well do exactly the opposite—that is, raise costs and increase dissatisfaction. Instead of hitching our medical wagon to a star, you and your colleagues were hitching it to the ballot box.

In your meetings, the physician, when mentioned at all, is treated as a powerless pawn in the "health care reform" process (the term "health care" is frequently used—it seems to be more fashionable than medical science, or medical care). Reform of medical science is not mentioned. The connection is not made (or is discreetly avoided) that our medical science comes from someone, and is administered by someone called a doctor.

You are busy participating in one of these high-level discussions, when you feel a truly awful nausea. You hasten to the toilet, and vomit blood, and lots of it. You feel very weak and dizzy. Suddenly things have changed for you. All that high-level discussion has become academic. You sit awhile, notice you are thirsty, go to the sink and panic again. You are ashen. You need a doctor. You are about to experience what it is like to be a seriously ill patient. Curiously that was never discussed in your high-level discussions.*

* In spite of all the prating about the uninsured, still, even today, a seriously ill patient will be taken to a physician and treated whether or not they have insurance. Exceptions are rare. This, however, may not be the physician of their choice, and the very sick, frightened patient can become quite concerned about the competence of the physician who is or will be attending.

You, being an advocate of managed care (whatever that is—things are best kept a bit vague), and having your judgment impaired by blood loss, find your way to your car, and make the dangerous drive to your Health Maintenance Organization facility, (HMO). The place is very busy. You cannot find the emergency room. After an interminable wait, you finally get to the receptionist. She is either too busy, or not well enough trained to notice that you are ashen. You must have fainted. You regain consciousness to find yourself looking at the ceiling from one of those hospital carts.

You realize that someone is taking your blood pressure. The person is young, and does not bother to introduce himself. In fact he is neither kind nor clean. This is probably just bad luck. The HMO has a large staff, and you might have drawn a very personable physician instead of this one.

It hits you. YOU need a doctor, a good doctor, one that knows his business. You are frightened. Most importantly, you need someone who can comfort you (we tend to say a physician in whom you have "confidence"). And now you find yourself in the hands of a physician in whom you have no confidence, and you want the option of putting yourself in the hands of a physician in whom you do. That emotion-laden thought wells up in you.

Suddenly you wonder why this was never discussed in those high-level meetings about health care reform (indeed, what about health care needs reforming? Isn't it the costs that are the problem?) You may be looking death in the eye. At such a moment the monetary aspects of your situation are far from paramount. Nor will all the rules and regulations you would impose on the health care process change these realities.

You realize, shivering there, that your colleagues in those high-level discussions do not even know the problem. They have missed the most elementary aspect of what health care is about. You now realize it is a very personal, vital interchange between two people, one where patients must put themselves entirely in the hands of another, a physician. In that situation, and that is the real situation, that physician has power, a hell of a lot of power, and you, now, more than *you* ever realized, are at the mercy of that power, knowledge, integrity, and, you realize with a jolt, that good will.

Furthermore you do not know who this physician is. You know the HMO has a good reputation, part of which is that they are quite economical, but surely they would hire only competent physicians. You pause a minute thinking, "Who are they?" You also know if you died at the hands of this person, your heirs could sue and perhaps collect a bundle of money.

But for right now, your situation is very different. You certainly want to stay on the good side of this physician. You feel as if your life might depend on it; and it might.

Before even talking to this doctor you felt the need for another opinion, and you think back to the high-level discussions about how second opinions should be stopped because they were believed to have increased utilization without improving care. You curse under your breath as you realize you and your colleges have missed a most vital point.

Medical care is always like this. It is between a patient and a physician—often alone in a little room. And the only way a patient will feel comfortable in that little room with the physician is for that patient to be empowered to say "I want to see another physician," and be able to do so. Equally important, the physician should be able to safely and emphatically say, "You do not need medical care, go home and don't worry" (and say this with neither government, financial or legal intimidation).

In your present position, you now begin to realize that in the name of universal coverage (or perhaps political opportunism) you have deprived yourself, the physician, and this society of essential choices, and thereby disempowered all of you. It will be the patient who loses.

You are very sick and very tired, too much of both to be scared, so you boldly say to the physician now standing over you, "I want to see another physician." He smiles and says, "That is all right. You are in the emergency room. I have decided to admit you to the hospital, and you will be under the care of a different physician there. You have a seriously bleeding ulcer and you need hospital care." He turns and is gone.

Now you are really frightened, but you are also very sick and your judgment is impaired. The physician is very busy. Most HMO's are packed. You recall that your high-level discussion group advocated legislative measures to discourage an alternative, fee-for-service medicine, to help encourage (read force) prepaid medical plans. But waiting or overcrowding were not discussed.

It is clear to you, even in your sick befuddled state, that you need alternatives. You need options, or else you will be robbed of your power along with the physician. You begin to see how the power of the patient and the physician are bound together.

The physician returns. He is hurried, harried, and brusque. He tells you that your wife will be there shortly, and asks you to sign a form which he says will give him permission to start an intervenous solution. Even though he does not bother to explain to you why, or the imperative nature of the need for this solution, you sign the form.

You doze off and your frightened wife awakens you. She tells you the nurse has briefed her, and that it is best for you to relent and allow yourself to be hospitalized.

You are transferred to a hospital room containing two other patients. One is moaning, the other has a continual parade of relatives around. Your new doctor is kindlier, a young lady. Your nurses are excellent.

After a few days, your doctor tells you that you are continuing to bleed, and their tests lead them to believe the best course for you is surgery. She talks with you and your wife about procuring blood donors.

You ask her if this surgery is really necessary. She replies that sometimes it is, and sometimes it is not; but the surgeon that reviewed your case thinks it the better choice. You object. You say that no surgeon even looked at you. She says, "Yes he did. Remember that doctor that was in this morning?" You now recall. He did little more than say a brief hello. She acknowledges this, but replies that he studied your chart.

You begin to realize that the hidden agenda of your high-level talks was the joy of power, of control, and the making of the entire medical system to fit your ideas, not your knowledge or experience. It does not matter your opinions then were innocent and well-meaning.

Now more than ever, you want another medical opinion. It may be unnecessary. It may increase utilization without improving care, but you care. You realize the misuse of the word care. You have been receiving what your colleges called health care. It has not been given with "care," to you as another human being. Patients deserve such care. Patients had best not let this prerogative slip away. They had better demand it, for it is apt to be the first to go.

Prepaid health plans (which is what HMOs are called because the patient pays so much a year for whatever care the HMO doctors think they need) by their very nature tend to deprive the patient of reassurance. Their physicians are very busy, and their personal, emotional responsibility to you, a patient, while it exists is slight. Prepaid health plans operate what (in medical circles) is called a volume practice. You are beginning to understand what that means. We will leave you there to ponder your next move.

The point is not that all HMO experiences are this way, but many of them are. The point is not that all private fee-for-service medical care is reassuring, it is not. The point is, options empower patients.

Having an insured patient pay a part of the fee has already been proven a failure at controlling costs. The only way over-utilization can be controlled, is for the physician to be empowered to say to a patient—in a reassuring, tactful way— "you are not in need of medical service, you may safely go home."

Doctor and patient must care for one another carefully! No one else will—not an insurance company executive, not your political representative, not you attorney, nor any other third party. When the chips are down, only you and the doctor really matter insofar as your scientific medical care is concerned. In this vital aspect third parties show in their true colors; they are in the way.

■ *CHAPTER THREE*

Medical Insurance

Long ago, the AMA (American Medical Association) after fighting against it for years, encouraged medical insurance. They did this in part to counteract socialized medicine (I was told at the time).

Patients' emotional reluctance to pay, and the embarrassment of physicians to charge would be reduced. Physician-patient relations would improve; so would physician accounts receivable. Insurance would provide a bulwark against patient unrest, and counter the growing socialistic noises from the politicians. With the illusion that someone else was paying the bills, insurance would counter the threat of politicians who would buy votes with the promise of free medical care. Many physicians have always resisted medical insurance.

Physicians have never been renowned for their business or economics skills. Some of our leaders seemed even less talented in this respect. They failed to recognize these things:

1. Government was going to socialize whether or not it socialized medicine. More redistribution of wealth was on the way.

2. Doctors were letting the third party camel's nose under the tent. Insurance companies would be competing for their share of the medical dollar, and eventually for control. The government would soon be in the insurance business.

3. Insurance rates and medical costs were bound to spiral upward. Other then catastrostropic coverage, most medical insurance was unsound.

4. Naming their scheme insurance did not make it insurance.

5. Healthy competition among physicians to provide better service at competitive cost would be subverted. Even today, this is not generally grasped.

6. No one ever dreamed of the extremes to which the bureaucratic "art" of insurance billing would be carried.

Medical Insurance and Physician Competition

Why reduce your fees below the other physicians, and increase your services when both you and your competitor are struggling not with the patient for your fee; but with an insurance company? That company is paying you both the same fee for the same service. Better to outwit the insurance company, even though the patient paid a portion. Competing for patients by reducing fees came not to be considered because it was not required. Neither was collusion to fix fees, the insurance companies had already done that.

So the noncompetitive bias was built into the insurance system from the beginning; so were patient and physician over use. That is the way things have been for over forty years. Is it any wonder there is a medical cost crisis?

As the system evolved, and the battle of wits became more sophisticated, the sharp business and administrative personnel in insurance realized that while physicians were naive in some respects, they could not be outwitted easily on their own turf. This took place over years. These were years in which the insurance company would put forth one set of fee restraints, and the physicians being on the line, and knowing their field would simply work around them. (More of the same is now being touted as the solution.)

The patients came to be treated somewhat like a child who starts a fight between two parents, but is not included in the tussle. Physicians are now being put in this position by politicians, economics pundits, and whoever else with power and media exposure cares to get into the fray. Now it seems more like a group of jackals fighting over a rabbit.

Initially patients were told by some physicians that while they were liable for the fee, as a service to them, the doctor would bill their insurance company and then bill them for any difference. Other physicians required patients to do their own billing. Eventually physicians were required to do the "bookwork." Eventually they preferred to do it, developing insurance billing to an extreme of wasted effort which has reached its peak in our hospitals. This adversarial art has mushroomed to an extent believable only to a bureaucrat. The "providers" find esoteric rules to increase the bill; the insurance company employees find arcane ways to lower it. Now the present politicians would "streamline" this ridiculous mess as reform.

From early on patients were en masse, too powerful to battle. Physicians were wary of them. Patients had only to elect a liberal, and there would be another round of redistribution of wealth and government coercion. Also angry or disgruntled patients might sue. Patients and physicians were quietly being pitted against each other.

It is still common to hear the medical profession is no good, but my doctor is great. Patients have a colossal mistrust for physicians en masse. This continues to titillate some politicians and attorneys.

Early on, patient care became physician's third concern. Dodging malpractice lawsuits and the IRS became the first and second concerns. Malpractice and IRS fears generated physician resentment and overhead, which was expressed in a drive for money. As government generated employee costs and inflation increased, as taxes and penalties increased, as IRS threats and authoritarian regulations from almost every quarter increased, physicians reacted. If the IRS took half your income in taxes, and even then tried to beat you out of more, the obvious thing to do was to double your income.

Medical insurance was the obvious target. Another was a reduction in charity practices. Physicians became less kind, angry.

Patient and physician indulged in self-deception. Both knew the money did not come from these wealthy big insurance companies, they merely handled it for a substantial fee.

Deception and dependence seemed to be in the self-interest of everyone.

Some physician's fees were lower than others; but for those patients with medical insurance, this difference in fees did not matter much. If a family's medical insurance coverage was paid by their employer, and they were insured for a large percentage of their medical fees, this same percentage would be paid to any of their several possible choices of physician. There was little incentive to shop for the physician with the lowest fee for the best service. More physicians were utilized. Other factors became more important.

God help the physician who held out and refused to take medical insurance. Exceptions were those physicians with an independent income, a wealthy clientele or luxury cosmetic surgery practices.

So the health care insurance system took precedence over health care per se. Commercialization of an idealistic profession resulted. Now, many people seem willing to sacrifice quality to reduce cost. Until a serious illness happens to them, they have so little experience to go by.

More Early Effects of Medical Insurance

So insurance was thrust on the medical profession. There was no economically viable way a physician could refuse to accept it. All but a very few were drawn into the scheme. Some looked upon this as a conspiracy by government, forced on all physicians. Some thought it a God-send. Control and enforcement became the order of the day; and many physicians resented this bitterly. Again, fee differences as a competitive advantage, however, virtually disappeared.

Some insurance companies early foresaw a windfall. He who pays the piper calls the tune. The idea of a professional with so much earning power and so little business acumen, excited many an insurance company. They were in a no-lose situation. If medical fees increased, their premium increased, their float increased, their wealth and power increased. (By float is ment the amount of money in possession available for earning interest.)

To be sure, they had to keep their claims payments down. This was essential to build their census and, at the beginning, to build up their monetary reserves. This need for reserves tended to keep competition down. They struggled to keep physician fees down, they said, and even advertised that they were the ones most capable of managing physician charging. Early on they began to exert control and restrictions on their payment policies. This was usually done with the alibi that insurance use was exceeding insurance premiums.

However, their imperative was to maintain and increase their census and so maintain and increase their reserves, their float and their power.

Predictably, there developed a pattern where the insurance companies constantly complained that over-utilization of their medical insurance by patients, and overcharging by physicians were squeezing them; and that fee cuts and premium increases were essential. One saw the large new insurance office buildings, their many employees; but few ever saw the insurance companies' profit line. What is the take of this vast insurance complex? What was the growth rate of their reserves? Surely the float, the amount of money passing through their hands was enormous, the flow constant and predictable, The interest on the float high. For forty years there were no catastrophic losses. While insurance companies can fail from catastrophic claim losses, losses on investments of float and reserves are more common. What does this system cost us all? Everything was a moving target, hard to pin down.

All manner of moves and counter-moves ensued. Then the government entered the act with the beneficent introduction of Medicare and Medicaid. This government bureaucracy, as one might suppose, quickly developed its own power base; and joined not the patients, nor the physicians, but the insurance companies, and government can be expected to continue to do this. As power brokers the insurance companies had more savvy; yet the government had more punishing power, and was accustomed to operating that way. This was to work to everyone's detriment. Physicians are hypersensitive to this kind of treatment. Their response to threats of this kind was predictable—hostility and cynicism.

The Relative Value Fee Schedule

When insurance companies agreed to a unit value fee schedule, they gave physicians a tactical advantage. This was also called a relative value schedule, abbreviated the RVS. This seemed logical enough, and suited the bureaucrats. An elementary unit of value was established. This unit, it was agreed, would be a simple return visit office call. Then physicians, and others got together and expressed all fees in terms of multiples of that unit value. An appendectomy would be worth the value of so many units. Say an appendectomy would be worth twenty office calls, in other words twenty units. All these different procedures were listed in one large book. Each was given a code number.

The idea was if inflation occurred, or there was some other reason for increasing costs, the only thing that would have to be negotiated was the value of a unit. For years organized medicine and the insurance companies fought over the monetary value of this unit. It was not really changed for over fifteen years. Practicing physicians had little faith in either side, organized medicine or the insurance advocates. Insurance companies managed to hold the unit value at $5.00. Yet these were times of inflation, and somehow medical care costs were increasing. How could this be?

Physicians reacted in the only way they could, covertly. The solution was so obvious that it simply appeared. One example of what occurred could be called the "a la carte" method or itemized billing. While the insurance business and the government were concentrating on the money, while they were negotiating over the fee schedule, they failed to consider the number and kinds of procedures. The physicians had the foresight, perhaps it was luck, to increase the individual procedures. It was plausible.

A patient wants a minor surgical procedure, a vasectomy for example. In times past the physician would quote an inclusive fee. Now what does this entail? Well it depends. A vasectomy is worth so many units. But it also requires a complete set of tools. We call this set of tools a surgical tray. This tray must be carefully and expertly put together. It must be sterilized under exacting conditions, requiring special capital equipment. Surely the physician who was billing for a vasectomy would be entitled to bill for a surgical tray, gloves, gowns, face masks, syringes and needles.

Now all these are disposable. They are costly. Many things must be disposed of in different ways. For example, all sharp things must be disposed of differently. Bandages must be supplied. All this requires trained, expensive, sometimes unionized help. Now, some hospitals or medical school clinics even add a sizable fee for the temporary patient use of the clinic space.

In these days of lawsuits, the physician who does a vasectomy must be prepared to prove that indeed a piece of each spermatic chord was removed. These pieces carefully identified, are prepared in a way they can be imbedded in paraffin and cut into very thin slices. This is called a biopsy. These microscopic slides are in turn read by another physician. (Notice how these malpractice-fear driven insurance costs increase.) Now instead of a physician and his assistant to be paid, we have in addition a tissue technician, and a pathologist. A pathologist is a specialist physician who interprets the microscopic slides.

Doing even a minor procedure under local anesthetic entails risk. Trial attorneys have great advantage when a mishap occurs in an office surgery. Careful physicians bring in the services of another physician called an anesthetist to spread the risk. This doubles the fee, but the insurance pays the bill.

If keeping a surgically equipped room in one's office entails more office overhead, more capital equipment, and more risk, why not send the patient to the hospital day surgery unit and do it there? The hospital will probably bill the patient more than the cost of the original procedure; but, well it is not the patients money, the patient has insurance.

As the years and inflation went on, physicians began to work around the edges. They got more things included in the fee schedule. Examples included opening an abscess, applying a cast, taking an X-ray, surgical trays, bandages and so forth. On the face of it, these things seemed logical enough.

Physicians then concentrated on different kinds of office visits. There was an initial office visit, a specialist's consultation visit, a prolonged visit, a nurses visit as well as the simple unit value office visit. It came to pass that the simple office visit was rarely used. The more expensive ones became the rule.

Things were being done to pad the bill. Things were being done to counter the malpractice threat. Examples of countering malpractice threats while also padding the bill were X-rays, cultures, laboratory work, and biopsies. All could be easily justified for one reason or another. Often they were necessary.

The insurance companies would mark down bills; certain procedures were required. The bureaucratic demands escalated. Physicians responded in kind.

Medicare beginning with 1992 instituted a very complex new fee schedule to change this. They have discovered single item billing and inclusive fees. Yet they still bill from a book full of procedure-based fee schedules, leaving the trump card to the physicians and hospitals (redefining procedures in order to increase billable fees). The game goes on.

Companies advertised to educate physician office employees in ways to bill the insurance companies so physicians might get the maximum return allowed by the insurance regulations. Finally most physician's offices evolved to where they employed one trained person whose sole job was to bill the insurance companies to the physician's best advantage. From this evolved the ever changing itemized bill.

These forms were prepared listing all the physicians' proffered services billable to the insurance companies. The physician, after seeing a patient, would check off numerous categories, the sum of which would be considerable. Without insurance these amounts would never have been tolerated by patients, or charged by physicians.

Notice, again, the deception. Patients do not see themselves as paying, and physicians do not directly bill the patient, the receptionist does. Such deception and dependence increase costs.

By this time, nearly everyone had insurance. This had been the AMA's dream. For the patient's employers and the government who were footing the bill it was becoming a nightmare.

Of course these insurance companies were being squeezed (big employers were becoming alarmed), and who knows, perhaps part of insurance profits, the part that consisted of the amount taken in, less the amount paid out grew slimmer, requiring further raising of premiums. The float never faltered. The amount of money going through their hands, earning hefty interest, was enormous and increasing. (Imagine the annual float, the earnable interest, on one hundred billion dollars.)

The basic flaws in the system were compounding. Gradual but continual price escalation, helped by inflation, increased the incomes of both physicians and insurance companies. The restive patients were mollified by the illusion they were not paying the bill; and by the addition of prescription drugs to their coverage.

This folly was to spawn an industry, and a skyrocketing of drug costs. One hundred dollar prescriptions quickly became common. Pension funds bought heavily into drug company stocks. Other large companies were laying-off workers. Many were facing union leaders seeking more benefits, and attempting to maintain job security. Better health insurance was most sought after.

Medical Insurance from the Patients Viewpoint

From the patient's viewpoint, medical insurance early on was an enticing gambit with a bit of lottery thrown in. If someone in the family were to have a catastrophic or expensive illness, they did well. They not only had this security; but if they got too far ahead of their premiums, they could lower their requirements for seeing a physician. There is always something many of us would like to ask a physician about.

Patients would get a check-up and refill those prescriptions, have that benign facial nevus removed, go for those extra visits the physician had advised. Junior thinks he needs glasses. Mary has this constant runny nose. Perhaps an allergist would help her, even though we have heard they do numerous expensive tests. And so things went along this way for many years. Drug and hospital costs were outpacing physicians fees.

Costs at home escalated. Both parents got jobs. Neither could quit because little Jenny had diabetes now, and they could never get medical insurance again if they lost this insurance. Their employers would have liked an excuse to dismiss them, because the employer's insurance and pension costs were dissipating their profits. Some employers were driven out of business. Health insurance costs being paid by employers far exceeded their expectations and their budgets. There were now so many other employee costs besides health care. Regulatory agencies appeared from everywhere with distantly formulated, often ignorant and ill conceived regulations. Jobs were lost. An epidemic of layoffs and retrenchments ensued and continues.

Physician employee costs escalated alarmingly. So did taxes, and inflation, and of course so did fees for medical services. An attempt by a physician to discharge a marginal employee occasionally resulted in a lawsuit. Medical practice overhead skyrocketed. Employee, government, and malpractice threats all were economically and psychologically distressing. Physicians were told by their accountants to incorporate.

A host of hassles with the IRS and the government took place over establishment of physician pension funds. Physicians were not allowed to have a pension fund unless they included their full time employees. This led to an increase in part time employment. This permitted some single mothers to supplement their welfare checks with part time employment.

As time went on, the pension plan investments of many physicians had not turned out well. Physicians were poor investors. Family costs were increasing. College costs were escalating. Many children would be unable to attend college, some for financial reasons, and others because they were unable to meet the academic standards of the crowded state schools. Physician's children were among them. Because of these things and others, physicians embraced insurance. Some saw it as a windfall. Others saw it for what it was. Neither group had power to change it.

Many physicians retired early. While patient fees covered malpractice premiums, the invention of punitive damages left deep pockets sitting ducks. Many less fortunate left private practice for positions with less risk of personal and financial catastrophe.

Times Get Tough

About this time the average family reached the limit of its spending ability. If prices of some consumer items raise enough, consumers will no longer buy them. However, if the prices of some items raise further, these consumers cannot buy them, no matter how much they need or want them (depending on the level of money circulation). House rent is an example. No matter how nice a rental or a market of rentals, the middle class producer simply cannot pay beyond a certain ceiling. The provider of this commodity must be aware of this constraint and stay within that range.

Somewhere along this time line of ever increasing medical insurance costs the average producing privately insured consumer over-reached his spending ability. So did many employers. For even some large, affluent corporations, medical insurance or medical and hospital costs were becoming their largest labor costs. The populace had been trained to believe the worst. Half truths flowed. Those who could not pay for catastrophic illness care must go without such care! Catastrophy seemed just around the corner. Some panicked. The AMA and others fanned the flames. Few challenged these half-truths. Meanwhile, as costs escalated, we were all becoming at least underinsured.

Cost shifting became the fashion. Government would force our employers to pay for this "essential" medical insurance. Few things are less essential than medical insurance. What is essential is quality medical care for everyone.

Some insisted that employer-provided medical insurance was their right. Others argued this was the most equitable way to provide care. Small business panicked. The politicians were there to help? Employers took on, or were forced to buy into, this ever escalating system. Although sophisticated, they were amateurs at the game the medical insurance people, and physicians had been playing for years. Whatever the reason, it became ever more politically expedient to require the employer to pay for this increasing medical insurance cost. I predict this will be the greatest folly of all.

Things have now become imperative. Someone must support this essential, ever costlier medical and drug establishment. While investors were scrambling to buy drug stocks, physicians, medical equipment suppliers, pharmaceutical and insurance companies were sharing ever increasing amounts of the take. Employers are busy passing along their inflated medical care costs and reducing the number of their employees.

Government and the media were blaming everyone else; and insisting that more of the same was the way out of the mess. The media has read recent election results to mean that government must step in and solve the medical care crisis. We have no medical care crisis. We never had better medical care. We have a crisis of third party interference from people who know not what they do. Government will solve this problem, it says. How will it do this? In my opinion they don't have a clue. What a colossal politically opportunistic presumption.

It took some of the big corporations several years to realize the alarming extent of what was happening. This was especially true of those who were hooked into providing this kind of assurance for their pensioners too. As pensioners age, large medical care expenditures approach certainty. Everyone involved with medical care soon learned this. Many of these companies are now discharging employees, cutting back, and taking charges against earnings. Government was busy, they said, making more jobs.

The AMA continues talking about the uninsured and the underinsured. Once more, another few years of this and we will all be underinsured.

But Is It Insurance?

What is the problem here? Medical insurance is not insurance. One might give it the name assurance, reflecting the fact that it is illusory and political. It is such an aberration, it needs a new word to describe it. What then is insurance? The dictionary does not help much. If one needs indemnification against the occurrence of some act, and is willing to pay for that indemnification, is that insurance? No. Carry this supposition to the limit. Suppose that act is certain to occur. There would be little use in the exchange of funds. To the extent that the act is unlikely, to the extent that the probability of the act occurring can be ascertained, to the extent that a risk can be spread, shared, then a monetary risk can be appended. This is a complicated way of saying what everyone knows.

It makes sense to insure your house against fire. First, you have theoretically no control over the event starting payment. Second, the event is unlikely. Third, you have reasonable assurance that if a fire did occur the insurance company would have the funds to pay. This is so because many others whose houses will not burn down have also paid the insurance company. Finally, it is likely the insurance company will make a profit. This assures two things. The company is likely to stay in business and continue to insure your house. Second the insurance company will not raise your premium much. It is elementary that the insurance company is not in this for it's health.

Now consider medical insurance today. Here are the reasons why it is assurance, not insurance. The Policy holders can evoke payment at will in a rather high percentage of uses. A much smaller chance of use is beyond their control. Compare this with a health insurance policy that was evoked only after the first twenty thousand dollars had been spent by the policy holder. (Back in the days when twenty thousand dollars would buy a lot of medical care.) In this example of high patient co-payment, sometimes called catastrophic insurance coverage, a great percentage of the use, if not all, was beyond the control of the policy holder. There is in this latter instance a built-in control against over-use. Note too, that the likelihood of use is low.

The theoretical deterrent of patient co-payment in our present medical assurance schemes has not prevented patient abuse for a number of reasons. The main one being co-payment is usually too small, and may be waived by the physician. Waiving the co-payment is often in the physician's best interest. The expenditures are to some extent controlled by the physician. However by denying the patient use of the insurance, the physician risks offending the patient, and deprives himself thereby. These two events are unlikely.

Most patients act as if this assurance-insurance were not a cost to them, and seem to make no connection between their over use of the policy and its escalating costs. This latter leads us to the most senseless trait of all. The person evoking payment from the policy is not, nor will be the person who pays for that policy. It would tax one to set-up a better plan for misuse. This arrangement boggles the mind. It is flagrant folly! There is indeed a built in temptation, if not incentive for over use and hence escalation of premium costs. One marvels that it has taken so long to reach this crisis of medical costs.

Examples from the Doctor's Office

There follows some actual examples: The physician has told the patient he will withhold a thousand dollar test, and try some cheaper tests first. "Doctor, I can have that magnetic resonance imaging scan, I have insurance." "It is all right doctor, I can return once each week for the next two months if need be, I have insurance." "Doctor, please do not freeze this off. My insurance does not cover that, cut it off, I don't mind. My insurance only pays if you cut it off." "I appreciate your warning me that this prescription will be very expensive doctor; but it will only cost me two dollars. I have insurance." "Would you write me some pain pills for the house, doctor? My insurance does not cover non-prescription drugs." You can guess how the physician will respond.

Consider another type of actual example. A person following a severe febrile illness develops intense shoulder pain, and generalized persistent weakness. An orthopedic surgeon consults with the patient for seven minutes, orders several expensive X-rays, and the bill reaches several hundred dollars arrived at by adding the insurance codes for the procedures billed. The patient subsequently passes through five other physicians, never spending more that fifteen minutes with anyone, each of whom bills using several codes, all including the maximum full consultation code. Expensive diagnostic tests are done, three of which cost about one thousand dollars each. Surgery is performed to correct neck vertebral defects noted on the tests. This, with the mandated limit of three day post operative stay, costs ten thousand dollars. (This three day limit quickly came to cost as much as the previous longer stays.)

Finally after eight months of no relief from the presenting symptoms, the patient is referred to a medical school clinic. The physician there spends an hour and a half with the patient, calls in another specialist who gives the patient some injections. The combined time spent with the patient is a bit over two hours. The patient is given a prescription costing less than ten dollars at the university pharmacy. The patient improves the next day and is well within a month.

When Medicare is billed by a physician, as a check on that physician, Medicare sends the patient a form letter with the fee codes and the amount the physician requested for these. The amount Medicare pays is usually substantially less then the fee listed in the physicians' code book stipulating the agreed upon fee. This amount is what the physician would customarily bill. Medicare then pays the physician eighty percent of this *reduced* amount. If the patient has Medigap insurance, that may pay the difference remaining between what Medicare pays and what the physician had billed, if not, the patient pays the difference.

The patient in the story above received such a letter and noted that the physician at the Medical school in the foregoing example had billed Medicare for the patient according to the RVS code for one consultation only. The amount charged was one hundred twenty two dollars and eighty two cents. Of this Medicare approved sixty dollars and twenty five cents, the amount medicare actually paid, eighty percent, was forty eight dollars and twenty cents.

The point is that at present most medical care is being paid by creative billing and creative paying. There is little relation to anything else. If the physician is excellent medically, but is poor under the scrutiny of the insurance billing bureaucrat, that physician does not get paid. It pays physicians to learn creative billing. Were we in a responsible competitive situation, it would pay physicians to get results.

One more example: A patient was sent to the hospital outpatient service for nerve conduction tests on his arms. The nerve conduction measuring apparatus costs about two thousand dollars and has a seven- to ten-year useful life. The neurologist during the ten minutes with the patient touched the patients arm in four places recording the conduction times in milliseconds. The bill for this short interlude contained six different codes and amounted to six hundred and seventy dollars.

What Has Medical
Insurance Wrought?

Medical insurance even in its early years, did much more than delay socialized medicine. Medical insurance destroyed the free enterprise, partially charitable, idealistic, medical system of that time. Few people realize even today the far reaching effects this one thing engendered. There was more. Medical insurance together, with the promotion of monetary redress for what the courts called negligence, and years of confiscatory taxation have left medical practice, and physician attitudes totally changed. It is a rare private practice physician over forty who is not angry with a bitterness that has been swallowed for years. This costs patients dearly.

County medical society meetings that had heretofore consisted mostly of scientific topics changed to heated discussions over regulations, medical political arguments, lectures and threats from government and political types. The long time customary joint annual meetings of the local medical society and the local lawyer's bar were discontinued. Many physicians who have been in practice for years do not even remember these meetings.

During my years as a general practitioner in a small town, it was customary at Christmas time to clean out delinquent, unpaid bills from the accounts receivable, mark them paid, and add "Merry Christmas." This always brought a rash of partial payments, marked "Thank You." The ministers and poor elderly were routinely treated free. What has happened to patients and doctors since?

Today's medical insurance is a bit like the game of old maid wherein the object of the game is to not get stuck holding the old maid. The old maid in this case is the medical insurance premium. The employers are being stuck with the major cost of private medical insurance. Like the old maid this cost is being surreptitiously passed around. The producer, whether the politicians call them the poor, the middle class, or the rich, pays the bill. The consumer will eventually be stuck with it as these escalating costs trickle through the economy.

Is there anyway to avoid medical commercialism? Indeed medical care, regardless of sentimental dreaming involves enterprise, work and risk. It requires capital. The simple truth is the costs must be paid. The aim should be to make this medical economy as efficient as possible. The nature of the doctor-patient relationship lends itself uniquely to the substitution of other values in lieu of money. Rewards such as prestige, excellent working conditions, complete assurance of lifetime security, enjoyable doctor-patient relationships, and reasonably affluent life-style could substitute for more money. If this could be traded to the consumer for assurance of lifetime medical care, it would be a good deal for all. Perhaps there is a way. Who will lead it?

Medicare and Medicaid are little more than a back door socialized medicine complete with a maze of regulations and threats of punishment. Money flow is allowed to pass through the hands of the payee, the physician, and the insurance companies. As a result physicians, insurance companies, the pharmaceutical industry, and the biotechnical industry are thriving. Some patients have been given the keys to the candy store. Other workers, the self employed and some employers may not be so fortunate.

Patient insurance premiums are certain to escalate to where it will be necessary for the government to take them over. Physicians are given a fading illusion of independence. This ostensibly is better than socialized medicine. One thing for sure whatever socialized medicine turned out to be, the malpractice threat would not be tolerated by a government run medical care bureaucracy. It would be interesting to see our two greatest power brokers square off.

Whatever happened, socialized medicine would remove the freedom of choice from both physician and patient. Most visible would be loss of physician incentive. Few laymen realize how much drive a physician must have. Less visible would be the slow change in the quality of our medical students.

Medical insurance has evolved into resisted bureaucratic control of physicians, but not in patient compliance. So far the physicians are holding their own. Patients never had it so good; neither have the drug companies. Both have exaggerated expectations. Neither can be sustained.

Just as years of inflation created a way of life now requiring major readjustments, so will any profound change in medical insurance. Medical insurance has done this. It has helped to create a flourishing commerce, dependent on ever increasing Medical fees. One might view the system as being far over-leveraged. Where will we get the money to keep this thriving commerce going?

Our problem is more than a crisis of medical care delivery, much more. It is a reflection of a frightening perversion and deterioration of order. We live in an era of deceit and dependence. Worse, both are calculated and cultivated. We live in a culture where the envy and hostility toward wealth, toward success weighs in heavily as one of the facts of a case. There is an ever increasing disregard for the rights of ownership, a frightening disregard for the rights of the enterprising, for the successful producer, whom envy has robbed of justice. We even now have a term for these people. Deep pockets they are called.

What matters is persuasion of the masses, politicizing. The congress gets passed an IRS overhaul, usually called a simplification that requires mass adaptation, often at great expense. Then it thinks nothing of changing the law a few years later and making the change retroactive! It is a wonder we have any consumer confidence at all. Even worse, it is a wonder that people still have the incentive to struggle, to attempt to adapt, and to start a business. Is it any wonder we have creative insurance billing, and great patient dependence on medical insurance? Increasingly, we are developing a dependence on medical insurance where someone else pays the premium.

The above is about what is happening. This book is about a viable alternative—a workable solution.

The Cost of Hospitals

Turn to the hospital. In light of today's system, let us examine a bill for use of a hospital outpatient surgery room for a simple surgical procedure done under local anaesthetic. The patient was in the hospital for less than an hour. In this instance, the bill depends on the procedure and not the time. The bill for the room only is eight hundred dollars. Medicare will pay 80% of what they will approve. This will amount to about one fourth. You pay the remainder. Who do you suppose pays the Medicare bill? You do. Oh, I know the rich pay most of it. Baloney. There are so many more of you, that you do. You pay the tax that pays the Medicare you are so generously allowed to repurchase. Then you must buy medigap insurance as well to help pay the widening gap that Medicare does not pay. If you are not old enough for medicare, you contribute also through your social security payments that are so conveniently held from your paycheck.

God help you if it had been a real operating room. I realize the hospital is crawling with employees, unions, social security, industrial insurance, yes, employee medical insurance, constant risk of lawsuits, OSHA and environmental protection regulations. The list goes on. Nevertheless $800.00 for an outpatient surgery room for an hour is still a lot of money, and one has no idea what the doctor bill will be.

Indeed, as was illustrated before, were one to go to the real operating room for an hour or so routine surgery, nothing fancy, together with the three days hospitalization postoperatively allowed by today's DRGs (diagnosis related groups), the bill would be above $10,000.00. Furthermore, if you have never seen the new hospital bill, you are in for a wry laugh. It is all itemized billing. This means $1.50 for a spot bandage; $3.00 for a 5 mgm. sedative, etc.

Back to that $800.00—or the $10,000.00. Now it is obvious, with all this escalating cost, that Medicare coverage will soon not be enough. As could have been expected, Medicare costs, regardless of how fast they are escalating, are not keeping pace with Medicare expenditures. Nor will they ever be. Whatever is driving this racing engine, it will probably continue. So you and many like you have purchased medigap insurance to cover the difference. In the hospital, frequently even this is not enough. For a $10,000 hospital bill, backed up by a popular medigap policy, the patient was still out of pocket about $700.00. These figures come from an actual case.

They depend entirely on the amount and type of medigap coverage carried. Some medigap policies pay all of the difference depending, of course, on the premiums.

Reducing the Cost

In trying to reduce the cost of medical care, it is elementary that we should ferret out and remove all nonproductive expenses. Not only charlatans, but anyone who draws money from the system without contributing a commensurate amount, must be removed. Patients must be kindly and wisely counseled to prevent over utilization. Certainly half-million dollar plus annual insurance executive salaries and other abuses are true of some aspects of the medical insurance companies; but not all.

One cannot blame an insurance company because someone is foolish enough to misuse it. There are definite problems for which we can in part blame the insurance system. We cannot blame it for just being there doing it's work. There are some kinds of employee medical insurance that work very well. They do a service for society. Medical insurance for judges is an example. To force employers to provide insurance for their employees is a very different matter.

In an attempt to avoid socialized medicine (read centrally-controlled authoritarian medicine) medical insurance has become exactly that. Patients have been enticed to relinquish responsibility for their medical care. "I have insurance. That entitles me to care. Here I am. Take care of me."

Physicians have been enticed to give up aspects of their responsibility. As an example a physician might think thus. "Mrs. Jones is a fine person, and a good friend. Her large family are fine people and good patients. They work very hard for what they get. Why not write her a prescription for a pain-killer for the family? What does it matter to her if I do these diagnostic procedures, even though they are more for my interest, my income, and safety from legal entanglement, than for her benefit. They will not bother her, and she has insurance. It is no money out of her pocket." Note that both physician and patient have relinquished an aspect of their responsibility to each other and to society.

The Insurance Billing Bureaucracy

The insurance company is not privy to what goes on between Mrs. Jones and Dr. Smith. Although they know in general that such things go on. They must just figure it in as a cost of doing business, while looking at their bottom line. The insurance company is a bureaucracy whose interests are to make a profit.

When it gets Dr. Smith's bill for Mrs. Jones care, someone on the staff looks at this piece of paper. This person has a set of duties, and a procedure for performing them. This insurance employee is not privy to the conditions, the reasoning that led Dr. Smith or his insurance expert to submit a bill of this size for Mrs. Jones care. The insurance bureaucrat that must pay the bill, remember, can have no direct knowledge of Mrs. Jones case or Dr. Smith's thoughts. This person has another method which must be interposed between physician and patient.

The bureaucrat's job is to process that piece of paper, within certain rules that have been sent down by superiors. So these insurance employees really have no idea what happened before an action displayed on a piece of paper crosses their desk. They have no concern with what will happen after it leaves. Their concern is that the rules set out for them are followed. That bureaucrat's action is final, unless someone higher up preempts that action.

For a client to appeal to this bureaucrat to apply judgment to the overall medical aspect is useless. The bureaucrat has no basis for judgment except within the sphere of the actions assigned. This is of course the definition of a bureaucrat. This blindness could extend up through the hierarchy of the entire bureau, possibly through to the top of the governing body.

For persons interested in teaching physician's insurance helpers, the extent of this blindness would be important to know. It is just possible that many governmental regulatory agencies work in the same way. It would seem almost impossible for these bureaus to create such outlandish regulations any other way.

This is the basis of creative billing. This is another important basic defect in the medical insurance system as it operates today. Not only do we have assurance instead of insurance in most cases; we have perversions of accountability.

Dr. Smith's insurance employee has taken a course, a rather expensive instructional course, lasting sometimes for days, where this person was taught by one of the former supervisors of these insurance company bureaucrats what to serve up to these bureaucrats to get the maximum return.

Dr. Smith also knows it is difficult to get individual attention. Physicians and nurses are just too expensive to employ in the large numbers that would be required.

So Dr. Smith adapted to reality and hired that insurance person. And so the game goes on. Medical insurance as it is used today, far from being the solution is part of the problem.

Industrial Insurance

There is much talk today about creating jobs. Few things have done more to extinguish jobs than industrial insurance as it is abused today. The average person has no idea how much this adds to the cost of labor, even worse how much this abuse deters the hiring of people, not just because of cost, but because of risk and bother. Their exists no effective control, no brake on this abuse. The industrial insurance premium for a roofer, for example, in some states is forty percent of the roofers wages. False claims are common. It is not uncommon for a worker to work for an employee for years, then after some altercation or discharge from employment, file an industrial claim for some alleged injury.

In some states, a worker with an alleged injury can go from physician or chiropractor to physician or chiropractor until that worker can find one who will submit a diagnosis satisfactory to the worker. In some states a worker can see as many as fourteen of these before the claim can be closed as without merit. That is to say a worker can see a physician or chiropractor who submits a diagnosis of injury, the insurance company can then send the worker to the insurance company's consulting physician who rejects the claim, and the worker can repeat this entire expensive process fourteen times. No punishment or financial deterrent is brought against such a worker or their attorney to my knowledge.

It is common gossip that to go to court against a worker is almost a sure loss for the employer. Whether this is true or not, this gossip spreads. And in a real sense, industrial compensation injuries give rise to a form of contagion, where one worker observes a fellow worker get a large financial settlement and that worker is apt to try the same. This is also true with aliens.

Many employers who hire illegal immigrants do not realize that aliens can sue and collect for real or alleged work-related injuries. An illegal worker legitimately wins a big settlement. That person can return to his home village financially well off for life. Others in the same village note this, and come to this country to work with the sole purpose of collecting a similar settlement.

It is folly to expect medical or industrial compensation insurance companies to regulate overuse or over-litigation, because of the nature of their premium structure, wherein it is easy for them to cover increased claim expenditures with fee increases. Industrial insurance companies base their next year's premium IN ADVANCE on the basis of the previous year's claims by that particular client. They are continually auditing clients to be sure they pay sufficient premiums, so they have no real financial incentive for such control. Industrial insurance companies do have strong incentive to collect every dime of premium they can extract. It is in this way, through nearly instant premium fee increases, they counter the huge payouts for the many justified, unjustified even frivolous lawsuits that have plagued this industry. It is in this way that they maintain their billions of float money, and build their beautiful big office buildings.

As with auto accident insurance, or product liability suits, many plaintiffs who sense the chance of a financial windfall are willing to malinger or near-malinger to win a lawsuit. This is common knowledge.

Of course there is a need for such insurance. Of course their are legitimate claims. Of course they should be litigated. That in no way detracts from the points made here. If anything, it increases the magnitude of the moral error, and the need to somehow control the litigation excesses.

To my knowledge, what actually happens concerning control of suspected claims abuse is a rare check by someone who has an interest, a job description to determine misuse by the provider. I have never read of any charge of abuse or misuse brought against an attorney, although I am sure this has occurred. Not only are those policing this area spread thin, to my knowledge, they do not have sufficient ability or franchise to prosecute malingering, courtroom abuses and opportunism.

There is still considerable risk for a layperson to try to expose someone. Some of these plaintiffs' attorneys often have considerable sums invested in their clients, and they are not about to lose this ventured capital. During the long wait for a monetary court settlement, often client and attorney become more like business partners.

What agencies are responsible here, if any? Who if anyone can bring abusers to account in the face of strong legal opposition, such as threats of defamation of character suits, and powerful organized opposition. This information is no secret. Many know about it only too well. So far, all seem powerless to bring about real reform.

Considering the medical provider aspects, their are entire tiers of providers, usually physicians or chiropractors. There is a group who rapidly push patients through, treating them for extended periods. Money is their game. There is a group of dedicated physicians who have the ability and integrity to give a just informed medical opinion. How is the patient to know in whose hands he or she finds themselves? Outcomes research, mentioned in the introduction and described later, is badly needed here.

A Worker's Compensation
Insurance Example

Consider an example. A person reaching far overhead, managing some heavy boxes, suffers a muscle sprain in the muscles of the neck, arms, and back, resulting in severe persistent arm, shoulder, and back pain associated with headache. Such a headache is usually due to occipital muscle spasm (back of neck). Muscle and associated fibrous tissue pain is so severe and so persistent, that it really seems much worse than it is. Severe pain that persists for five or six months is enough to alarm anyone.

This patient goes to their chiropractor, they get the usual X-rays, are told they have a subluxed vertebrae and more treatments are advised. The person is unable to work, and gets no better. The husband thinks something more should be done. They go to an attorney who recommends litigation. Now the action begins. On hearing of this, the industrial insurance company immediately changes from a treatment to an adversary stance.

Understand I have no proof of this. It may not be so, but in many years as a physician I have seen these same effects appear to happen again and again. It makes sense that the referring insurance person would refer to the source that best suited the purpose at hand. If such a situation is nothing else, it is an adversary situation. This is a shame.

The patient is notified to appear for a consultation examination by a physician in a nearby city. This person is their "hatchet man." While the physician may well be expressing an honest opinion, there is a history known of this physician's opinions about such matters. This doctor tells the patient there is nothing wrong with her, and to return to work. Even though this is what they do in the army with a similar case, perhaps, this does not go over well here.

This is an example of how important it is to get in the correct hands if you happen to have a complex or unresponding industrial injury. Go to the best specialist you can find. Chances are good the industrial insurance company hangs on that person's every word, and will do exactly what that specialist says. These insurance companies are starved for input from physicians of ability and integrity.

This is not to imply that the employers are blameless. Some are heartless and need a dose of employees' rights. All this is a ghastly business to many physicians who prefer to have nothing to do with it. The same goes with other accidental injuries. The system is fundamentally unsound, heavily politically motivated. Those who misuse the system flagrantly often have the political and legal muscle in place before beginning. A few who abuse the system are caught. This is not easy.

The more common and more subtle abuses, the persistently painful knees, backs or necks, these people who are no longer able to work and are drawing compensation or waiting for there "settlement" are so common most of us know of one. Some are indeed unable to work, yet this is a relative matter. Many an Army recruit, would love to be in their place. Some win large sums in court aided by medical experts receiving thousands of dollars a day for their testimony, and by lawyers risking their capital with the expectation of large fees.

It is no secret the industrial insurance program could stand improvement. This kind of thing could save us all millions were it made part of the Safety Net Hospital-Clinic system.

Some workers with injuries become hot potatoes for their employers. The very efforts of activists have often been unreasonable and thoughtless enough to backfire and produce the opposite effect intended. So often an employer, or supervisor who would with compassion help an injured employee to find a competent physician is instead frightened by the prospect of unreasonable consequences, and is relieved to pass the injured person and the contingent responsibility to the most available healing facility. Frequently this is one who has a sign posted in the workplace.

Although well meaning, the heavy unreasonable hand of OSHA has occasionally become a frightening menace among those who must endure it. Industrial accident law is similar. It is written by and for the legal and insurance professions. A supervisor or employer never knows how opportunistic an injured employee will become. So these unreasonable rules produce fear as they were intended to do. This does not bring about intelligent compliance.

Objective, experienced specialists in psychology, suitable psychological testing, medical experts in disability and rehabilitation whose mandate is to steer the alleged injured back to work or to health would go a long way toward a solution. Many are employed now. Hopefully they will be used more and more. Removal of the hope for monetary rewards and contingent fees would save the society billions. When these same experts operate in an adversary situation where the climate is to win or lose money, the system is doomed to fail. Many of those involved know this. What they do not know is how to stop the entrenchment.

A simple solution would be to have all such matters handled by the SNHC (Safety Net Hospital-Clinic) for "free." An accurate determination of ability to return to work, and return to work quickly (just as was learned with combat neurosis), coupled with some counseling, and without the expectation of monetary reward, would be good for all. This monetary reward virus would be difficult to eradicate, but it could be done. The society could come in time to view such problems as entirely medical matters, not at all legal ones. Expectations could be changed over time for the benefit of all.

Utilization Review

Consider another example. Consider an insurance person who starts a utilization review company. Whether this is a person who became experienced in the insurance billing game by working for an insurance company, or for a physician is immaterial. Of some ethical significance, I suppose, is whether that person was trained at that employer's expense. Is that utilization review person an adequate mentor?

Does a utilization review person sit in while the patient is getting their proctoscopic exam, take a look down the proctoscope, and with medical knowledge decide that the physician was justified in biopsying what the pathologist later decided was a benign polyp?

No, these persons are paper shufflers who believe they can make more money by being self-employed. Even if they were physicians, they could not have been privy to why some medical decision was made. Who will pay this extra cost? Can such people make enough money for themselves, and save enough money for their employer to reduce the ultimate medical cost? Only some middle management paper shuffler could believe that. How could anyone believe that, unless they believe either the physician or the insurance company are real crooks. There may be some, but not enough.

Only if there are some really big physician crooks out there would this begin to make sense. Such acts by employers are surely acts of desperation. Perhaps they were partially right. More likely we have a plethora of petty crooks on all sides. Sadly each is driving the other's petty crookedness. The crooks out there are not just the patients and the physicians, they are those in the middle, skimming off a bit too, having no business being there in the first place, who think they can outwit and control.

The basic immorality is the attempt to control and coerce in the first place. The underlying mistake is the wedge this drives between physician and patient. The people who are being taken are you and me. The people who are wrong, are those who did not foresee this in the first place. Perhaps they were dulled by power, or power and ideology. Perhaps they were dull in the beginning before they came to power. Their answer is to control by decree from a distance and to institute this incrementally.

Consider the notion of medical rationing. What a can of worms this could become. One regulatory excrescence will pile on another. And today's politicians, what do they know about medical science? How can they be best advised? This problem can be worked out best by physician and patient, trustful and responsible each to the other.

What Are We to Do?

Only physicians and patients working together, trusting together, can do this job. This can best be done in the absence of outside interference, and with a facing of facts by physician and patient alike against the background of free competition and a medical care safety net. Only in this way can patient and physician alike be forced to each face up to their responsibilities. The patient must pay the rightful cost and the physician must charge a realistic fee. Patients must be able to rely with confidence on the physician's judgment, and the physician must be able to rely on the patients maturity and good sense.

If one thinks about this, it is difficult to come to any other conclusion. This mutual confidence can only come through physician and patient trust; and each must have the freedom to go elsewhere. Any third party's best interest is to denigrate, to exert a bit of control albeit subtly, even unwittingly, into the trust between patient and physician.

No third party can possibly know the details of the patient's experience or the physician's knowledge and skill. Patient trust and physicians' professional ethics holding that trust to be sacred is the only way medical care can be practiced. Those who try to drive a wedge between patient and physician should be recognized for what they are. They are opportunists at best, regardless of how well meaning they may be or appear to be.

Cost shifting by such third parties continues to try to paper over these realities. Naturally it is to their advantage to sell the idea they know best, and to instill the notion the physician or the patient are perhaps suspect. The stupidity, the political opportunism, the hope for something for nothing that brought in a third party payee in the first place is an example of the irresponsible and short sighted greed and opportunism that is at the bottom of all this aspect of the "medical cost crisis." This greed, this opportunism, these irrational expectations exist on all sides. First recall that all this started because physicians' freedom was threatened by government socialists.

Yet there is a need for a refuge, for a source of care for everyone. That is what the sections in this book about "A Solution" are all about.

■ *CHAPTER FOUR*

Risk

We must recognize the interdependent complexity and implicit uncertainty in such a process as any professional doctor-patient interaction. And we must find pragmatic ways to cope with this fuzzy information thrust upon us by reality. When we seek to assess biological functions precisely, we are confounded. Like the future, no prediction can be made with certainty. We are confounded by our need for simplicity, for certainty, for we are far from knowing all that constitutes a living organism. Uncertainty, risk and just plain bad luck (whatever that is) haunt us. Both patient and physician face risks.

Risk is the likelihood of an untoward event. Said another way, risk is the probability of an untoward event given a set of conditions. Used as a noun, risk is the state of being exposed to injury, pain or loss.

The attempt to remove risk below what is realistically practical is expensive and futile. For the medical care system, the false presumption that no risk is acceptable has been stimulated mostly by the intervention, the intrusion of powerful third parties who have deftly shifted the attitude of the public on this and similar matters. Medical care costs have risen astronomically as a result. The subterfuge of zero risk is one of the most used and most costly of polemic deceptions. (Polemic refers to winning thru argument, thru debating and such adversarial skills).

Risk is reality. Risk in connection with human lives is particularly important because risk cannot be eliminated. Risk follows rigorous laws. In any act, what risk there is, there is. It does not matter whether a dime or a life hangs in the balance.

Mistakes will occur. Yet risk reduction is essential. We can assess, even quantitate the risk in a given situation, depending on our ability, given that situation, to assess conditional probabilities. A conditional probability simply means given this, what is the probability of that.

For example, given it is September, what is the probability, the chance, the risk of rain? What is the probability it will rain, given the condition it is September?

Expressing risk in terms of conditional probabilities enables us to use more precise quantitative expressions (through the use of a mathematical expression called Bayes theorem). With today's computers such important calculations are done easily. For example, you are told you must have an operation. Now you can know in exacting numerical terms the risk to you of your physician doing the surgery at your hospital compared with the norm, or even compared with that hospital down the street, or in the next town.

Carelessness in medical practice is not condoned in any form. Care, concern and strict accountability are essential. Yet risk cannot be reduced below a certain point; and as that point is approached, risk reduction becomes more costly and uncertain, and finally impossible to reduce further.

Today, when a catastrophe happens, regardless of the risk assessment, whether that be the space shuttle, the Valdez oil spill or some untoward medical care result; someone must pay; and pay means much money preferably, of which thirty to forty percent goes to the lawyer. There is a pathological aspect of this culture that goes to work to find a victim to blame, regardless of how far fetched; so long as an insurance company or some deep pocket can be hooked for this money.

Corporations that lose a lawsuit simply pass the loss back to the stockholders, or their customers. They add it to the cost of doing business, or the corporation declares bankruptcy. No individual in the corporation is stuck; but the winning lawyers and plaintiffs get their windfall. You and I of course ultimately pay the bill, even though it is indirectly removed from us.

Risk Assessment; Risk Zones

Given it is possible to precisely calculate the risk, risk can be expressed as a number. Then this number can be compared to some other risk number. These risk numbers are relative terms. They need to be referenced to something. As mentioned above, we should soon be able to express physician's performance quantitatively—as a number. We might say your risk from gall bladder surgery is 2, your risk from driving to Chicago 1, so your surgery risk is twice that of driving to Chicago. This may seem elementary unless one realizes the great precision with which these numbers can now be derived.

What is the conditional probability this patient is an average risk patient given the set of conditions, the variables, this patient presents? What is the personal risk for the patient? What is the personal risk for the physician? What about this patient or physician increases or decreases the risks involved? Given this physician and this set of environmental conditions (in which the doctor will perform the procedure), what is the probability the outcome will equal, exceed or fall below the average risk for the area? What is the probability of unforeseen or chance conditions affecting the outcome? That indeed is the risk.

Even simplistic examples like the risk of driving across a street, at once bring to mind complications. What kind of driver? What kind of street? These apparent defects are more easily surmounted than one would expect, even though the risk assessment becomes more complicated.

Consider another example, given this automobile, on this highway, in this weather, with this driver, what is the probability, the chance, of this type of accident? Notice there are really three sets of conditions. One set which we might call the "state variables," concern the auto, the highway, etc. Then there is a set of outcomes: There is a chance of this type of accident or that type of accident. Finally there is the set of prior conditions. What is the chance that things we already know for certain will effect the outcome? Perhaps the driver is ninety years old. All this information is entered into a computer spreadsheet and "worked-over" (parsed) by a computer and some mathematical wizardry into a number. A complex risk assessment of this type may fill a large spreadsheet matrix of many thousand cells.

This science of risk analysis, along with outcomes research, is now being introduced into medical quality control practices. As with many endeavors, these performance profiles will gain in accuracy and acceptance. But before this science can advance, punishing, adversary proceedings must be radically altered. Once this risk for the physician is removed, more open approaches to individual physician shortcomings can be made, yet stringent methods must be used to assure physician skill and accountability.

Lying in bed at home in a quite village, one is in a very different risk zone than flying comfortably first-class on a transatlantic flight, or lying on an operating table. We must become more aware of the practical aspects of this reality.

Their is a heavy storm at sea, even though the risks change appreciably, it does not necessarily follow the captain becomes any less competent—especially any more culpable! And so it is with the practice of medicine.*

So risk can be expressed as a number. And, for every increment in risk reduction beyond a certain level, the effort and the costs go up increasingly. These increasing efforts yield ever decreasing increments of risk reduction, until the risk reduction beyond some practical point is illusory. Ample illustrations of this may be found in today's private hospitals. Treat enough people in or out of a hospital, and there are bound to be mistakes. There are bound to be errors, injuries and deaths. We all accept this when we get into an automobile. Wash enough dishes, and you will break one. Was that negligence? When does it become punishable negligence? What would, what should such punishment accomplish?

There is no doubt that all untoward occurrences should be minimized. Every effort should be made to do so. But there is no doubting reality either. Too often junk

---

* Those who prefer a mathematical treatment of this subject should see Kaplan S., Frank M.V., Bley D.C., and Lindsay D.G., COPILOT, AN EXPERT SYSTEM FOR REACTOR OPERATION-AL ASSISTANCE, USING A BAYESIAN DIAGNOSTIC MODULE, in Reliability Engineering and System Safety, vol.22, p.411-440, 1988. Related references are listed in the Suggested readings.

science, and determinations based on the current fashionable or powerful hysteria prevail over medical fact, or even reality.

It bears repeating that an inordinately high percentage of money and effort is spent trying to make some of these misconceptions about risk appear true or believable. This is a cost of medical care that should be curtailed. A high percentage of all effort, a high percentage of medical cost is spent in this inefficient way.

Over-training is another aspect of this issue. The multitude of efforts to prevent, to anticipate, defend or cover-up what is or may appear to be an error demands a price in morale as well as money. Malpractice litigation introduces a need to cover-up mistakes, and it is entirely inadequate at prevention of them.

All this is a tremendous deterrent to the development of accurate risk assessment, good medical quality control, and prevention of potential harm due to ineptness. This is not to imply that ineptness and callousness do not occur. They do. There are crazy doctors out there. The medical profession is in the best position to detect and correct this, however.

When physicians can be shown statistically their skills are subpar, they can be convinced of the need for retraining in deficient areas, or the acquiring or changing of specialization, or the removal of themselves from clinical medicine altogether. (There are plenty of other non-clinical positions for physicians.)

A psychological atmosphere of idealism can be cultivated for the good of all. It could slowly come to replace the atmosphere of fear and hatred poisoning doctor-patient relationships now.

Introducing monetary punishments, financial opportunism, adversarial situations, no matter how modified, have failed and they will fail. Instead most physicians need rather to come together, and in a non-punitive inquiring manner face up to their position in a risk assessment, or some aspect of outcomes research. Outcomes research means inquiry into such things as why is the mortality rate from a given procedure higher in some hands than in others, whether this be a hospital, an individual physician, or even a given geographical area?

There are other risks for the patient, depending on the seriousness of that patient's reality situation (meaning how serious that person's illness is), and the risks implicit in the necessary diagnostic and treatment procedures. The patient is scared, and may have a very good reason for being so. For the patient is cognizant of the risks even if this is subliminal. When we are patients, we ask "How serious is this, doctor?" "How can it be stopped?" "Should I get a second opinion?" "Who should I see?"

Fear arouses fear. These days the physician assumes risks too, sometimes these are in proportion to the patient's type of illness. But there may be risks for the physician that have nothing to do with the reality of the patient's illness. Is the patient hostile? Of a personality type to project blame? Is the patient a bit paranoid, dependent, suit-prone, seductive, violent?

Sometimes in today's medical setting, the physician is as frightened of the patient as the patient is of the doctor. Let such a couple get into a really tight, serious medical emergency, and the physician's fears of the mounting risks may hamper his coolness, his ability. This is frequently in proportion to that doctor's sensitivity. This may feed back and arouse patient fear and hence increased risk.

The patient has so little help available to furnish accurate information about that physician's technical competence. Once assessed, how can this risk be minimized?

We will discuss practical aspects of this later when the idea of double TRIAGE is developed in the section about solutions. These very important aspects of medical care seem to be overlook in today's third party obsession with money, with insurance. One wonders why.

If the legal forces have the power, the polemic upper hand, why not develop a situation where both types of behavior coexist as competitive alternatives? Let the type of quality control and outcomes research introduced above flourish in the Safety Net Hospital-Clinics. They become a refuge for patient and physician alike. Let malpractice control exist elsewhere among the other medical care options as it now does. Then over time observe the results.

Chance, Risk and Responsibility

A physician acquaintance had an appointment to perform a minor office surgical procedure on a patient that he had known for years. The patient died of an acute coronary occlusion minutes before getting in the car for the quick drive to make the appointment. One could build a plausible and instructive scenario around this had the patient died just a few minutes later on the office operating table.

Now to other examples. The outpatient, the hospital patient, the accident victim etc. are treated as if they had no responsibility in their illness. Patients may be endangered if in the hospital the atmosphere prevails that no patient is responsible to watch out for hazards themselves.*

* See Feilich, B. THE DEATH OF A BABY: NEITHER FORGIVEN OR FORGOTTEN, in Letters to the Editor, JAMA 1992; 268:1413-1414.

Now, at your great expense, the hospital must treat you constantly as a potential lawsuit. They know full well that mistakes will happen; or the appearance of mistakes will happen. You are surrounded by staff people, who treat you as if you could not be held accountable or responsible for anything but the bill. That too my be covered by insurance. Again to your great expense, you are surrounded by a myriad of overlapping liability insurance policies, and by a host of college degrees. Chances are good that you are surrounded by many more employees than are necessary.

Suppose a person choked to death on a piece of meat while eating at home. That person perhaps had a couple of drinks before eating. Suppose the same thing happened in a restaurant. Suppose that person, completely sober, and having taken no medicines did the same thing their first preoperative night in a hospital. Now the risk of dying would have been lowest in the hospital; but the risk of a lawsuit would have been highest there. In each of these situations the choking could have occurred in an unguarded instant. In the hospital, however, the expectations have been pushed to such unrealistic heights that every patient is expected to be guarded every second. More than one person, then, is at risk: the patient, and those caring for the patient.

Putting aside for the moment the notion of incidence, physicians, being human, will make mistakes, just like we all do. No amount of training and care can eliminate this completely. One-half of all surgeons are sued for malpractice sometime in their career. Because of the nature of their work, some of these mistakes will cause death or some other catastrophic result in rare instances. For the individuals involved, of course, it is not rare. How are we to handle these facts of life? The answer is to develop a situation that minimizes these risks, including adequate accountability to be as sure as we can they are minimized. Then we must all face the fact that this is the best we can do. We can only minimize the risks.

Consider the uncertainty implicit in making a diagnosis. In medical diagnosis there is little certainty. Does this patient with an acutely painful belly have appendicitis? The physician is never certain. That physician's situation at any point is best expressed as a probability. We say he or she has X degree of confidence. As time progresses, each new piece of evidence (or lack of it) can change this degree of confidence in a given diagnosis. How much of the patient's money should be spent for more tests? How much risk is there in waiting, in not waiting?

That degree of confidence can be expressed as a number. That number brings together all the many bits of information and judgment calls made and focuses them into a useful quantity. Each new bit of evidence or lack of it will move the physician toward certainty along some course.

For example we calculate one course of action and so have that number. Now we carefully gather the bits of information of another possible course of action and focus that into a number. One has now but to compare the two. The trick is how to bring these bits of information together with a spreadsheet and Bayes theorem.

One of the virtues of the Bayesian approach is that this mathematical formula explicitly tells us, quantitatively, the degree of certainty (or uncertainty) present at any stage of the endeavor. Another piece of information might radically shift these numbers. This can be shown dramatically if the computer program is also designed to redraw a graphic representation of the situation each time a new piece of information is added. Remember certainty is not guaranteed, only a clearer view of the degree of certainty or uncertainty. At what level of certainty is one to assume a given risk?

Who Takes Risks?

Who wants to take any chance with their life? The answer may startle you. The answer is everyone. Everyone who gets into a car, an airplane, on a bicycle, on a motorcycle, into a bathtub, anyone who crosses the street, anyone who swims. Common sense would tell you that we could arrange that list in order of relative risk. Such risks are perceived as reasonable for reasonable care will minimize them, whereas for a physician many malpractice risks are not considered reasonable at all in the sense they are not neutral, reasonable care will not minimize them.

We build wide divided roads and require speed limits to minimize the hazards of driving. We could minimize further the risks of death on the highway by requiring all trucks to use separate roads. This society has decided for many reasons not to do this. In this sense we are putting a monetary value on a life. We could stop all risk from driving, of course by discontinuing all driving. Should society say that physicians should not presume to take a life in their hands, and forbid all medical care? Should physicians be kept in a position where they avoid all risky medical care? We are moving rapidly toward this even though we as a society believe that doing this would increase the risk of loss of life.

Where is the optimum risk zone? How is it to be achieved? How are we to deal with this problem? Medicine's problems are not unique to medicine alone.

They are aspects and reflections of emerging widespread problems of the society. Any cure for the high cost of medicine must see medicine's ills as a symptom of widespread defects and misdirections of contemporary society. Certainly all parties desire to minimize the incidence of untoward events occurring within the medical care situation.*

The Concepts of Risk Zones and Risk Limits

There is little awareness of the possibility that there now exists the ability to arrive at precisely developed risk zones within which reality is accepted. From this, risk limits can be calculated, which then become guidelines to help assess incompetence more accurately. We can greatly reduce medical care risks by more effectively removing incompetents of course, yet we must be more cognizant of the shifting risk zones that are an integral part of medical practice. All this has a direct bearing on costs as well as safety.

Examples of Zero Risk Damage

Years ago, as a family physician, I helplessly watched as a pregnant mother and her young son both died of polio within a week.

It was spring, our children were dying of polio every summer. A polio vaccine saved fifty thousand lives the first year it was introduced. It was hastily introduced after

* See "The Double Edge of Knowledge," JAMA Aug. 14, 1991, Vol.266 No.6, pp.841

it's discovery by Jonas Salk, because we knew many would see their children die in the next summer epidemic. However, one life was lost from a reaction to that vaccine out of an extremely large number of immunizations. Does it make sense to sue and permanently damage a company that made the vaccine? That is what happened.

Thousands of children would have died without it. There are many of you who remember this era. That vaccine was made under strict standards laid down by a government body. Standards, I am told, the company pointed out to the governing agency were inadequate; but the vaccine had to be distributed quickly. There were severe risks in either direction.

The enormous financial success this concept has brought some trial attorneys is balanced by the loss to society. That was just the beginning. Over the years, similar law suits have followed. Vaccines for our children are very difficult to get manufacturers to make now. When they do make them, ninety percent of the cost goes for malpractice protection. This zero risk concept has not only made it nearly impossible to get vaccines made for our children, it has spread to the entire medical political arena. An acceptance of the concept of the practical use of carefully calculated and developed risk zones is urgent.

The dangerous retrovirus know as the HIV which causes what we call AIDS is spreading. There is no known cure. There is no prevention. I am told a prominent drug company now has a promising vaccine for AIDS. They refuse to start human trials unless and until they are given iron-clad indemnification. But no one can control all of the legal profession's trial attorneys. The country is power-less. No one is willing to assume the risk.

A drug has been discovered which effects remission of that terrible mental disease called schizophrenia. Its effects are miraculous; but in rare instances it causes destruction of the patient's white blood cells. The company who markets this drug would not sell a prescription for it without including the cost of a mandatory white blood cell count. Much pressure has been brought on the company to discontinue this demand, and so lower the cost of the drug. This is another of the many indications of the practical damage to society the present malpractice litigation crisis is producing.

If the nation will not accept risk, then their will be vigilante type reactions that will reverberate throughout the society. You can begin to see some of the reasons for the high cost of drugs, and the virtual stoppage of live vaccines. Paradoxically, this insistence on zero risk has enormously increased the cost in terms of human life, as well as money. How much of a showdown will be required?*

* Kassirer, J.P. "Malpractice And The Quest For Certainty." New Eng Med J vol. 320, No.22, pp.1489.

CHAPTER FIVE

Doctors and Lawyers

Introduction

To reform our medical costs, we must first understand them.

Cutting costs implies sacrifice and change. Yet there is one area where medical costs could be cut nearly a third without impairing or denying medical care at all. This is the area of medical errors and omissions known as malpractice. That term and its popularization is itself a clever polemic ploy.

Being a very patriotic person, I have great respect for our system of jurisprudence, and I have an acute sense for injustice. When any of us feel strongly we have been bullied or unjustly treated, when we find ourselves caught in some mess, then the courts, and their attorneys are very essential. Also physicians are important when we need them. Both professions must be improved.

Some of my best friends are attorneys, my very best friend is a Superior Court judge, yet as I continued to study and to write on this subject, as I began to reflect over my past forty years of relations with these two professions, medicine and law, I was distraught at my emerging outrage. Worse, this feeling (more than I had realized) is shared very strongly by most every physician with whom I have talked.

The whole of medical practice, of Doctor-patient relations have been distorted, skewed by this aberration, through most of my lifetime. This has been true here more so than in most any other country.

As some politicians, economists and a myriad of others join some insurance meddlers, and begin to back physicians into a corner with their sundry schemes dictating what this esoteric medical field should constitute, if they finally draw real fire, bitter resistance, it will, I predict, evolve around the malpractice issue.

As I worked on this book, it became obvious that medical cost reform was only one aspect of the problem. The medical cost crisis coexists with a legal cost crisis.

There also is a loss of public confidence, and a public cynicism born of a hopelessness, that only gross injustice can bring. I was surprised to find this so strong among the business groups with whom I talked. Yet, it will do little good to smear accusations.

The Game of Court

In a fairyland we shall call Always Ever Land, The Game Of Court is played. This Game Of Court is often played for power and money. It requires two or more victims. It is played by three people called lawyers, one of whom is called a judge. The court is their playpen. They are quite familiar with it, and in fact get paid well for being in it. Anyone else (even to some extent what is called an expert witness) is an outsider, especially the victims who must pay dearly for being there. Their are twelve conscripted players. They are called a jury. In Always Ever Land, the jury, with the judge's guidance has the ability, usually based on the emotional aspects of the proceeding, to decide anything. They can do this, no matter how complex the presentation, and regardless of their education, intelligence or attention span, and especially regardless of their hidden agenda. The lawyers try to determine these hidden agendas each for their own purpose. The judges may have a hidden agenda too, hidden even from themselves; but important stuff for the trial attorneys of the area to determine.

The lawyers are the persuaders. Their job is to persuade the jury, and/or the judge that they each are the one with the correct argument. This may have no basis in fact since the lawyers pride themselves on being able to take either side and win. The opposing lawyers may be friends, but when playing the Game Of Court they play the Game Of Adversary. They take pride in this duplicity.

To win means to convince the jury your side is correct. This is called justice. The game is played for control and money. In Always Ever Land, power will bring you money. But because of the Game Of Court, money without courtroom power brings one vulnerability.

One way to get a substitute for power may be purchased. This is called insurance. In Always Ever Land to have money is looked upon with "enfavor." "Enfavor" means disfavor arising from envy. Those who are most free in one sense are those with no money to lose. The successful producers tend to work themselves away from liberty.

Contingent Fees and Quality Medical Care

Contingent fees as used in this book refer to the present practice of taking a *substantial percentage* of the plaintiff's winnings, depending on the outcome of a trial.*

What contingent fees really do is give lucrative business opportunities to some attorneys. I am told they usually select those malpractice cases which promise a large monetary return for which they are willing to take the financial risk. Contingent fee-compensated plaintiffs attorneys become in a sense venture capitalists of the court room. Once having risked their capital, such attorneys are under pressure to recover it. That personal financial stake in the winnings is exactly the source of many abuses, and it is about this situation, it is within this context, that the term contingent fees is used herein.

Were a not-rich patient to have a desperate case of compensible error due to frank medical negligence, but winning that lawsuit would gross less than $250,000.00, I am told many such patients would have a difficult time finding a plaintiff's attorney to take the case. Like any venture capitalist the reward must be great to justify the risk. Whether the plaintiff is poor, has very little to do with such case selection or refusal. This is about financial opportunism.

Trial of tort cases by jury is not perfect, but it is the most entrenched and lucrative process found to date. Add to this the contingent fee practice, coupled with junk science, and we have evolving an institutionalized major

---

* Any codifying of legal procedures, affixing a fee for a given time or procedure, similar to the medical Relative Value Fee Schedule might still be called a contingent fee, if this fee were assessed the losing party only. That is not what is meant when the words contingent fee are used in this book.

disruption of our social order. This has direct bearing on the increasing cost of medical care.

It is discouraging to write about what contingent fee tort abuses are doing to much of society. Most of us already know this. The problem is we are powerless to change it. The problem is power. Peter Huber* said something to the effect that this is a profession bent on control, that their thrust was starting fires, not extinguishing them.

Lawyers are only human. They naturally act in their own best interest, and they have ways of rationalizing that what they are doing is for the benefit of the patient and of society.

The legal profession and the medical profession tend to attract students of very different personalities, persuasions and personal goals. Both professions charge too much, put too much emphasis on monetary gain, and not enough emphasis on their idealistic roots. A more responsible social order would correct this.

Often attorneys are in a position to benefit from exploitation, pitting parts of society against each other, even changing cultural mores. Often they are in a position to benefit by duplicity, by creating complication, waste and delay. This and crowded court calendars have the unfortunate result that many such trials are held years after the events in question. For the attorneys' purposes the actual medical events themselves often have little usefulness. Their job is to build a plausible argument.

For physicians and their patients such action is a very big step in the wrong direction. As science and technology advance apace, much of our legal process has been outmoded when applied to these areas. Much of the legal

---

* Peter Huber, GALILEO'S REVENGE: JUNK SCIENCE IN THE COURT ROOM, BASIC BOOKS, 1991 PP. 22-23.

profession have reacted to this, as they have in the past, by ignoring scientific truths. Clever lawyers invent ways to start and to win lawsuits.

Under the common law Frye rule, (1923) determination of what is appropriate scientific evidence is based on scientific evidence arising from a theory or method *generally accepted by the scientific community*. The Federal Rules of Evidence of 1975 appear to reject this. A recent Supreme Court Decision would appear to burnish these Federal Rules a bit.*

In the malpractice arena, injury, untoward events, and physician incompetence are monetized by this system; yet doctors are not sued for incompetence, they are sued for negligence. What the court does, then, is first determine the presence of what it calls negligence; and then it determines how much money should be paid to redress this. The lucrative presumption is that any redress can be reduced to some large monetary sum.

A psychotic obstetrician-gynecologist removed a woman's uterus and then, for no reason, removed a part of her stomach. Being a bright paranoid schizophrenic, he retaliated with defamation of character suits against physicians and staff members' attempts to remove him from the hospital staff, and revoke his license. Eventually the woman sued for malpractice and won. The issue of psychosis, medical license removal, and commitment were issues that remained for other proceedings. During all this time he continued to practice.

* Interested readers should refer to Bernstein, D.E. JUNK SCIENCE IN THE COURT ROOM, Wall Street Journal, March 24, 1993., and also to an article in the Journal of the American Academy of Science as follows: Koshland, D.E.JR. GET RICH QUICK SCIENCE, Science, vol.259;1993,p1103.

Nearly the only aspect of medical science involved in this comes from the adversarial exchange between what is called expert witnesses. These are sometimes professionals, including physician witnesses who play in the game for money.

Would it be better to outlaw contingent fees, and produce a fee schedule for attorneys similar to the one developed for physicians? As you perhaps chuckle over this naive question, realize how your mirth illustrates the difference in political power of the two professions.

If contingent fees are so essential for the legal rights of the poor, the development of a safety net legal service similar to the one postulated for physicians later in this book would care for the poor and many others as well, and offer a valid alternative. The law should be about civil order, and of course justice, not about windfall monetary awards for attorneys. We are moving in the opposite direction. This is a system that is well along the way to redistribution and brokerage of the nations wealth and prerogative. This system of course is banked by the insurance industry, a most fortuitous symbiosis.

Anyone who attempts to solve the medical cost crisis must have powerfully effective strategies for solving these types of plaintiff attorney crises.

It makes little difference to a physician whether that attorney is on the defense or plaintiff side. They are both lawyers. The medical-legal defense attorney (usually hired by an insurance company) must win or lose at The Game Of Court. The real medical facts of the case may well be beyond the players of this game.

Consider an example. A physician being sued for an outrageously incorrect reason—that of being the deepest pocket—was instructed by his insurance-company-appointed defense attorney, at one stage of the proceedings, to answer only yes or no. The doctor was disciplined not to appear to instruct about the facts of the case, but to let the attorney win the case. The attorney cautioned he would interrupt the proceedings by calling for a recess if the physician disobeyed those instructions. It is painful for a physician to realize that in court the real facts of the case may be considered irrelevant.

There is no way a monetary award to plaintiff and attorney can punish a physician correctly, retrain, improve or remove that physician. If the patient suffered death, or debility, or pain; money does little to really redress this either. Perhaps the error or omission could have been prevented. At present bad physicians are practicing when they should not be, and good physicians are being harassed for money.

A physician truly guilty of an egregious act is most certainly a menace. Attorneys or malpractice trials really do not have the ability to know, or to determine whether a physician is a menace. They restrict themselves to the point of negligence charged. Why do you suppose they persist with this, plus the contingent fee-money redress formula? One reason is they manage to "convict" many excellent physicians who just happened to be in the wrong situation at the right time, the attorney collects the insurance money and both physician and attorney continue on.

Top-notch physicians in our medical schools have more risk exposure to these lawsuits because they deal with more difficult or desperate cases. More and more physicians are quietly backing away from these desperate situations. You will never know if it happens to you.

The tendency now is to charge a physician just days before the statue of limitations expires, and drag the pre-trial proceedings on, giving more lawyers work. The actual trial may well be held years after the episode in question. The aim of each side is to manufacture an argument for their benefit.

Remember what happened is not necessarily actually what was reconstructed in the courts often years later, nor do the decisive actions that convinced the judge or jury necessarily have any connection with what really happened. Nor are they any measure of physician competence, as has been shown time and time again. What really happened may well be beyond the ability of every lay person in the courtroom to understand. Expert witnesses know this; so do attorneys. The whole thing is about money and control, and the sacred adversarial process.

Almost without exception, that money came from the physician's insurance policy, paid for more or less directly from a portion of every patient's medical fees. Patients are the monetary victims of malpractice litigation, physicians are the emotional victims.

So malpractice lawsuits only make physicians practice defensive medicine, for which the patient pays. How can judges, attorneys and juries set standards for medical care, when even a physician of another specialty would be hard put to do so? Now we are contemplating empowering insurance companies to set standards for our medical care.*

If this business were stopped, there would be no decrease in the quality of medical care, none at all. More than likely an improvement would result. This would be an improvement in the quality, mind you, not just the cost.

---

* Whether this is done directly or slyly, incrementally, indirectly, the result will be the same, Patients will be shooting themselves in the foot.

Quality of medical care would be far better assured by a viable, term-limited peer review group; consisting of physicians, nurses, knowledgeable hospital staff, and lay people, perhaps patients who had undergone similar procedures. The virtue of their purpose, and utility of their training and experience is obvious. This notion is developed in the solution section.

This peer review group should be freed of fear of the costly defamation of character lawsuits that hamstring them now. Such groups, would work in close coordination with state licensing boards, medical speciality licensing boards, and experienced arbitrators who are physicians. The group should be structured, insofar as possible, to achieve a non-punitive atmosphere so necessary for allowing problems to be worked on openly.

While the adversarial approach has utility in many disputes in our courts, in medical situations, better results evolve from an atmosphere devoid of histrionics, sly deception and melodrama implicit in an adversarial proceeding. Remember, solving medical problems, even medical disputes are often scientific matters and are best handled as such.

Such peer groups would be better able, to determine a physician's competence and the nature of that physician's actions, if the investigation were conducted promptly. A peer review group can look into that physician's past actions with more perception. The precise extent of that physician's training can be assessed. Data as to that person's scholastic, clinical ability, and character throughout the long period of training, if relevant, would be available and more easily evaluated by such a group.

Prevention too must be emphasized. The emerging outcomes research, followed by correction of physician defects detected in advance in a non-punitive atmosphere offers real promise.

This emerging interest of physicians in outcomes research and investigation should add credence to accepting physician peer review as a method of solving disputes between patients and physicians. Outcomes research means where one physician or group of physician's results (outcomes) are compared with others.

The Expert Witness

It is unlikely that expert witnesses in an adversarial situation are totally candid and objective, regardless of which side they represent. They are polemicists with medical knowledge which they can use or withhold, working in an adversary situation, moving to the baton of the attorney who hired them. Does anyone really believe these experts would offer the same information in an actual medical consultation among physicians?

Again, Peter Huber* indicates that the law discriminates poorly between the opinions of charlatans and Nobelists. Attorneys are frank to declare they would not go into a lawsuit with an objective, uncommitted, expert. In an adversarial situation, an impartial expert witness would be a risky liability.

Expert witnesses are expected to earn their pay. As mentioned in Huber's book, expert witnesses may not work directly for a contingent fee, but these experts are contingent fee players nevertheless, and they know it. Their continued employment and re-employment by

* Loc. cit.

another client depends critically on the strength of the support they can supply. The expert's clients gradually learn they cannot risk going without him or her, for the opposition will surely hire that expert's mirror image clone.

One can find an expert witness, often a physician, who will testify to almost anything. It is not the case that one can get an expert witness to lie. Perhaps the facts presented to that expert contained a little constructive fudging.* So indeed, might his or her testimony. Or maybe this is not the case at all. It is simply a matter of finding the expert with the desired belief. Often it is merely a matter of searching a data base to find a physician, a healer, a nutritionist, a naturopath, etc. with the opinion required, who believes what he or she is testifying, and who can present it convincingly.

Life Is Not the Game of Court

In stark contrast to the legal realm, the physician moves in an entirely different world. A fundamental problem at the bottom of much of the medical care crisis is the lack of appreciation by the populace of this most basic fact. Science and the law do not have the same paradigms.† They might as well be on different planets.‡

* See Mark Twain's delightful essay on lying.

† The term paradigm is from Thomas Kuhn's book "The Structure of Scientific Revolutions."

‡ Those interested should read Pauker, S.G. & Kopelman, R.I. "How Sure Is Sure Enough?", New England Journal of medicine, March 5, 1992, Vol.326, No. 10, pp 688-691. It is worth reading not to understand technical details; but to serve as an illustration of how physicians think.

Life is not the Game Of Court, even though the main players would have it appear to be thus. Not only is a physician's aversion to harming another human great, but there is a very good chance that one of that physician's peers or students will have been on hand at the time. There are few pressures like having to face trained physicians and nurses, competitors, who read your hospital charts, who work with you, are always around you; and who have no interest whatever in covering your mistakes.

Will one physician testify against another if they think there has been incompetence? Absolutely! What an experienced physician who was there thought was wrong, and what a plaintiff's attorney wants to believe, or would have us believe was wrong, are two very different things. Otherwise there would be no case. The physician who witnessed the situation realizing the complicated nature of the events is no fool. That person knows full well the court is an adversary proceeding and some "expert" can make an easy distortion, twisting his or her testimony.

That one physician will not testify against another is not only a plaintiff trial attorney's propaganda. It is a common attorney contrivance to justify keeping those who might testify against that attorney away. It is also a slogan. Slogans here mean sound bites of the court room. They are half truths the legal profession repeat so often they believe them themselves.

Picture some professional polemicist pandering and preening before a group of conscripted lay people, a jury. The jury members are listening with various degrees of attention and understanding, to various degrees of truth, half-truth and distortion, about some event that happened perhaps years before.

From this, jury members are trying to decide some convoluted technical medical issue. The cultivated intimidating air, the protocol, the pomp, does little to sharpen the wits, nor increase the technical acumen of the participants, even though it lends a subliminal but false sense of competence. The authority, the power is real, and it should be respected. It should be strictly reserved for the benefit of society.

Probably none of the jury possess the basic science background necessary for even an elementary understanding of the complexities, judgments and risks implicit in this one issue presented, One wonders how but by power and skillful manipulation could such a travesty ever come about.

The situation has worsened in the past fifty years, and most physicians have neither the time, the interest, nor the ability to fight it. Physicians have been naive enough to give away their power.

The important social issues, then, are not really about how much money a plaintiff and the attorney deserve, or even whether malpractice requiring negligence was committed. Notice the denigrating connotations of the propaganda words "committed," "malpractice" and "negligence." Some attorneys have a way of stirring the dust, then complaining that no one can see.

To the physician, the issues are: Did an act of incompetence or carelessness occur? Or was it a chance occurrence? Could it have happened to anyone? Does it bear on that physician's present or future competence? (Remember there is no certainty. Caring for serious illness is a risky undertaking.) Will money really right the wrong? Once again, this is not a cover-up, of course cases of real negligence occur, and once again a peer review group can dispatch them just as well, usually better than a medically unsophisticated lay court.

Once an act is alleged to be negligent or mistaken, the medical peer reviewers are concerned about a far wider scope of concerns. An important question is how can we as a group of physicians prevent this from ever happening again? This is most definitely the issue, one in striking contrast to the court. Another is why and how did it happen? But this too is not the issue before the courts, and that is exactly the problem.

But physician's issues don't stop even here. Most physicians disagree with the present scope of what is called negligence. The instructions to the jury about the definition of negligence start pure and clear, and then they begin to stretch out like a cloud of smoke until the definition covers most any medical errors and omissions issue that has been presented before the courts and lost.

So physicians' concerns transcend the courts concerns. They seek to know, to better physician ability. The whole thrust of medical science revolves around just such scientific idealistic concerns. The teaching, examining, and licensing functions of the medical profession are without peer.

The medical profession has a long history of performing unpleasant autopsies on persons to study problems having no connection with the courts, to get answers for themselves. To seek what went wrong and why. What went wrong here has a far wider scope than whether some physician was culpable. What was the disease process? What can we learn to reduce further human suffering, and to prolong life? How could another death or untoward result like this be prevented? Such a concern is not only paramount, it is an honored tradition.

Searching for answers to improve medicine flourished at the time of the Salem witch hunts and the McCarthy trials. And it still flourishes as today's courtroom excesses continue.

Win or lose, a malpractice suit smears that physician. The lawsuit is frequently announced as front page news in smaller cities. An acquittal or settlement, if announced at all, appears on the back pages.

Fewer of our young are becoming proficient in the scientific way of thinking, and more are going into less demanding fields, cultivating skills of persuasion, of acquisition, thus lacking even a concept of science. Yet this is truly the age of science and technology. It is an age where more and more is being validated by experimental verification. Complexities undreamed of by our forefathers can be built-up bit by bit, by one ingenious experimentally verified truth fitted to another.

Most physicians want to have respect for the law, and for a just order. But alas, the law has already become far removed from the fundamental tenants of science, especially medical and biological science, and is apt to remain so. In many ways science has a more progressive, superior methodology for the uncovering of new knowledge, and for verifying truth. Yet it is difficult to stay abreast of the rapid developments in medical science even for those in the field.

Science and the law must coexist. It would be for the good of all if this relationship were a mutually helpful one. At least neither should exploit the other. This will take great effort. Each must avoid condescending closure of the mind. Knowledge is power and scientific knowledge is the most powerful at this time. Science must appreciate the law, and lawyers must appreciate science.

Consider another way to approach physician account-ability to patients. Separate physician culpability from patient harm. Handle them separately. Again, let physicians, the defendant physician's true peers, judge and punish. They can know or determine best not only what the defendant physician did; but what he or she lacks, and what it will require to remedy the situation for future patients benefit.

Now consider the patient. Is the person simply ag-grieved or disgruntled? Is this problem a result of prejudice, a misunderstanding, greed, or is there a genuine gripe, an injury, or some combination of these? Perhaps an arbitration body composed of local physicians and local patients and or experienced arbitrators could determine that issue non-punitively, including what should be done about it.

Except monetary exchange would not be the only solution. Nor would the hidden agenda be monetary ex-change. The participants would strive to determine the best way to redress the aggrieved, and to asess the com-petence of that physician. Protection of the populace and care for the patient (plaintiff), not enrichment of the game players would be the aim.

Malpractice Suits at Charity Hospitals

The Los Angeles Times on March 1, 1992 contained an excellent article about medical malpractice suit losses of the Los Angeles County Hospital system. The article criticized the County Board Supervisors for not having a more direct hand in these pay-outs. Some of those criticized said in effect that such matters were too technical for them. They were honest and they were correct. The politicians were criticized, and physicians were criticized directly and indirectly. What the newspaper thought the County Supervisors would or could do about this, other than review the cases, was not stated. Certainly politicians do not understand the many complex technical issues. Certainly the political misdirection and many make-do jobs could not be changed. Too many political debts were being paid.

One wonders about the judges who presided over these cases. The paper made no attempt to name or state the number of the attorneys or judges involved, nor did they name or state the number of the physician defendants.

No indication was given that physicians in the county political system were capable of serving to prevent or battle these lawsuits. Were they working to rectify these admittedly technical matters?

Not one word was written criticizing the excesses of the tort system. Only by implication was there any indirect reference to the defects of the malpractice law system, or how the system might be preying on a teeming charity hospital.

A study of the plaintiffs would have been informative too. According to the paper, the Associate Chief of Staff of the hospital said the staff physicians wanted to keep the lawsuits out of public view. He said the county would have difficulty retaining its staff if it were to identify the doctors who were sued. He was very correct in part. I, for one, would like to see the physicians identified, and as much information as possible about the entire mess brought to public view.

I suspect the number of physicians sued is in fact kept from physicians to give them an illusion of security. If the hospital physicians, especially the volunteer teaching faculty, knew this was going on, many would quit. Many may quit as the result of this newspaper article.

If society is to develop an effective Safety Net Hospital-Clinic system, almost every aspect of what goes on at most present day big city charity hospitals need be taken as a lesson of what not to do. It epitomizes much of what is wrong with the care of the so-called uninsured today, due mostly to political control of medical problems; yet the scientific medical care is first class. The patient load is enormous, but this is not the physician's fault.

Concerning the Los Angeles County Hospital, hundreds of volunteer physicians from all over the Southern California area work very hard to care for its patients. They donate their services to teach, and so the poor receive medical treatment. At the same time a group of malpractice attorneys is skimming millions of dollars from the system.

The millions are desperately needed by the sick and the associated private university, the University of Southern California Medical School, and others. They are barely able to afford to continue their teaching and research activities. Recently USC was forced to close its medical library for lack of funds. What would happen if this training facility simply quit, and went elsewhere for its clinical facilities?

To stand in front of, or wander through the five-story Los Angeles County outpatient building while the clinics are in operation, is to see for oneself what no amount of writing can convey. The masses of people, crippled, bewildered, many not speaking English are waiting outside. Inside there is the same, plus the smells, the fear, the suffering, the futility, the impossibility of caring for this swell of humanity with the present system. The outpatient system according to the Times sees 10,500 patients a day!

The obstetrical service would be more instructive, but an observer would be in the way, especially if they became ill. Women deliver their babies in the halls because the regular hospital beds are full. Women come in off the streets in labor who never had a prenatal visit. Many alien mothers are there in labor, desperate to deliver a U.S. citizen. Tiny premature babies, many doomed to die an expensive death, are born, often to irresponsible mothers, and to careful County Hospital nurses.

Perhaps it would be too much to ask anyone to spend even an hour in the emergency clinic. It should be required of every malpractice case jury member. Emergency is always busy because many irresponsible poor, rather than bother with preventive care, rather than wait at the clinics, perhaps feeling unable to get through the eligibility checks, present as an emergency. By the time they present they are often indeed an emergency.

Suddenly, on this steady swell of patients, intrudes a wave of real emergency patients. Often battlefield conditions instantly take over. The smell of blood, raw flesh and death surrounds one. How is this described in a courtroom?

According to this article, Los Angeles county spent nearly one hundred million dollars on malpractice cases during the past three years. In this three years, 1,364 malpractice claims were filed against the county. A total of 549 cases, some dating back several years, are pending. One-third of the malpractice pay-outs exceeded one hundred thousand dollars each. How many of these cases were won on settlement, never going to trial?

In 1991, the Los Angeles County hospital had 181,000 admissions, 40,963 deliveries, and 317,576 emergency room admissions. It had 3.8 million outpatient visits. In the year 1991, it paid 26.5 million dollars in malpractice costs. New York city's similar Bellvue hospital, with 242,972 admissions, 30,662 deliveries and 1.1 million emergencies in 1991, paid 53.5 million dollars in malpractice expense. In other words, the Los Angeles County Hospital delivered about 112 babies a day, and admitted to the hospital nearly 500 patients a day. The hospital handled in its emergency room on average 870 patients a day. It is of interest to note the differing distribution of patient load between the two hospitals. It would be interesting to calculate the malpractice cost per patient on each of the services. Some statistician could have a field day with all the raw data available.

There is a desperate lack of adequately trained physicians work under what at times can only be described as battlefield conditions. Many of the old volunteer faculty have already been driven away, and many of the interns and residents lack adequate organization and supervision. The thing feeds on itself. How much of this is evident in a courtroom? The newspaper, not the courts, brought this problem to public attention. How much interest do the courts have in solving this problem? Yet, this is a medical problem in the hands of a political process, and a political problem being thrust onto physicians only when it is convenient. Only those actually on the front lines really know the situation well enough to improve it. They have been avoided so far in the attempts at reform.

Look in the mirror to see who pays the costs of this charity hospital care, and of these lawsuits. You will still miss the wrenching of the gut most physicians feel at the ever crowding, at the steady decline.

Malpractice awards underwent an explosive growth during the 1970's and early eighties. These lawsuits have leveled off recently according to this article. Nevertheless, the cost of malpractice settlements and court costs have multiplied seven fold in the past decade to a projected 38 million dollars in 1992. This is more than Los Angeles county paid last year to resolve all other types of litigation combined! Awards and settlements climbed from 5.5 million in fiscal 1980-81 to 17.4 million in 1988-89, $23.7 million in 1989-90 and $26.6 million in 1990-91.

Perhaps this observation will convey an idea of how little real medical facts matter in prevention of these lawsuits. In an excellent teaching institution, according to the Times, four million seven hundred thousand dollars was spent for a private consulting firm—a professional risk management company—to run Los Angeles county's malpractice defense program. Think what *one hundred million dollars* effectively spent on hospital improvement would have achieved: retraining physicians if they were at fault, or correcting the medical delivery system if that were the problem. In fact, money should have been spent, earnestly and effectively, to find and correct all faults, to correct any defects, and especially to prevent whatever was real and preventable.

More about Malpractice Lawsuits

Malpractice suits, not infrequently are caused by a variety of chance circumstances, or by someone disgruntled, or perhaps a savvy person who brings a medical situation to an attorney because it can be won or settled. Or they are caused by an attorney who seeks out such a person, as in the case of the class action suits so popular today. The attorney believes he or she can massage enough money out of the case to make it financially worthwhile. That is the basis on which many of these cases are taken. Most cases of real physician incompetence or abuse are never brought to court. There is no doubt there do occur flagrant cases of abuse that do come to trial; but even if the physician loses, nothing happens but a redistribution of money, mostly from the involved insurance companies.

Extracting money from insurance companies solves little. Many cases are brought to court not to win, but to force a defendant to settle for some sum of money. Such settlement is made by the insurance company in most cases.

The defect is apparent. The emphasis is on money. Little is done to prevent the defendant physician from returning to practice; even if that physician is psychotic, crazy! Not enough is done to determine if what that physician did was just one of those things that could happen to any competent physician. Not enough is done to determine if that physician is a serious menace, one likely to repeat the error. Fortunately the State Medical Licensing Boards are becoming increasingly more vigilant.

Some ambulatory paranoid schizophrenics are quite intelligent and clever at evading detection. Such a person is often adept at legal maneuvering. Psychopathic personalities can be equally dangerous, especially if they are physicians or plaintiff's attorneys.

Physician cannot win this battle alone. Protection from the irresponsible aspects of what is going on must await patient forcefulness. Patients should reexamine the acceptance by society of these practices for they affect patients too. Physicians have amply proven their inability to counter them alone. If nothing else, patients must come to realize it is they who bear the cost.

Only those trained and practically versed in the medical profession, in medical science, have the ability first to police their own profession, and second, to adjudicate the highly technical matters required to judge the merits and fair disposition of disputes that evolve out of technical medical actions. Hired witnesses, physicians included, in an adversarial situation before a lay jury in today's court rooms are not able to do this.

Coercive Advantage

One privilege, one license given to attorneys is the power to subpoena, to summons, to sue. This is a very powerful coercive advantage from which not just physicians, but the populace as a whole does not have adequate protection. As the number of attorneys increase, the danger from abuse of this coercive advantage power increases.

Once a malpractice related subpoena or summons is handed to a physician, or to anyone, that immediately, and by arbitrary fiat, gives at least two attorneys a lucrative job. There are those who say that someone must first come to the attorney with a grievance. This is only partially true. It is the attorney's decision to exercise this power, this license.

In frivolous and baseless, even malicious medical malpractice suits, insofar as I know, physicians are not allowed to recover from the attorneys responsible even the cost of their forced defense of such a suit.

Even when a malpractice suit is particularly malicious and or, groundless, physicians are often so glad to be out of the Game Of Court, they are content to be free of the whole mess. In the event physicians are determined to get redress, and are willing to return to the one-sided (law is for the lawyers) Game Of Court to get it, they find in most cases their insurance companies are not, for they have spent enough money. Money is all they have spent; they do not share the physician's anguish. It is all in a day's business for the insurance company.

Although many malpractice insurance companies say they will fight and not settle, most malpractice insurance companies will even settle a totally groundless malpractice lawsuit. This simply makes economic sense, again economics is the sole determinant. (Making lawsuits expensive is favored by the courts as a way of deterring lawsuits, it also increases settlement amounts).

Growing Scientific Complexity and the Law

Physicians have a fetish about truth, about what is so, and why. So we have our peer review journals. These publish only those reports of scientific experiments reviewed and approved by peers unknown to the authors. No doubt this reduces the homicide rate. (The rejected authors are sometimes quite unhappy.)

Physicians are quick to label proffered experience as anecdotal.* A proper study must have controls. There must be placebos, if a drug is being investigated for efficacy. Placebos are some "ineffectual" substance like sugar pills made to look like the real remedy being tested. A double blind study means that neither the study subjects receiving

---

* Grimes DA. Technology follies: The uncritical acceptance of medical innovation. JAMA. 1993; 269: 3030-3033.

the treatment, nor the persons administering the treatment know placebo from the real thing.

Science is the most effective method of understanding and manipulating reality known at this time. In the past it has tended to shun complexity, believing complexity could be dealt with by breaking it down into simpler units. It is doubtful if this linear simplistic approach is sufficient for biological processes.

The harder sciences like physics have their problems too. Quantum physics has turned upside down some of our cherished, long held theories or beliefs. Our savior is the concept of chance. But now we slip over into belief. To not believe in belief is also a belief.

But how can nonlinear complex events and dynamic processes be measured? If scientific truth depends on reproducible experiments, and these in turn depend on quantitative measurements, how is one to quantify complex physiological processes?

Conventional measurements are inadequate to characterize complex structures and so are most statistics. Then the mathematical and spatial notions of fractals, and the concepts of chaos theory evolved, describing a new way of thinking about spatial arrangement and time in complex nonlinear dynamic systems. These also cannot be adequately measured, ordered, or validated with mean and variance statistics. Concepts for measuring such complexity are being worked out based on concepts from chaos theory. Medical science is now busy constructing nonlinear models of basic mechanisms.

Do you think a jury can understand this stuff? It has real pertinence in the sudden death syndrome, a natural for the malpractice-suit courtroom.

The hard physical sciences and medicine are gaining more in common. Practical applications in fluid balance, cardiac and renal physiology are examples. No mention has been made of chemistry, which is an advanced and most important esoteric science. It is used daily in medical practice. It is misused daily by many in law and government.

Defense attorneys have contempt for physicians who try to "educate" a jury. This makes a physician appear an arrogant know-it-all to a jury, when such a person on trial had best appear a supplicant. (Who would say this ancient verity is not so?)

In a sense, many trial attorneys have discovered there is no truth. Any notion they can get by a jury and a judge, if it remains unchallenged, is not only so, it may in time become accepted as fact, and it may become accepted as legal precedent. More pernicious, any notion attorneys can get into the cultural consensus or lexicon, even if untrue, becomes not only accepted as precedent; but is no longer questioned by the society.

One distortion can be built on another, until it infects the entire body politic. A similar situation was true of religion in the dark ages. Misuse of aspects of asbestos exposure, disinformation about Agent Orange, silicone breast implants, Sucaryl, etc. most anything that can be called a chemical are examples that have misled the public into believing what is not scientifically valid. Junk science is fast becoming our most dangerous hysteria.

Aspects of these problems are complex scientific questions that have no business anywhere they cannot be decided in careful, non-adversarial inquiry. A type of trial where customarily one side must be declared winner and the other loser benefits society not at all in these arcane situations.

Take for example silicone breast implants. There is much more to this problem than whether silicone is good or bad. Suppose there is accumulating evidence that only in a rare individual, some unknown kind of allergic process (for want of a better descriptive term) is operative. Why should millions of dollars hang on some judicial pronouncement monetizing this individual or class of individual's problem? Why not compensate those who can safely have implants but are now estopped by the prior suit?

What is needed, for the benefit of all society, is continued objective inquiry, careful calculation of risk, and informed consent about this risk. If inquiry can proceed without fear of financial opportunism, a test may be found to determine who has this idiosyncrasy to be harmed by silicone implants and who does not.

In this age of science, some plaintiff's attorneys are spoon feeding us their own tort truth. This would be humorous if it were not so economically damaging to the culture. The society is literally being divided into those who have a science education and those who do not. Some of the latter are opinionated university professors in non-scientific fields.

A tort trial attorney can take a professor who is earning fifty thousand dollars a year, and give that professor the chance to earn two hundred thousand dollars a year in his or her spare time, and an expert witness is created.

As medical science grows, as it demands more in precision and competence, it gets beyond the abilities of one person to achieve expertise in the entire field. The torch of medicine is carried by many specialists. Many specialists are unfamiliar with each other's area of expertise. This to date has been mankind's way of coping with scientific complexity.

The more technical and complex an issue becomes, the more fertile the field for growth of legal distortion and deception. Yet the power and arrogance of some trial attorneys and judges makes it impossible for them to see they are not competent to decide disputes of this nature. They will become less so as science becomes ever more complex and specialized. The legal profession should be aiding and abetting a society that can better handle this growing reality. To do this they must give up much pretense—and much money.

Perhaps the legal profession should ask itself these questions: How is one to earn respect and power? How is one to be wise? How is one to bask on their pinnacle of wisdom and respect in the face of a world view so very different from reverence for the past, for pomp and procedure? In science, one discovery can destroy overnight some of the never-questioned notions of a Newton or an Einstein.

These very different viewpoints have been building for centuries. Science has always disturbed those accustomed to wearing a mantle of power and control, a power that resists disagreement, even in a democracy.

Today an honest adjudicator is subjected to clever specialists, each slanting their information to win the argument. While this may work in criminal and other cases, in medical and scientific areas it is the foundation of fallacious precedent, tragically incorrect decisions and of unnecessarily increased medical care costs. Worse, these incorrect decisions are preserved or tolerated.

With respect to those who must fill these very responsible roles, we must ask the question: Are we coming to an end of our traditional legal jurisprudence effectiveness in esoteric complex scientific matters? If so when and how will society get this powerful legal-government system to correct this error? Indeed we have a legal crisis.

Sadly, some contingent fee malpractice, product liability, workers compensation, and accident compensation lawyers (and perhaps others) with their Game Of Court are no longer the keeper of the keys of justice. It is not just that this aspect of the legal profession cannot unlock the inherently convoluted esoteric problems inherent, nor have they dropped the keys. They have melted them down and sold them.

Some Malpractice Trial Myths and Deceptions

- No risk is tolerable
- Abuse of the notion of informed consent (Complete informed consent is impossible, physicians always fail)
- The thing speaks for itself
- Medical charts are an indication of practice quality
- Medical charts are evidence of what actually happened
- Negligence is an indication of practice quality, or of that physicians ability
- A bad result is perforce a compensible error-especially in the case of newborns
- Someone else can be forced to pay for most of the harm that befalls us
- Malpractice litigation improves medical care
- Fear of litigation makes for better care and protects patients

- Malpractice litigation does not increase medical costs
- Malpractice suits involve a low percentage of physicians
- The THREAT of malpractice does good, not harm
- The deepest pocket should pay, regardless of how tenuous the connection with a case
- If a visible bad result can be presented properly to a properly selected jury, the case can be won regardless of the facts, especially if the facts are complex
- If one wins, justice was done
- A lay jury or judge listening to the adversary system work over a complicated medical case, or any complex technical esoteric matter are quite capable of reaching the correct decision

Recognize that as these perversions of truth penetrate and permeate the culture, they damage the incentive of those they directly victimize. They distort the judgment of the masses of people. Certain realities compound this. Fickle juries, envy, illiteracy, a culture of poverty and dependence on government are some of them. A sad part of all this is the subliminal cultivation of a people, softened by hope for handouts, often unable to distinguish deception. In a democracy this is dangerous.

A Procedure-based Fee Schedule
for Attorneys

Perhaps it is in the nation's best interest to develop a procedure-based fee schedule for attorneys similar to the one developed at Harvard University, and put into use for the medical profession. In court cases this fee could be affixed by the judge, hence subject to judicial review. (In the case of punitive actions, a few weeks in jail would be a better deterrent than punitive monetary damages—at least, no percentage of a punitive damage award should go to the attorney). Such an act would force a codification of legal procedures, and require a hard look at what is the value an individual attorney earns by performing a given procedure. A unit value could then be developed. In the case of private legal consultation, the client could be given foreknowledge of the applicable fees.

There would be considerable room for individual variation so competitive alternatives could work to the advantage of the consumer. Such a fee schedule could be refined and purged of abuse over time. Most important would be the return of the legal profession, as a group, to a more idealistic, realistic set of expectations. Such a fee schedule should be based on objective definable criteria, such things as education, achievement, professional knowledge, skill, risk and training.

Once a unit value was standardized, each legal procedure should be identified, delineated, variations accounted for, and a relative value rating attached. It would be no more difficult to do this for legal charges than it was for medical ones.

Time and expense are not satisfactory, since they are easily inflatable and do not reflect efficiency. Differences in ability would be reflected in the procedures as is the case with medical care.

The idea is to encourage a reasonableness and economy, a turning away of many of the legal profession from the lust to win a windfall, the aggressive drive to win the money. Perhaps this would then be replaced by more pride in negotiating skills and the idealism inherent in the profession.

The concept of an idealistic humanistic moral code should at least be reintroduced to some of the profession as an aspect of their professional code. The aim is to replace chicanery as a pragmatic modus operandi.

An alternate additional option, a system of socialized law, a safety net for clients and attorneys alike should be devised similar to the one recommended in this book for physicians. Clients could use the Safety Net Courts, and avail themselves of such a service in every county.

This would meet many of society's needs. It would give attorneys who preferred a more thoughtful life style a refuge also. In such a Legal Safety Net, attorneys would work for a salary, with excellent benefits as described in the section on the Safety Net Hospital-Clinic. Benefits can include academic and teaching aspects, perhaps a chance to review and enhance ethical and moral values or a step toward a judicial appointment. This could lead the way to correction of serious social ills.

Such a safety net would be most important for much of family law. Many poor divorced mothers with children and with non-supporting, not-affluent ex-spouses have no legal representation, regardless of the legal aid existing. Such a refuge could work with the medical safety net to better handle not only family law, but accident, worker's compensation, and similar claims not requiring medical expertise, for the benefit of all.

Such an institution might become equally inviting to a type of client looking for a negotiated solution rather than a court room battle, or for clients seeking protection from such battles forced upon them.

The work of the legal profession should be steered from lucrative sham fighting where attorney and client seek not so much justice as a monetary windfall, to a situation where disputes are settled as efficiently as possible. This does not mean there should be more legislation and fewer trials. It means trials would be less tipped in favor of the legal profession, especially in the area of redistribution of wealth, the unfairness of which dampens incentive.

Rather than striving to engender controversies for attorneys' profit, legal reform should result in a profession that changes the culture toward prevention, negotiation, compromise and simple, inexpensive non-punitive solutions that work as well. Legal reform should achieve less civil disorder.

As we rapidly approach serious overpopulation, duplicity, aggressiveness and ruthless domination become more dangerous almost daily. This is not off the subject. Physicians face daily these ills in physical form, and they must cope with real trauma and death resulting from ever-increasing violence for which the monetary cost is borne insensibly by everyone.

Attorneys and Liability Insurance

Consider the subject of coincidental collusion. Is there a chance monopoly or just a symbiotic relationship between attorneys and insurance companies? There are several branches of such insurance. If there were less legal threat there would be less need for the varieties of liability insurance and liability umbrellas now being sold. The market is huge. So is the float. Would these companies have an interest in keeping the status quo? They are an ever-present (perhaps unwilling) deep pocket, if only for the float. Industrial insurance float alone is in the billions of dollars. Very lucrative, even if the insurance companies pay out every dime of premium on claims. If there was a threat of much less need for such insurance, how do you suppose these insurance companies would react? On whose side do you suppose they would join in a struggle to minimize the lucrative aspects of this legal license or coercive advantage?

Just as there exists a mutually beneficial relationship among lawsuits, trial attorneys, and liability insurance, a similar relationship is developing between physicians and health insurance. This is becoming another spiral. As physicians' fees increase, health insurance premiums rise. As health insurance premiums rise, the insurance company's float and hence their power increases. The resulting escalation in medical costs make insurance companies' ever-costlier services more necessary. The bottom line: Insurance companies profit from more money, not less of it. Higher premiums or greater census or both are required.

Consider "managed competition" in this context, applied to either attorneys or physicians. Setting up a monopolistic insurance system that would control physicians or attorneys will make matters much worse. Does throwing attorneys into this mess help to clarify the point? Do you think attorneys would ever stand for such a shift in power and prerogative? Would government even consider it? Why then do you think such a thing should or could, be forced on physicians? The answer of course is power.

Again, visualize the spiral. Lawyers succeed in putting together plaintiff and sympathetic judge and jury resulting in ever-increasing monetary awards. This results in increasing insurance premiums, which results in larger awards and so it goes.

Most attorneys serve a valuable function in our society. Certainly we cannot, nor would we want to reduce their social value, for example the culture needs all the help it can get with juvenile crime.

While the problems and inequities mentioned in this chapter apply to the medical profession and their patients, they, of course, apply to others as well. It would be best if those attorneys involved would recognize and control these problems and these inequities themselves. Just as physicians should correct their excesses themselves. There are surely cases that need to be sued, injustices that should be resolved in the courts. As with medicine, we are not talking about the need; but about the cost and the curbing of abuse and injustice.

CHAPTER SIX

The Problems

Summary and Conclusion

To clarify our approach to a solution, keep in mind the problems. The problems are these: Well-meaning third parties who offer plan after plan, do not understand the psychology of physicians, nor do they have sufficient experience with the actual doctor-patient relationship, or with medical practice to really know the problems. They make more trouble trying to solve virtual, fantasy problems that occur to them. These of course necessarily reflect their bias and lack of first-hand knowledge.

As you might have suspected by now, doctors deeply resent such outside control. Nothing will destroy the quality of medical practice more quickly. They feel this way first because only they know medical practice. In other words, they resent control from above because to them, in the essential technical areas there is no above. This may seem arrogant; perhaps it is. It is also a fact. It is also a fact that physician power is feared and resented; all the more reason for maintaining physician idealism and esprit.

But when the chips are down and things are real, and physicians are fighting for a life, very vital decisions must be made and made quickly, sometimes in the face of considerable uncertainty. This uncertainty is so often increased by damaging third party threats and regulations made by those who can know little about the actual situation.

Especially in these tight spots, unless you are a physician, you are part of the problem, not part of the solution. Furthermore, one never knows when a tight spot may occur. In an instant, a simple injection may eventuate in a potentially fatal, totally unexpected, anaphylactic reaction (shock with fatally low blood pressure) where every second counts.

Any attempt to conscript physicians will be regarded as enslavement and never forgiven, no matter how silly this may sound to those not involved. Regardless of how many favorable examples can be derived from other countries, that resentment will echo for generations. Those who feel they know best, those with a penchant to control, those political opportunists desperately seeking a cause, may resent the raw presentation of these facts.

The reader is referred to Tanner* as an example. This is a compilation and brief review of various plans for "health care reform." What is meant by health care reform emphasizes costs. Quality generally is taken for granted. This of course is the first mistake. The report bristles with sentences concerning control. The government will con-

---

* Tanner, Michael; HEALTH CARE REFORM: THE GOOD, THE BAD, AND THE UGLY, from Policy Analysis, number 184, Nov. 24, 1992, Published by the Cato Institute.

trol the physician, the insurance companies, patient access, medical care costs.

"Must be required to," "Every resident of the United States would have to," or some variation reoccurs repeatedly, as does the word regulation. The term "Managed competition" and the word envisioned occur prominently; but never does the word OPTIONS occur.

Every problem is between a sick patient confronting a physician for care. To be sure this seems obvious. It is obvious. That is exactly the travesty. The essential aspect of a successful solution is not to lose sight of the obvious while indulging in visions of being mighty. Indulging in visions is all that remains for those ignorant of the essential technical issues, as well as the administrative aspects required, for these too are closely tied to the technical issues.

If people misstate the problem in the beginning, they are obviously unlikely to develop a good solution. Much is said about the problem of the uninsured and underinsured. That would indicate the problem was not only lack of insurance, it would indicate that having insurance is important in the solution. That is simply incorrect, given the present meaning of medical (health) insurance.

The truth is, many vested interests cling to the health insurance notion because it promises to be more lucrative. In fact this very aspect of such insurance is what is participating in the medical cost spiral. This lack of control at the source allows what I have called perversions of accountability, and sooner or later reality will reveal these perversions. In free markets such things quickly come to light, and are as quickly extinguished.

We are seduced by the illusion of certainty, of security that health insurance seems to offer, especially if someone with deeper pockets can be made to pay.

So the financial extremes of the ever growing and increasingly irrational actions of some courts and some clinics have vastly increased some insurance business. This increasing concentration of wealth for insurance companies makes them similar to banks, but with a captive clientele of ever wealthier depositors. Then this plethora of deep pockets grows on itself.

Now imagine what would happen if we passed control of physicians' fees to this insurance business. A bit like the fox guarding the hen house, wouldn't you say? Is this being seriously considered? It is already happening in the case of Medicare and Medicaid. Incremental control (gradually put in place bit by bit) is constantly operative in these government programs. No one profits except some insurance companies.

Note how *something* has alarmingly increased the cost of medical care and lawsuits and the clout of insurance companies. Speaking of clout, *employer health insurance costs are merely passed back to the worker or consumer. The control and power however, pass to the employer or other third parties.*

In the case of health insurance, as much is spent now on third-party administration costs as is spent on physicians' fees. Again, the cost of legal involvement in medical care is hard to estimate, because of malpractice threat costs, physician cynicism, malpractice insurance administrative costs, the overlap of medically-related product liability suits, etc.

We must stop the fear of patients they will someday be unable to afford necessary medical care. We must stop the fear of physicians they will someday be conscripted or exploited.

"Am I underinsured (against physician's fees)?" This is such a perversion of our real set of problems. The physician is asking the same question. "Am I underinsured against my patients?"

In summary, what really are the problems as seen from a physician's viewpoint? We have spent chapters detailing them. Yet, the problems are more than cost. A related problem is access. The problems pragmatically, are these. A person becomes aware they are sick or injured. They hurt, and they are frightened. Who should they see? This in itself is a major dilemma for many patients. Once they select a physician, once they are seen, are they relieved, are they satisfied, do they feel better, are they wondering if they should consult another physician? Do they know what to do next? These problems will not be solved by more general physicians, or by the many forms of managed competition. You may say everyone knows these are really the problems. The concern of society is how is one to pay for this? What is our cost problem?

THE COST PROBLEM IS THAT MEDICAL CARE DELIVERY IS MOST INEFFICIENT, AND HENCE NOT AT ALL COST EFFECTIVE. THE BEST SOLUTION WILL BE TO INCREASE THE EFFICIENCY AND PRODUCTIVITY OF MEDICAL CARE DELIVERY WHILE MAINTAINING ITS QUALITY, GIVING SATISFACTION TO BOTH PATIENT AND PHYSICIAN. THIS IS BEST DONE THROUGH A VIABLE COMPETITIVE MARKET WHERE THERE IS A NICHE, AN OPPORTUNITY FOR **EVERYONE**, INCLUDING THE OPPORTUNITY TO FAIL.

Beware of the person who mouths or writes the words "must be required to." No patient, no physician, *nor you,* want to "must be required to" do anything when it comes to your personal, intimate, vital, perhaps dangerous medical care. Must be required to pay reasonable taxes, practice responsible medicine and not overuse the system are "must be required to" enough.

We must create solutions based on viable competitive options. We must provide for those unable to pay for their own care in a manner we would all be willing to use ourselves.

While the so called managed competition ideas have remained vague to date, this book has and will refrain from attempting a rebuttal. The purpose of this book is to present an original workable solution based on experience. There are plenty of critiques of these managed competition plans whatever they may be.

Yet years of experience with people, rich and poor, slightly ill and very ill, and experience with physicians as well, merits the following comments. Perhaps anticipating some of these problems will result in a better outcome, if such an outcome is indeed put upon us.

Remembering the book has emphasized insurance as a problem, not a solution, consider these following points:*

The plans so far include a "basic plan," this will soon come to be the "poor people's plan." It will likely suffer the fate of Medicaid, where these recipients were promised a great deal of services, but the money was not there to furnish them, and the paperwork was more time consuming than the patient care. As a result many physicians refused to see these patients at all. Some doctors saw them for free because it was easier. Some physicians set up practices solely to treat medicaid patients. Specialists referral was not quickly forthcoming.

I predict this whole scenario will be played out with the addition of more strict rules imposed by a "must be required to" government. Eventually, this will quickly, at

* See also Rice T., Brown R. Holes in the Jackson Hole approach to health care reform. J.A.M.A. 1993;270:1357-1362. This is one medical journal article every layman can and should understand. None of its authors have an M.D.

the scene, act much to the detriment of the patient confined to basic care. Those who can afford it (about two thirds of the population) will quickly opt for better care plans, especially if they are or expect to be heavy users of the system. How this problem can be surmounted is detailed in the solution herein.

So these plans will not assure patient access and quality, especially for those with only the basic plan. Cost control means nothing without *access* and *quality* including ready access to specialists and costly technology when this is imperative. Why are we considering such a inept mess? Is this due to ignorance, innocence or deceit? It does not matter, the affect will be the same.

Sooner or later we must return to trusting our physicians to furnish us health care, otherwise we must train those we can trust. Certainly the solution is beyond the many well meaning meddlers now trying to solve the problem by applying more of the problem. We must give them credit for starting the ball rolling, however. If only they would sit back and watch awhile. There is a solution in this book. It is by far the simplest, the most workable. But it must surmount the special interests who may not know or care. It surely can be improved over time especially if we give what belongs to the medical profession— the real practicing medical profession—back to that medical profession.

Who wants to be restricted to marginal medicine? Who wants to be in a tight spot and find themselves restricted to marginal medical care for whatever reason? Health care costs will rise for the excellent reason that health care is rapidly becoming better and more essential, just like our autos. Health care costs will rise for this reason regardless of the system. If you cap or control these costs the lines will only lengthen.

Such practices, however politicized and glossed, if restrictive, may not bother the mildly ill. For those who become very ill, these practices may become fatal!

CHAPTER SEVEN

Developing a Solution to the Medical Cost Crisis

Humans need time and room to adjust to change if they are to embrace change rather than tolerate it. We should leave the present system mostly intact, and change by adding options. Then allow the systems to compete and adapt over time.

So we should divide the solution into two parts. One part would be the status quo, which would be allowed to evolve within the framework of contemporary progress and new ideas. This would happen presumably within the constraints imposed on private or insured medical care.

A second part would be the development of a refuge for patient and physician alike, distributed throughout the land. They would be free to all patients, the poor and millionaires alike! The only requirement would be they be sick. Please do not put down the book. I am noted for my Scotch parsimony. There is a way this can be done sensibly.

These Safety Net Hospital-Clinics (abbreviated SNHC) would be constructed to function well in the midst of our contemporary capitalistic, drug, biotechnical, and private medical care delivery systems. As these new approaches developed, neither method could avoid changing and reacting to the changes that were taking place in the other.

Inspired methods to reduce expectations for monetary compensation need to be effected.

Also the Safety Net Hospital-Clinics will handle the acute care needs. There will be no more driving an acutely ill person from emergency room to emergency room to find one that will accept that patient.* Eventually even ambulance service should be included. Yet there will be the freedom for development of competitive options.

Within these SNHC we would do the following:

1. **Reduce incentives to run up the medical bill.** Analyze medical visits with an eye to reducing rather than increasing costs, and number of visits to do the job. Put the emphasis on results rather than profit. Physicians do order unnecessary tests whether they get paid from them or not. They may do this to protect themselves against malpractice risks, but they also order tests to increase their certainty. It is a fairly accurate generalization to say the better trained and more experienced physicians are, the less they tend to do this.

2. **Reduce frequency of patient visits**, based on real patient need only, determined by expert diagnosis and referral to personnel who then can afford to take time with a patient.

3. **Introduce a new form of TRIAGE**, going to great lengths to provide the very best scientific medical care for

* Hospital emergency rooms by law must treat all patients present-ing—if they have the facilities to treat that patient adequately.

all socioeconomic classes. As you will see, this system would be very different and more efficient than the present gate-keeper idea. A gate-keeper is employed to monitor the flow and or referral of patients to reduce cost and load on the specialists. They are often a general physician or nurse. To get to your favorite specialist via your employer's insurance, sometimes you must first get around the gate-keeper. It is the hope of the gate-keeper's employer that the gate-keeper will be able to care for the majority of patients that present. Much depends on that professional's level of competence and on the patient load, for the gate-keeper is rarely employed just to screen patients.

4. At the same time, we would **reduce complexity and manage costly and capital intensive procedures more parsimoniously, and more efficiently.** This does not necessarily mean expensive capital equipment would be used skimpily, rather such equipment would be used intensively.

5. **Delegate many aspects to less costly personnel; but the ultimate of medical ability would be brought to bear at the point of delegation.** Utilize computers in innovative ways. Much of this technology remains untouched. Remember computers now can talk from vast dynamic knowledge bases. Sophisticated computer use is now happening in some of our teaching hospitals.*

6. **Require help and input from the patient and the family.**

7. **Put the emphasis on excellent working conditions**, safety security and employee status and *esprit.*

* See Waldrop, M.M. "PARC Builds a World Saturated with Computation." Science.261 17 Sept. 1993 pp 1523-1524.

8. **Emphasize early accurate diagnosis followed by comforting, less costly reassurance and patient education.**

9. We should **require more patient responsibility**. We should curb patient abuse of the system, and educate patients about how to be better patients.

10. We must **curb or eliminate abuses by third parties**.

11. We should **require expertise and accountability.** We should develop individual physician risk factor profiles, and actively conduct outcomes research. Why are outcomes at this place, or by this person better or worse than elsewhere? The medical profession should be on the forefront of this developing science of risk assessment and of outcomes research. We must train and test so that we recognize who knows what. Then put them in a position to operate efficiently without harassment.

12. **Attract top quality personnel** to this safety net, in part by freeing them of the many damaging and annoying factors that have weeded the small business culture. These experts delivering care should be cloistered, surrounded and protected by non-monetary rewards. They should be free to do their job of developing and delivering excellent medical care. They should then be held accountable by their peers to do just that—deliver excellent medical care.

13. **These Safety Net Hospital Clinics should become** not only a refuge for patients and excellent physicians, they should become **think tanks** and places to test far more than medical research. They could test questions such as these: Will a large sample of patients fare better or worse free from malpractice litigation? Can accountability and a high standard of medicine be handled

by the different types of administrative and adjudicative peer arbitration proposed?

14. Why not **require the many distant regulators to test** *and be tested on* **some of their own regulations at the SNHC?** Interested parties should read McGovern*

15. We can believe **there are physicians and other technical people who prefer to work in such an atmosphere as the Safety Net Hospital-Clinic.** Consider the great difference in income with little difference in training, or quality input into the system between a M.D.Ph.D. at the academic research bench, and a similar M.D.Ph.D. in an executive sales capacity for a big drug company. Their wagons are hitched to different stars. Each has for them a satisfying life.

16. **The SNHCs would be clinical teaching hospitals**, with all that implies. They should be kept that way. Yet every clinical teacher must have as their primary purpose patient care.

Other Aspects of the Solution

The three essential elements, patient freedom of choice, practitioner freedom of choice, and a healthy enthusiasm for competitive alternatives must remain guiding principles. Understand that there will never be financial equality. Another guiding principle is excellent scientific medical care, available to all regardless of ability to pay.

---

* "A POLITICIAN'S DREAM IS A BUSINESSMAN'S NIGHTMARE," by Senator and Presidential candidate George McGovern, written in the Manager's Journal of the June 1, 1992 Wall Street Journal, wherein by recounting his failure at a small business, he describes what it is like to be on the "other" side of those regulations that seemed so sound to a politician.

Decisive commitment and enterprise are imperative. These essential ingredients are usually missing in government where compromise and persuasion rule.

We must first acquire and then use highly educated people parsimoniously yet effectively, with minimum regard for their political connections or their buddies. We must decide on alternative systems. Remove impediments. Start things going within general, well-thought-out plans of action, operating within established principles, formulated by those who know the area of expertise involved. Once derived, they should be followed, yet always remaining open and adaptable to change.

The essentials are personnel, infrastructure, supplies and equipment, training, growth and maintenance of the art and science of medicine and its associated disciplines. Preach preventative medicine; then act. Think through new systems from the ground up. List all aspects of medical care. Then work to reduce the costs in each. We should then apply both monetary and non-monetary rewards for service.

Move from the status quo to both old and new systems while providing for a smooth transition, keeping in mind the inertia inherent in the current practices, the buildings, the education, the attitudes, the expectations, the entrenchment.

We must be aware of what would impede change. For example those committed to the status quo, such as high-income physicians, and those with heavy, financial, political or educational commitments. To succeed, besides persistence, it will be necessary to anticipate the powerful entrenched forces who would lose money or prerogative as a result of the Safety Net Hospital-Clinics. These may be the very politicians who are advocating changes in the medical system to help those who cannot afford medical care. This endeavor should remain non-partisan.

Those in power must understand the necessity of separating the situations requiring scientific evaluation, such as medical practice, from matters best handled by litigation through opinion, persuasion and debating skills. The courts must come to realize they have no business attempting to enforce accountability in certain scientific areas, and allow the SNHC to use a viable alternative to their domination, if only as a test.

If we are truly interested in assuring that no one suffers bullying or injustice, then both medical and legal professions had best recognize their limitations. This includes reduction of income and other expectations as well. If we are to effect this change, many sectors, many people must adapt to these changes.

At the SNHC, technical accountability and individual rights would be assured by peer review. It is only natural that some attorneys would oppose the loss of this lucrative source.

Professional hospital administrators also interested in non-monetary remuneration would be useful and necessary.

At the top, and in all matters having to do with physicians, a physician with active practical medical experience would have term-limited authority. There would be one exception. That is, the administrative staff, as well as the patient, would have the prerogative to charge physicians with wrongdoing before the highest governing councils of the envisioned SNHC system.

Patient-Physician Relationships

How many patients feel the need to like their physician, need to feel the physician has a personal interest in them? How many patients want the ability to pick and choose among physicians? How many patients would be bothered by being assigned a physician? The success of health maintenance organizations answer these questions in part. Most health maintenance organizations now in operation in this country simply assign a patient to a physician. Patient tolerance would indicate they do not object; or they are willing to accept such assignment as a trade-off for other perceived advantages. This is not entirely true.

About 85% of our visits to the doctor are for common things. These are quite familiar to the well-trained. These could be handled quickly and efficiently, with little cost once diagnosed, given the right circumstances. The patient would be sent home reassured and satisfied by a medical care system structured to motivate both patient and physician to deliver and accept this cost effective care.

Continuity of care is quite another matter. Most patients would object to being seen by a different physician each visit; or even each illness. Reasonable continuity of care is not difficult to achieve for most health maintenance organizations. It would be made essential at the SNHC.

Patients now are conditioned to accept referral to several specialists. A higher percentage of patients self-refer to specialists these days. Again if the patient personally dislikes that specialist, most would want the option of seeking another. This desire might not be available from most "controlled medicine" schemes including present day HMOs.*

It is attention to these aspects, easily overlooked, that could make a great difference in the acceptance by patients of these Safety Net Hospital-Clinics. It is not uncommon for patients to visit a specialist or a generalist they personally like when "the going gets rough," even though they are entitled to similar care from their health maintenance organization.

This aspect is not meant to denigrate HMOs. It is simply common sense. If suddenly things look very serious for a dear child, or anyone, their is a human tendency to quickly forsake the rather impersonal HMO and want to rush to the "BEST." That is an emotional reaction and it is a very human one. It is a simple truth that there is great need for personal comfort in medical care, and no political scheme will ever change that. All of us who aspire to this presumption of changing our medical care delivery should be ever aware of that most fundamental and ancient of human needs. Comfort was essential, long before scientific competence was ever considered, and it remains ever much so today.

Our nurses are such a valuable adjunct in this important area of personal comfort, if only they will continue to see this art for the value it holds, and if only they will be permitted to practice it, and to develop it. But they must be recognized and valued for this, yet they must tenaciously insist on this value and purvey it. Now is a time

---

* When physicians refer patients to another physician, as they did in only 6.7% of the time in 1991, they usually give the patient three names to choose from. However about 24.5% of patients self-referred to specialists in 1991. From Schappert, S.M. National ambulatory Medical Care survey: 1991 Summary. U.S. Dept. of Health and Human Services, Advanced Data, No.230, March 29, 1993.

when all of us must resist domination in medicine by those who know not of what they speak.

Likewise, the freedom of patients to move in and out of the Safety Net Hospital-Clinic should never be hampered. While at the same time, great effort should be made to supply the healing and comforting essentials. These two are the very essence! Freedom to move and care. Patient and physician must care for one another carefully.

If they can afford it, patients should be free to move elsewhere at any time. For those who cannot afford to leave, every effort must be make to supply these essentials discussed just above. Great respect must be accorded patient prerogative.

Variants of real honest to goodness insurance policies could spring up around such patient concerns. Even so, patients would acquire a competitive advantage. Everyone would know the SNHC was there for anyone.

CHAPTER EIGHT

The Safety Net Hospital-Clinics: An Overview

This book emphasizes the importance of a number of solutions (competitive options) existing side by side, permitting development of competitive advantage, and the freedom of choice for everyone. The option posed here is a locally controlled system of Safety Net Hospital-Clinics throughout the nation. These could be built in part on the infrastructure of the present county hospital systems; but with great physical and administrative changes. There could be a hierarchy leading from the small county hospitals (or their out-reach facilities), through the larger ones, to the medical school teaching hospital system.

The emphasis would be on idealistic medical care for all regardless of ability to pay. There would be no means test (proof of inability to pay), meaning anyone could come and receive care if they were willing to wait their turn. In time, efficiency and productivity could be increased and patient waiting times reduced. In general, those with money are busy. The poor have time, as do the majority of retired people.

Those with money might well be attracted to other alternatives; however many such patients would come for honest, objective referrals to private physicians. One of the questions patients now have is who would be the best physician to see for their particular problem? Patients who would prefer to continue to consult their private physician, and are told they need surgery, could well use the SNHC for a second opinion. One of the important functions of the SNHC physicians would be to maintain close ties with the private practitioners of the area. Many of these private physicians would be part-time teaching volunteers.

These hospitals would have a permanent staff whose duties would be patient care with some teaching and research and management of the part-time volunteer clinical faculty. There would be interns, residents, a nursing teaching staff and student nurses. This situation is very enticing to many physicians in a way that is hard for most lay people to understand. The organizational details follow. (See also fig. 2, page 193).

Many of the routine medical duties would be performed by a staff of interns and residents (specialists in training). Residents would be more geographically distributed than they are now, yet there would be many more opportunities for training primary care physicians and for specialty training.

As mentioned above, there would be an attending staff of volunteer physicians to help with inpatient and outpatient care and teaching. They would receive the chance to "keep up." Any teacher learns as well as teaches. These volunteer physicians would hold positions of prestige. This would give them some competitive advantage at their home office. They would be allowed to volunteer one half day a week for as little as three months a year.

Family physicians are more economical than specialists only if there is a shortage of specialists, and only in a fee-for-service-practice. Even then specialists are often more economical. Specialists have become an economic problem for insurance companies, not a medical care problem for patients. This system would train many more of both specialists and generalists in a cost effective manner, upgrading the entire standard of medical care. Such a system would aid in specialist distribution throughout the country as well. Sufficient numbers of residents would opt to stay on (if there were vacancies in the SNHC) or locate in the area after their training.

A better system would evolve if each county (or practical geopolitical area) had autonomy, so that each unit had an individuality. One would then have many tests of this idea, and variations of it; and perhaps avoid problems inherent in central control.

The full-time staff positions would be paid in monetary salary about the same as most HMOs now pay their physicians. Non-monetary remuneration will be elaborated later. The residents and interns would require whatever is the going rate, which would be considerably less than the staff physicians.

These hospitals would be a home-away-from-home for physicians. They would be places where house staff and volunteer physicians could have a meal at mealtimes, or a snack at any hour, and sit around the table and talk shop. Local private physicians would be welcome to these sessions. The hospitals would be kept clean, and up to a high standard everyone would respect and patronize. They would welcome the poor and be geared for the middle class.

Yet they would necessarily be short on the amenities, and sometimes crowded. Volunteers of all kinds could change this greatly for the better. These SNHC would allow many patients the healthy trauma of associating closely with those unable to pay for their medical care.

Economy, and efficient professional administration would be essential. Yet, the level of ancillary help, drug and equipment use intelligently managed, and the level of hospitality and camaraderie for the staff and local private physicians kept high. Nor should these institutions ever be allowed to become a "make work" or a politically-controlled environment.

As with physicians, ancillary employee selection and job security would be given careful attention. All employees, including physicians, would be instilled with the notion of economy. Extensive use would be made of disciplined part-time semi-volunteer or volunteer help. Dilettantes would be quickly weeded out.

Still, because of careful selection and careful control of expectations, the employees and the physicians would maintain a high degree of esprit. All patients, all people, would have the security of knowing no one would be without high quality medical care for lack of ability to pay.

There would, of course, be an emergency unit which would take only true emergencies. TRIAGE, delegation and discipline would be applied. At the discretion of the emergency room physicians, patients not considered emergencies would either be reassured and sent home, asked to return to the next day's clinic; or sent to an on-site all night clinic. There they would be seen by an intern or resident for diagnosis and treatment or consultation. Only when necessary would they be admitted. (Today, such patients are often admitted overnight for legal reasons with the hope some insurance will pay.) Patient overuse would be controlled by physicians on the basis of medical need, not by insurance, political or legal considerations.

An acceptable realistic level of risk would be established, carefully calculated, hence quantified, and made public. Anyone could check the quantified risk associated with any given procedure or medical action by any physician. For the benefit of those for whom the numbers would be meaningless, numerical values for common risks would be available for comparison. This is easily within the competence of contemporary risk assessment procedures.

The medical cost crisis would be over; and the competitive alternatives now in place could continue. Any change must come about in this way. There is too much vested interest, too much power entrenched, to allow the system to be wrenched free of the status quo. This would best be done by allowing competitive alternatives to sort themselves out over time. No one has the foresight, the grasp of the global problem to do this by fiat. The insurance companies, the HMOs, the preferred providers, the private physicians would feel a ripple, not the jolt of a wrenching change. There would be physicians for whom this type of practice would have no appeal. There would remain plenty of alternatives.

Great competitive pressure would be put on all other hospitals, and on all expensive diagnostic and office procedures as well. Medicaid, aid to needy children, and other such programs, tracking insurance payments, Medicare's struggles over fees to private physicians, insurance fraud hassles, employment of investigators, many other entanglements, all would dissolve. Why? Because anyone presenting for care, showing reasonable decorum, would be treated in these hospitals-clinics—anyone.

The cost savings from removing the need for third-party red tape would partially meet the cost of this open door policy. There would be less need for heavy advertising expenditures by drug companies because of strict formularies and computer-controlled mass purchasing. The dispensing of a drug with the associated computer record would at the same time issue the order for the purchase from the supplier. Such computer software is already in use. This immediate response would reduce inventory. This is simply an example among hundreds of what would be done to improve efficiency and lower cost while upgrading quality.

Far too much of the present day high cost of drugs is wasted on promotion, the stocking of large inventories of many varieties of the same or similar compounds, and on drugs with minuscule differences exaggerated for marketing purposes.

Drug companies' marketing efforts would change from expensive sales people visiting physicians offices selling physicians a brand of drug, to confronting a buyer of a large organization. That buyer would have science and economy in mind. Such a buyer would buy in large quantities from the most sensible supplier. Concerning drugs, we have much to learn from present day retailing technology. The cost savings would be tremendous, as would the required evolutionary changes in the drug industry.

In the opinion of some, these changes will reduce innovation in the drug industry. They will not. In fact the drug companies need to be rescued from their marketing excesses. These run the gamut from "selling" a physician a drug, to costly public relations releases. The latter help to keep their stock price elevated. The drug market bubble, even with today's insurance excesses, is becoming dangerously enlarged.

For once, patients and physicians would have solved the embarrassment of fees. Each would improve in the other's eyes, and humanitarianism would increase all around. Tensions would ease, work would be more pleasant. Decisions would be made, and procedures recommended and carried out strictly on the basis of medical need, not medical greed. Costly demoralizing medical defensive procedures would slowly diminish as the perceived threat of litigation diminished. These hospital clinics would be fountainheads of preventive medicine and public health.

If this system were so good, perhaps all physicians would want to join. To the extent that this were so, we would have backed into a new type of medical care delivery. EXCEPT, any patient or any physician would be free to leave at any time.

Undoubtedly, there would always be a sizable pool of fee-for-service physicians, patients who can afford to pay, people who prefer their insurance, their trial attorneys, and their physician. Just as there would be healthy competition, with no one able to corner the market, there would also be freedom from coercion.

What, in more detail, is this concept of making the SNHC an innovative refuge for patients and physicians, and a haven for the ancillary medical worker as well? First, this would involve observation and data gathering concerning how aspects of the present society are impinging on the cost and delivery of medical care. The SNHC would be a place where actions not available in the other medical care options could be carefully and ethically studied.

The SNHC could accomplish several things at once, not the least of which would be the chance to develop better means of medical care, including physician and patient protection. From the beginning the system would have the mission of proving itself. This too is an advantage.

The issue of medical errors and omissions is a case in point. The SNHC would provide a very valuable test were it allowed to be an island permitted to practice a different procedure for these problems. Any outcome of such actions, so long as they were carefully done, would be of great value to society. The scientific establishment might in time opt for a radically different procedure for settling patient grievances. Perhaps scientists would not find the ancient legal traditions, or even the present peer arbitration the most effective, and variations would evolve.

About Safety Net Hospital Care

At the SNHC, as here organized, one could give a superior scientific and technical level of medical care to all patients, once they presented themselves and took other reasonably responsible steps like returning for appointments. How then would medical care differ?

In a private practice there might be fewer patients around. There might well be fancier surroundings; but rarely will there be fancier medical equipment, or better, more honest medical care. There might be a change in the atmosphere however.

There would be no less solicitousness, but not that connected with monetary need. Those who require this could go elsewhere. Remember, the SNHC would not dare alienate many people, for it could not afford to have too many people paying taxes for medical care they would never use for sure. Remember also the appeal of this system is it would always be there if needed, it would not intrude if not needed. These are the realities that would govern both partners, the care-givers and the patients. Kindness and compassion would be a firm operational principle, for the simple reason they give both physicians and patients benefits.

The difference is that little attempt would be made to sell the patient, or to meet the patients expectations in areas outside the realm of sound scientific medicine. The difference refers to physician time and frills. It refers to a tightly run organization with very different goals than a fee-for-service practice. However, high physician and ancillary personnel ability, with all that implies, would be an essential administrative policy. Physician time would be used efficiently and effectively for best patient care.

Perhaps an extreme alternative would be a fee-for-service physician in an expensive neighborhood. This physician would serve the needs of those people who value their ability to pay high prices for the best. What is the best? Such physicians have the job of selling this type of patient that from them comes the best medical care. A bit of merchandising will be required. This merchandising may involve different things, only one of which is scientific medical knowledge and skill.

Consider this aspect of medical care: It applies to any profession. The consumer is unable to assess the technical aspects of that professional. That is why professions must govern themselves. The chances are that those top scientifically in a given medical field will be in or near a university, or a big charity teaching hospital, not necessarily pandering to the rich, since their major motivation is not money. A physician having a wealthy clientele would tend to have values similar to the patients. Some of these physicians, indeed, may be the nation's smartest medically. Certainly such patients would be spared no expense to provide them the best their physician knew, plus the appurtenances such patients would associate with the best.

Effects on Patients

There would be none of this fear about paying for and obtaining treatment for catastrophic illness, now so well propagandized. The patient need not fear being unable to afford ordinary care either. The Safety Net Hospital-Clinic is always there as an option. Patients would have the opportunity to see for themselves what aspects of it they would care to use, and so would the physician have options. It is exciting and instructive to imagine what would happen.

Catastrophic care insurance companies would have more options also. Some patients might want to supplement their need for a SNHC visit with some form of insurance. An HMO could carry this catastrophic care insurance to cover itself for major claims or those it must refer out, until it gained a large enough membership to underwrite these itself, or it could make arrangements for joint care with a SNHC.

Patients could go to a private physician of their choice, and also use the SNHC for their more serious illnesses; or they could do the reverse. They could purchase catastrophic care insurance instead, and go to the SNHC for their more frequent medical problems. These possibilities would tend to lower catastrophic care insurance premiums, and make such insurance possibly more specific, or specialized. Payout limits might be set as is now done with liability insurance.

Patients with severe chronic illness, or for example, parents with a diabetic child could go to the SNHC. The chances are good the child would soon find a niche there, and be quite happy. In any event, patients and parents would know they were getting the finest scientific medical care even though the frills might be absent. Parents of such a diabetic child, for example, would not be afraid to change jobs for fear of losing insurance benefits. Employers would be less burdened with the complexities of providing medical care for their employees and pensioners. Employers, especially small business employers could use more of their assets and efforts to regain our place in the world productive scene.

Effects on Other Aspects of Medical Practice

The use of template progress notes and surgical procedure notes derived through evolving systems engineering, will improve efficiency. So will direct patient computer interfacing. The SNHC will be striving constantly to improve its medical science. It will be striving for ever greater efficiency and cost effectiveness in its medical care delivery. Interconnecting computers, computer bulletin boards, early incorporation of digital technology, wireless communication, televideo, high definition television, efficient dissemination of patient information, and electronically transmitted scientific publications can all be used to improve inter-facility communication. While costs will always be a factor, elimination of direct financial considerations and more sensible approaches to accountability will make possible new ways of medical care delivery that can be passed on to the private sector.

We have led the world in many medical innovations. We can do it with this one. The honest truth is, there is no really satisfactory medical care delivery method in the world. Let's make one.

The SNHC and the Private Physician

How will such a revolutionary thing as advocated here affect the remaining medical profession who do not want to work in these free Safety Net Hospital-Clinics?

Private practitioners may not be subjected to anymore competition from the SNHC than they are now from existing HMOs, charity, veterans, military and teaching hospital-clinics. That is, unless these Safety Net Hospital-Clinics begin to offer a better, new, and innovative arena to match the scientific progress in medicine today. Then both patients and physicians will flock to them. Private practitioners could be expected to alter their actions to compete with these SNHCs if a competitive threat presented itself. The rising tide of HMOs and preferred provider organizations are a much more competitive threat to private practitioners at present.

Once the SNHC is in place and functioning properly, an entirely new form of adaptability confronts private physicians and their patients. Let the private physician face the patient and the patient's pocketbook with no third-party intervention. It is exciting and instructive to imagine this. It is almost novel, so long have we bought the propaganda about the terror of being without health insurance. Of course few of us would pay for medical care if we thought this stance of being entitled to medical care insurance paid for by someone else would get medical care for us free. We started out, remember, to help those who could not help themselves.

For many physicians, the safety net idea, if it can be organized as proposed, will offer a haven rather than a threat. Many physicians might flock to the SNHCs to escape the present problems, and to trade high gross incomes for more security and less hassle. It would not take much arithmetic for private practitioners who can really look at the bottom line to realize the trade-offs are not bad. Many staunch supporters of the status quo might come to realize this in time. If not, they would still be free to practice as they choose.

Will private physicians be required to pay taxes to support their competition? Yes they will, and so will patients pay for a service they may not use. Both would still have the assurance they could use the system if they ever had to. Knowing good medical care is always available is valuable security to us all. Also, physicians will be paying taxes to help handle a vexing problem that has been thrust on them by a society that has never asked the same of any of its other members.

The SNHC innovation has the advantage of disrupting the status quo gradually since it coexists with all other forms of medical care delivery from the onset. And so it allows these other aspects of medical practice to evolve in ways not appreciated before. This would tend to minimize the costs of this change. Still, physicians will pay a price for this promise of freedom. The strategy of government threatening a given group of citizens to where those citizens can be stampeded into accepting less than they had wanted in the beginning, then incrementally adding more demands over time, has become all too familiar.

If everyone opts to avail themselves of free medical care, would this not force "socialized medicine" on all the other medical practitioners? This is doubtful. Everyone will not avail themselves of these Safety Net Hospital-Clinics, at least not at first. If whatever happens meets with majority physician and patient preference, that would be just great, no matter what it is called. The goal is free satisfied physicians and patients, both with viable alternative options.

It is those who are in real need, from whatever walk of life, who avail themselves of this refuge, who will be helped most. Many middle class citizens, knowing the SNHC is there, and perhaps testing it occasionally, will then see that medical insurance makes no sense.

Those who can force someone else to pay their premiums can be expected to continue along the status quo. The hope, the intent is that all of these systems will stand or fall each on its own merits, free of coercion and third party exploitation, and free of government inter-ference, with its entrenched penchant for regulation and redistribution of wealth.

Some Problems and Some Advantages

The Safety Net Hospital-Clinics must be protected from becoming a dumping ground for hopeless defects, cocaine babies, addicts and such, even though they could well have a hospice wing. They must be protected from encroachment by healing professions less able scientifical-ly, even though they may be far more expert at marketing.

Only by the most thoughtful mass cooperation of voters can we keep government's fingers out of that portion of the income tax payment reserved for operation of the Safety Net Hospital-Clinics. There is the danger Congress will put all manner of conditions on this money before passing it on to the states. Somehow this must be prevented. These funds must be kept out of federal and state budgets, and put directly in the hands (and the well publicized budgets) of the professionals operating the local Safety Net Hospital-Clinics. One innovation would be for Congress to require itself to obtain its own medical care at the Safety Net Hospital-Clinics.

Once the public understood the tremendous competitive advantage and the security value to everyone of the Safety Net Hospital-Clinics, even though an individual never used them, it would be difficult for politicians to find an opposing majority. The knowledge that anyone could use these SNHC, and the power this would give patients, would be sufficient to make the open, honest, efficient operation of them a concern of all patients. And we are all potential patients.

Instead of social service workers being occupied with the task of deciding a patient's ability to pay, they could turn their talents to diagnosing, for each poor person, why that person is poor, and attempt to remedy that on an individual basis. Valuable knowledge could be acquired through careful documentation of both successes and failures.

Highly medically specialized TRIAGE workers would quickly route patients to the best source of medical care or social service solely on the basis of medical and psychologic criteria. If the patient had no medical problem, they would be reassured and turned away, effectively and with power. The entire system would be run by physicians and ancillary medical persons, in a disciplined, professional and economical manner.

The Power of the Safety Net Hospital-Clinics

More than a refuge for medical care, the SNHCs would give patients without a knowledge of medical science a chance to compete for better care on more equal footing with physicians. There would always be other physicians the patient could consult for free, even for just another opinion at the SNHC. Many people who can, will seek medical care where they can be more demanding. In some ways most private patients are not demanding enough, because they feel powerless. Many feel they have no alternative to the present medical care delivery system, or if they do, they are not aware of it.

Suppose when you went to the physician or pharmacist, you asked first the cost. Suppose you said, "That is too much. I will not pay that much." Suppose you said to your physicians before they handed you a prescription, "How much is that medicine going to cost? Can you give me a cheaper one." Suppose you said to your physician "No, I will not go to that hospital. I have shopped around, and hospital X in the nearby city is much cheaper and more efficient."

Patients would have an advocate in the SNHC. Suppose you knew that in an emergency, in a financial bind, or through your preference, you could always go to the Safety Net hospital or clinics for free. Even if you would rather not go there, think of the competitive advantage it gives you the patient. Suppose you, or a large group of you went to your employer and said "I realize that as a group we get cheaper health insurance rates, but I want to be responsible for my own medical care. As seductive as the idea of someone taking care of me is, I want to be responsible for myself. Instead of the premium cost you are paying for me, pay me that as a salary increase." Suppose you went to your Congressman and said "You give my employer an income tax deduction to supply me with medical insurance. That is unfair. It robs me of the options I might have. It robs me of self-responsibility. I want that money tax-free, so that I can bargain for my own medical care—besides I am already paying for care at my SNHC."

Instead of being virtually forced to go there (because that was how your employer was insured), suppose you went to the local HMO (Health Maintenance Organization), and you said, "I want to sign on as a patient; but I want a trial period first to see if I like the service to which I am committing myself, and to see if it meets my needs. I may not personally like any of the physicians that would be caring for me. Further, if I do agree to stay with your plan, I want the right to see the physician of my choice, unless in rare instances this is impractical." I would like a list of the physicians on your staff who might be caring for me, this list should include their training and resume.

Suppose indeed. Does this illustrate how patients have lost their bargaining power. Can you see how subtly insurance has diminished this right? Who is helping insurance companies do this? Why?

Now suppose masses of the public did just what you might have done, even though they were not sure they would want to go to a clinic at a Safety Net Hospital-Clinic; but *they could if they had to.* See what power the SNHC system gives you, the patient? Finally, if you really do not like your SNHC, you with others can get together, raise a fuss and get it changed to better suit your needs, even your expectations.

What about other physicians who do not want to be associated with the SNHCs? Will they not resent and perhaps sabotage this Safety Net idea? Perhaps they will. At first it may be like the Boston tea party to them; a radical gesture unlikely to gain acceptance. But if it happens to gain wide acceptance, as I believe it will, the more adaptive will take notice. Many will look at the idealism implicit in this notion and change. They will adapt. As they do, they will begin to feel the greater freedom. Once they do, once physicians and patients resign their desperate hold on the status quo, improvements can occur.

Once physicians change, they will change in many unforeseen ways. With this plan in place, they would be freed from this responsibility, this guilt hanging over them (abetted by government), that they owe a debt to society, to the poor, the inept, the helpless. (The truth is we all do!) They will be relieved because they will know that no one will go without medical care, and no one will conscript them either. They will work with the knowledge that fewer patients will resent, albeit covertly, what they pay their physicians for medical services.

It is my sincere belief that after a time, both physicians and their patients will be better off. They will be free. Free of many subtle shackles that have been binding them for some time.

■ *CHAPTER NINE*

Triage and Delegation

TRIAGE means the sorting of patients. It was used in a war situation where a person, usually a physician, sorted patients according to severity or type of injury so the patients could be routed to particular destinations, or given on-the-spot treatment. Some variant of that is often used today in crowded emergency rooms. TRIAGE is used here to mean a very different form of gate-keeper, so a word different from gatekeeper was chosen. If a physician's sole motivation is quality of patient care, then much medical cost can be saved by conscientious TRIAGE and delegation, at considerable advantage to the patient.

There is a much better way to TRIAGE for our purposes than is commonly employed, if sufficient medical personnel exist. With increased skill and knowledge comes the ability to make rapid judgments that are accurate in a high percentage of cases. Instead of on-line screening by the less skilled, why not put the most skilled on-line to rapidly divert patients to their best destination? Better yet, have general physicians quickly do the initial new patient contact, and TRIAGE to the specialty TRIAGE. This double TRIAGE system is illustrated by figure 1. At first glance this may sound inefficient, but read on.

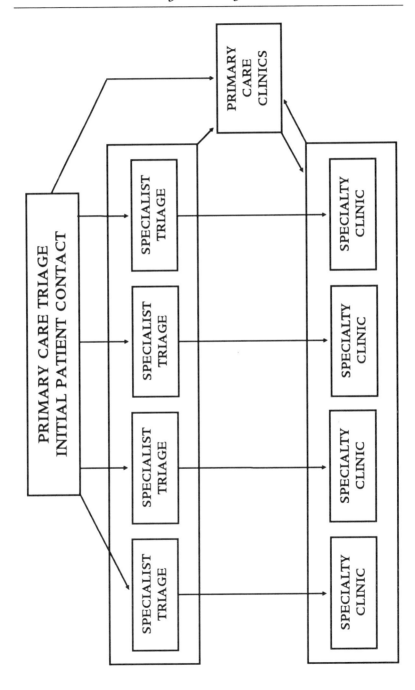

Ninety percent of what a physician sees in a day's practice consist of no more than fifty different conditions. Roughly eighty percent of what a physician sees every day consists of no more than twenty conditions. (This narrows even further in today's specialty practices). Of these eighty percent, an aid can be trained to meet many of their common needs, **once these are accurately determined**, and if this delegation to an aid were followed and carefully supervised.

Conscientious TRIAGE is one of those changes to which we must adapt if we are to reduce costs, yet maintain or increase quality of care. The importance of personal physician-patient relationships can be preserved too. The trust of the patient would need to be earned in all situations.

Triage and the Safety Net Concept

The mandate of the Safety Net Hospital-Clinics is to give the best scientific medical care to the sick with economy. Again, one must first determine who is sick. Who needs attention, how soon and where? Some will need emergency care, some patients need acute care which may or may not be immediately apparent. Some patients appear for emergency care by design as a quick way to enter the system.

Many patients will require follow-up by clinicians, public health specialists or ancillary staff. Without the constraints imposed by a finance requirement, many of these out-patients and even in-patients may be treated at home or use new kinds of medical half-way houses. Charitable organizations and volunteers will eventually play a part in this aspect, too.

Persons without social security numbers will require a numerical identification, prerequisite to entering the system. Many who do not understand or speak the English language are seen daily by our charity hospitals. They must be fitted into a TRIAGE system.

The patient would see an initial receptionist who merges this patient into the system as an identifiable entity whose record is always immediately available, and capable of being retrieved quickly from anywhere in the nation. The technology exists to do this, and there is precedent galore in the present hospital systems, (meaning the system would have an easy beginning and time to evolve). All it would need is dedication, good will and freedom from interference.

At this first contact, the first sorting would take place. Most patients would be able to sort themselves given the opportunity. An example would be patients returning for their second appointment who would already know where to go. Only new patients (those who had been previous patients, and were returning with a new illness, or those on their first visit) would require initial contact decision and direction. First visits comprise about 16.4% of expected patient visits. (According to the 1991 National ambulatory Medical Care Survey cited herein).

The patient is first screened by general physicians who quickly route them to individual specialty screening clinics. There a member of each specialty quickly sends the patient to their final destination. TRIAGE would be a chore rotated among the physicians. *Every member of all the clinical specialities, including general physicians, would serve a turn at being a TRIAGE physician for their particular service.*

This rotation would be continuous. Each physician serving on the TRIAGE service would do this for a short time, for example an intense day or half day. The more advanced residents could also serve a turn as a TRIAGE physician.

Some may ask why this first sorting by a generalist to a specialist? The traditional way has been for the generalist to use the specialist as a consultant. This has not worked. Many times the specialist feels like an ace pilot on the ground, by radio, directing a pilot in the air.

This is what is happening. The generalist, rather than the patient, is choosing the correct specialist, so the specialist's talents are used efficiently. (Keep in mind both of these at this point are only TRIAGING, even though final dispositions may be made.) The specialist contact is the **diagnostic decision point**. It determines the final destination, which may well be to a general family physician.

When a specialist sends a patient to a generalist with a presumptive diagnosis, this may also upgrade the training of the generalist. Good physicians are students all their lives. Good medical practice is best wedded to good teaching. Such a situation is the ideal. This may need to be compromised in less populous areas.

Remember the specialist has seen the common things in their specialty too. This person has had three to five years of extra training in the recognition and treatment of those conditions. The specialist then should be more efficient at knowing what to do, and deciding who can most economically do it, given the exception of those conditions that the initial screening generalist finds obvious and routes directly.

An example might clarify the reasoning for this double TRIAGE. Fifteen to twenty percent of patients seek medical attention for skin diseases. Dermatologists have been shown to be cheaper than generalists in the long run, even though their fees are higher, because of the greater precision of their diagnostic and treatment skills. A good dermatologist can diagnose many skin conditions at a glance, conditions that would be an ongoing problem to many generalists.

Similarly other specialists can put their skills to quick, efficient use when screening patients. This does not mean the dermatologist would refer all the skin disease cases to the dermatology clinic. The TRIAGE dermatologist would know whether the patient had a favorite family physician, and that dermatologist would be in the most cost effective position to decide whether to send the patient directly to that family physician, or whether to route the patient through the specialty clinic.

The TRIAGE specialist is also in the best position to know what initial diagnostic procedures should be ordered, and accompany the patient to the final destination. Should further initial testing be indicated, only those diagnostic procedures that were quickly apparent would be ordered by the TRIAGE physician. The results of these tests would become available for the physician at the patient's final destination. The TRIAGE physician must also decide whether the patient needs care that day or at a later time.

There would not be time for extensive activities, except there would be time for merited quick dispatch in the case of minor concerns, where a quick diagnosis, reassurance and dismissal were all that were necessary. These concerns, of course, would not be minor to the patient, and this would be respected by the medical and ancillary staffs. Time for reassuring instruction is so essential for good patient care. Once past the decision point this could be given by ancillary personnel efficiently and effectively.

Again, such patients, after accurate diagnosis, might be referred to specific ancillary staff where patient education, explanations, reassurance and detailed instructions would be given. This most essential part of medical care would not be neglected by the SNHC.

Such delegation could markedly reduce the cost of medical care with little (if any) difference in safety. These sessions would teach, as well as give patients comforting instructions and reassurance. Regular sessions with the referring physicians would also teach the ancillary staff, hence continuously upgrading the effectiveness of a trained ancillary staff. They could form the basis for a new type of continuity of care. This type of efficiency becomes practical once the money is removed from the system.

Enlightened management of patient telephone calls, instead of explicit or veiled discouragement of them, would also greatly increase efficiency, lower costs and provide greater access to patients. Much judgment must be used here. There is increased risk involved. It is not in the patient's best interest to do too much by telephone, because objective assessment of the patient's condition is more difficult.

Even though personal reassurance and education were performed in part by trained ancillary personnel instead of a physician, in time patients would come to know and respect their nurse or medical assistant. They might seek out this person by telephone, knowing they would be readily referred to the physician if any doubt arose. Remember we are referring here to the common conditions, those that while judged not serious by the TRIAGE system, caused the patient concern. Or we are referring to well-known frequent users of the system, such as those with chronic or recurrent conditions.

For return visit appointments, there would be a battery of ancillary care technologists, part of the initial contact technology. They would arrange the final destination or return appointments. This would be done most efficiently with computer assistance and hand held wireless communication systems to both human ears and to modems.

Given sufficient patient load, there would be special off-hours TRIAGE physicians, delegated from the on-duty staff, who would refer as they saw fit. They would protect the emergency service from being overrun by people seeking quick access via the emergency room. This would help patients with after-hours problems who would otherwise need to go to some private Emergi-Center. It would assure real emergencies of better attention.

The Safety Net Hospital-Clinics, then, would be similar to today's university hospital specialty clinics, with the addition of a special admissions TRIAGE clinic, and the absence of money or means test complications. (A means test decides whether a patient is eligible for welfare). The SNHC staff would perform a new kind of patient service not available in either today's fee-for-service or charity medicine. That is the problem of whom to see. The problem of whom to see would be solved for the patient by a TRIAGE system. It is important to have a plan for large numbers of patients because it is easier to scale it down than to build it up. Once such a plan is well organized and operational somewhere, it can be adapted by smaller facilities.

At the SNHC, the emphasis has shifted from randomly organized, more physician intensive, money driven, service oriented, conventional private practice to efficient, cost effective, yet humane use and adaptation of newer techniques for handling large patient loads with myriads of demands, where payment is not a consideration. What a freedom and boon to efficiency this gives. There would be, as well, constant emphasis on the use of forefront medical scientific skill and technology.

How does this differ from controlled medicine? First, it evolved from actual experience with patient care. This method was developed by a practicing physician with experience as a general physician, then as a specialist and a part time clinical professor in a university teaching hospital, and in a military setting, not by a committee of prominent lay people.* Secondly, there is freedom and there are options for patient and physicians. Care is taken to see that both are treated humanely. This introduces two important things. One is esprit. The other is competition, a market.

Control of Overuse

There is another important aspect of TRIAGE, really of all aspects of the SNHC system. These physicians are the first to confront patient abuse and over-use of the system. At every level of professional endeavor the staff must be upheld in their authority to dismiss a patient from care. The dismissing physicians must be protected from the inevitable legal opportunism, no matter how self-righteous it may be made to appear. Remember, the TRIAGE

* Or by politicians with a preconceived opportunistic agenda. These politicians must be given the credit for starting this revolution however. If only it will turn out to be in the patient's benefit. Remember we will all be patients.

physicians are there to assure that the really sick person sees a physician who has time for that patient. This is a very important innovation.

If such a system is to survive it must not follow the example of some of our public schools, where some teachers cannot teach discipline for fear of litigation or violence. A physician's decision that a patient no longer needs care must have authority. If this is decisively and objectively practiced and upheld at the outset, the practice will soon become accepted and the system will work. Physician accountability will be discussed at length later.

The Safety Net Hospital-Clinics will emphasize necessary basic medical care. They are there to provide a refuge for both patients and physicians, even though they will provide much more. Physicians (and only physicians) must be empowered to dismiss patients from the system for the sole reason they no longer need basic medical care.

Family Physicians and Specialists

This double TRIAGE idea leads to another aspect often misunderstood. That concerns the role of the general physician and the specialist. (This is repeated because it so commonly confuses.) Not surprisingly these roles differ depending on the economics of a medical practice. Some blame the high cost of medical care on too few primary care general physicians. That is simply incorrect, if only because it confuses medical economics with medical care quality. But that mistaken notion is the reason for all this confusion and attempted explanation. There are many names for the general physician, and there is some confusion about their training.

Clearly to be a "general specialist" is a contradiction of terms. One is either a better trained generalist (Sometimes the term family physician is used here) or one specializes. The confusion arises from the term "primary care physician." This simply means a physician (specialist or otherwise) who is commonly consulted directly (primarily). More and more specialists are being consulted directly as patients become more sophisticated, and as some generalists become better trained and refer to specialists less. Why should this bother anyone? One must consult the insurance bureaucrat for the answer to that. For those who equate medical care with medical insurance, and if insurance-bureaucratic-rules, seeking primarily to control costs, limit access to specialists, a problem can develop, because those specialists commonly consulted primarily feel discrimination.

Once again, medical practice is very complex, risk tolerance is necessarily low, and physicians are a self-demanding lot—and we must live with what this book calls third parties. We must also live with reality—yes we really must. So what's the point?

The idea was the generalists would initially see the patients, treat what they could, and send the others to the proper specialist. Theoretically this would lower the cost of medical care if the primary care physician charged less, and if that doctor was quick to refer the patient to the proper specialist. Several things happened to blur this idyllic picture, and some things already existed.

It is a truism that we do not know, that we do not know, what we do not know. Every physician, in fact, is concerned about completely missing something, simply because of not thinking about it, or not recognizing it.

This problem has certainly bothered medical students. Feeling inadequate when confronting a patient is very upsetting for a physician. Many young physicians were reluctant to enter a family practice residency, and tended to enter speciality residency training because they felt more adequate, more competent knowing one specialty well. Recall the discussion about risk and uncertainty. It takes a certain type of student to thrive in a family practice residency. I suspect it always will.

The notion a general practice is necessarily less lucrative than a specialty practice is simply incorrect.

Because some general physicians had more training, and because they were reluctant to refer away lucrative business, many general physicians diminished their referrals to specialists. Specialists reacted. Because specialists felt the need to provide more hands-on management in the case of some patients, or for monetary reasons, specialists failed to return patients to the family practitioner after that initial consultation. Caught in the middle, many patients continued on where they got the best results. Some people tended to continue choosing their specialist rather than relying on a family physician. This was especially true of those patients who had self-referred themselves away from their family physician. Other patients preferred their family physicians. This is as it should be and the process should be left to evolve.

As mentioned before, only 6.7% of referrals were from one physician to another in 1991. Specialists, in response, began to cultivate direct patient referrals, and many patients became more confident with their stable of specialists. Some specialities lent themselves to this more than others. This trend became more marked in urban and suburban areas.

So what happened? The hope was that the general primary physician would provide competent care for a majority of patients, thus sparing the cost, and reducing the need for more specialists; but so many specialists with good reason were calling themselves primary care physicians. Competent care must always be viewed within the context of what is available.

To repeat, in the present fee-for-service and insurance medicine, general physicians are not quick to refer away income. There is a tendency to watch and wait until a condition develops to the point where it is recognizable, or until it clears with time. There is a tendency to treat until it becomes obvious the patient must be referred, or until the patients themselves decide to see a specialist. While the general physician rarely puts the patient in jeopardy by such behavior, the cost is increased thereby, not reduced.

Now, should the patient self-refer to the wrong specialist, there is much less tendency for that specialist to cling to that patient, because of the restrictions on his or her general expertise, and because of the specialists psychological need for assurance. (It is said specialists know more and more about less and less). Specialists in such a case tend to dismiss the patient at once to the proper referral, often at no charge.

In an HMO, the tendency is for the general physicians to see a large number of patients per unit time—as many patients as possible is often encouraged. There are also specialists on the HMO staff. Rapid, efficient disposition of the patient is required. Physician time may be "wasted" by the patient's need to talk, to be listened to, and to be reassured, or to be instructed. This vital function is important for patients. Often this function was best served by a general family physician. All of these desirable things can be provided efficiently and effectively, but a different system is required.

This would not be a problem at the SNHC because the TRIAGE system provides more efficient patient assignment and more efficient expenditure of clinic physician time by relieving the clinic physicians of much patient load, giving these physicians more time with the sicker patients. Those not so ill or endangered, once this were accurately determined, could get their information and reassurance from ancillary personnel.

Finally, third parties are into the act. These people must get their information handed them from others, since they have no direct contact with patient care. They are often misinformed. It seemed logical for companies, saddled with ever escalating employee health costs, (refer to the chapter about insurance) to hire generalists as gate-keepers. This has been discussed.

The generalist gatekeeper notion, in my opinion, overlooks a fundamental fact of both medical quality and cost. Both are optimized if at the point of delegation there is applied the utmost in medical expertise available, for this requires the utmost in quick diagnostic ability.

Generalist gate-keepers have continued because no better method has been found to help reduce the implicit defects of the present insurance mistakes (in no way the gate-keepers fault), and because no one but the patient and physician know really what is happening. Referrals are reduced. Mistakes are difficult to ascertain, mainly because few are interested in looking beyond the cost reduction resulting from the reduced referrals. Many sophisticated patients feel trapped and frustrated. More and more have their stable of specialists in mind.

From this gatekeeper concept grew the misconception that generalists provided *adequate* care at a lower cost, hence specialists must be more expensive, and so we should have more generalists and less specialists. One needs a reason why specialists are more expensive. The "street reason" is specialists do more (unnecessary) expensive tests and procedures. This works well for it is difficult to prove or refute, and it presents a natural for politicians who can emphasize or remove that word "unnecessary" depending on the audience.

There are two horns to this dilemma. The general physician can more economically treat that great pool of common conditions in most situations; and also provide continuity of care. Yet, leaving aside the values of continuity of care, and acknowledging the general physician is well-trained, and able to care for the frequent common ills of a patient population, there is hardly a patient the primary care physician cares for that the correct specialist could not do as well or better. This is said from the experience of being a general physician for several years myself.

On average, the specialist's therapy is more precise, consuming less time and money, even though the specialist may have higher fees. The costly complex procedures are usually done from specialists decision anyway. Specialists can best decide when these need not be done.

So in the present medical practice environment, the general physician may not reduce the cost of medical care, but does provide a luxury, and the comfort of continuous contact with the patient and that patient's family, but may not provide for the continuous development of the best quality care.

Continuity of care can be provided by the specialist as well in some situations. Many patients go directly to specialists in some areas particularly. Many patients with chronic illness have a recurrent need for a specialist, and such care is often the most cost effective. Internists, Cardiologists, Pediatricians, Gynecologists, Urologists, Dermatologists and Orthopaedists are examples. Many of these specialists are now striving to be called primary care physicians also.*

Change the economic parameters a bit. Should the patient care be within a Safety Net Hospital-Clinic (or within a health maintenance organization), the economic incentives to hold on to a patient change.

In more remote areas, with today's transportation and communication, what is available may resolve to the expertise of the person at the point of decision.

Finally, once again, consider the scenario where there is no fee-for-service medicine, a situation with a large patient load of prepaid, or no pay patients presenting for care. Patient over-utilization and its control is a problem. Optimum accuracy and efficiency in determining the severity and acuteness of the presenting patient illness becomes crucial. For the Safety Net Hospital-Clinic, enlightened deployment of care resources, and first contact double TRIAGE delegation of the patient assumes more importance than ever before.

* General physicians saw 24.6% of patient visits in 1991. The above group of specialists saw 50.6% of patients in 1991. 6.7% of patients were referred from one physician to another. Taken from Advanced Data No. 230,1993, U.S. Dept. of Health and Human Services op.cit.

Competent efficient initial assessment assumes a new prominence. There is but one concern. Is the person sick? If so why? What is wrong? What needs to be done? If the person is not sick, regardless of how needy, the Safety Net Hospital Clinic is not the place for that person to be.

Who is to do this? How is it best organized? It is solving practical problems like these and making them work that will solve the medical cost crisis. Not only must more efficient ways of medical care be innovated, they must be made to work on-line in real time. It would seem obvious that physicians and patients working together would be the logical choice to do this. The hidden agendas of third parties should be brought to light, and the costly aspects eliminated if maximum patient concern and cost containment is to come about.

Some Examples

A patient appears with a dark mole on their face. The TRIAGE dermatologist takes a look and tells the patient not to worry, the growth is a harmless, unsightly, benign skin tumor. That physician tells the patient what to expect and forthwith sends the patient home, perhaps via an ancillary person who gives the patient a prescribed leaflet to further inform and reassure. The trained ancillary person listens to the patient as long as required. If that patient elects to have the growth removed for cosmetic reasons, other options are available in the fee-for-service sector. Remember: an extremely important role of the TRIAGE physician is that of reassurance and dismissal, but this implies an accurate diagnosis. A high percentage of patients need only that. To be sure, some will require referral for tests before that reassurance can be provided. There will be no need here for defensive medicine, for unnecessary activities to protect against lawsuits, or to increase the fee. There will be every reason to order whatever diagnostic procedure good scientific medicine requires and no more.

Another TRIAGE person may tell a quite sick, slightly febrile patient that they probably have a viral upper respiratory infection, one that has been going around. That TRIAGE physician has seen several that day. This patient is told they had best go back home to bed, drink lots of fluids, try not to spread it to others, and return to their assigned family physician or call one of the telephone advisors there if they became further concerned. Once this diagnosis is entered in the computer, that information goes automatically to the public health department. Next fall that patient will be contacted for a "flu shot."

A patient presents with a normal third pregnancy. The primary TRIAGE physician sends her to the prenatal clinic and her family physician.

The mission of the Safety Net Hospital-Clinics is the most efficient use of the medical facilities for the patient's best interest, and operation of these facilities in coopera- tion and friendly competitive association with the other physicians of the community.

Alternative Options

For people who want medical care another way, and who can afford it, plenty of other options exist. In fact alternative options are there for both physician and patient. This would be a major morale factor. Preservation of physician esprit and incentive is so important for good medical care. Good medical care will always be more than a job. Good medical care requires tremendous drive and energy. This requires esprit.

Finally, some of the smaller more isolated Safety Net Hospital-Clinics will need to adapt their TRIAGE methods to their facilities and resources, and to the availability of the more distant facilities with greater resources. Different kinds of alternative options within these SNHC facilities must be used.

CHAPTER TEN

The Safety Net
Hospital-Clinics

Some Ideas on Getting Started

The starting of something new and original is always fraught with doubts. Certainly there will be mistakes, sometimes deep discouragement. Much must be cut from the whole cloth. Many of us feel lost without a pattern. No amount of discussion and persuasion from a book will substitute for the actual story of courage, originality, and on-the-spot initiative required. The working together of patients and physicians itself may stir old suspicions and egos. What do business or administrative people know about running a medical enterprise; and what do medical people know about business? If not before, certainly as people get to the actual doing, these questions are apt to surface. One great help is to have access to those who have done it before, or at least have done something similar.[*]

Nonmonetary Remuneration

Medical school (from the beginning) imprints the value of non-monetary remuneration. The faculty, instead of more money, received status, stimulating working conditions and the opportunity to work at the frontiers of medicine. Such a faculty has the luxury of having specialists in training; young, top-of-the-heap physicians (called residents) to do the chores, so to speak. These residents learn by doing. They are taught by the paid, full-time faculty and a volunteer clinical faculty of practicing physicians. It is these residents and interns who do the common work, the day-to-day listening to and ministering to the patients. This makes for contented patients (who have many trained people to answer their questions, who are under virtual continual surveillance), highly-trained and motivated helpers, and a relaxed faculty.

So our medical school teaching hospitals create an environment desirable to most physicians and one of great benefit to patients. They create a faculty who are highly regarded, and thrive on this. They work for less pay, yet have great security. They have the opportunity to live and

---

[*] For this reason, interested persons should procure from the Group Health Cooperative of Puget Sound, 521 Wall Street, Seattle, Washington their booklet entitled "We Knew We Could Do It." This booklet chronicles in delightfully quaint ways the problems that a group of patients had as they began their own prepaid medical care cooperative, which then grew to giant size. It says much between the lines that is impossible to paraphrase in a book such as this. At first they grew too slowly; then grew too rapidly. Either was a problem.

work in a community of scholars. So they not only care for patients, train, discipline and motivate new physicians, they have the opportunity to add to future progress in medicine.

If there is a problem, a puzzle, a rare case or difficult procedure, one of the full-time faculty, or a volunteer teaching staff clinical professor is there to make the decisions or to perform the procedure, thus teaching the young specialists, who are growing in stature and ability. The patient profits from this constant high-quality surveillance. These same patients could be seeing these same residents in just a few years out in practice as full-fledged specialists. What better precedent on which to build a solution, a system of patient care for all.

Medical students, after four years of pre-medical college, get four intensive years of didactic and practical medical training in fairly large groups in a setting much like any other college, except that the tuition is higher. Upon graduation they are given M.D. degrees. After that, they are trained on-the-job in small groups. After the first year of this (the internship) they are eligible to take the examinations for their license to practice medicine in a given state. Most continue on as residents in specialty training or in Family Practice. It is important to distinguish a medical school from a teaching hospital. Some are combined.

Each SNHC should become a teaching facility, or if of insufficient size, a branch of one. This would be a feasible luxury for every participant, physician, patient and resident staff. Everyone would benefit from a clinical training facility for nurses as well. These would integrate with local colleges who would provide the didactic aspects of a nursing training program.

Medical schools and teaching hospitals could stand a little competition too, and the training of residents could profitably be more widespread geographically. Some would become settled in the area of their training, helping in the uneven distribution of specialist physicians.* Many of those desirable resident applicants could become part of a SNHC residency training program. The SNHC should become a teaching hospital center for training residents and interns because this would attract volunteer part-time faculty to the area. How this works is perhaps difficult for lay people to understand.

Patients too would benefit, for they must now journey to the medical teaching centers when they have a diagnostic problem not solved at home. They must put up with inconvenience, yet they have advantages too. Top medical minds will be checking and discussing them. This medical group is rarely in a hurry. They may call in another specialist, and another.

There are medical schools, which instead of having their own university hospitals, have an association with a county charity hospital. There are medical schools that have both. There are teaching hospitals not directly connected with a medical school. We have a long tradition of county charity teaching hospitals in this country. Bellvue Hospital in New York City, Cook County Hospital in Chicago and Los Angeles County Hospital are examples. Cook County Hospital is associated with the University of Illinois, and Los Angeles County Hospital is associated with the University of Southern California. Medical schools that own teaching hospitals also have residency

---

 * In the teaching hospital-medical school where I am associated, in one specialty residency three hundred applicants applied for just four positions. Even with duplication of applicants to different schools, there is still a surplus.

training programs and there are teaching programs associated with the veterans hospitals. Some large multispecialty clinics have accredited teaching programs. Numerous smaller county charity hospitals scattered all over the land have residency teaching programs in family practice.

At one time there existed a network of County charity hospitals in many areas throughout the country, with their associated outpatient clinics. Many of them are in existence today. Perhaps some of these could be adapted to become our first Safety Net Hospital-Clinics. Some have been phased out for various reasons, others are run down. It is time to revive them. These hospitals and their outpatient clinics were there to serve as a source of care for the poor. With a bit of fixing, they would provide quality care for everyone. Some of our private hospitals might choose to join this network.

We have a widespread network of veteran's hospitals and their associated clinics. Some of these are utilized somewhat inefficiently. We have a widespread network of military hospitals with their associated clinics. Contrary to the opinion of many, some of these military hospitals are among the finest in the land.

The utilization of our veteran's and military hospitals hopefully is and will be decreasing. They could be joined with a reconstituted system of County hospitals and their associated outpatient facilities (at least initially) until the infrastructure of the required network of Safety Net Hospital-Clinics is in place. They would be quickly convertible back to military usage in case of emergency.

We have a rosy yet worn promise of a future peaceful geopolitical coexistence. Political pressure exists for the reduction or alternate use of some veteran's and some military facilities. We have perennial political pressure to spend money "in order to make more jobs." While need exists for other infrastructure, there is also need for reduction of the estimated hundreds of billions spent on medical care. Some of this money could be used to develop the network of hospital and clinic infrastructure rather than divert a healthy portion of the money to the medical insurance companies to build their infrastructure and pay their large executive salaries.

The reader may think these County hospitals are dirty, rundown, depressing places. This is only partially true. Some are now quite modern and well-run teaching hospitals. While many think they would not want to go to these places, there are two remedies. (1) Clean them up. (2) Realize the scientific quality of medical care, the part that really counts has little to do with the physical decor. The system proposed would change them radically anyhow as they changed from "poor house hospitals" to hospitals we would all be willing to use with trust and appreciation.

There exists, then, a good start on capital structure for the creation of a medical care safety net system for all. This would include outpatient clinics and emergency room facilities. From this beginning, a permanent staff, similar to the medical school teaching hospital staff (detailed elsewhere) would be installed. There would be a full-time professor of each department, an associate professor, and so forth depending on the size of the institution and the size of each department.

There would be an excellent pension plan so staff physicians would not need to worry about extra fees and extra business ventures to provide for their old age or a suitable standard of living. There would be the privilege of working after retirement at full-time pay, if the hiring supervisory system judged the person capable, and a need for that person existed. Elder, capable physicians would be consulted and many would volunteer.

Much that would make this system excel would depend on subtle psychological factors, best judged by elderly, retired physicians from their unique vantage point of a lifetime of experience, those who are wise, idealistic, caring, and knowledgeable about medical science, actual clinical problems, and social problems as well.

With a volunteer clinical part-time staff, a reasonably well-paid full time staff, seeing patients, consulting and also training a resident staff (interns, student nurses, and residents) working at relatively low pay, there results an *unbeatable* medical care bargain.

There would be no thought of money (from patient fees or insurance hassles) in such a medical practice except in the cooperative effort of the entire staff to practice economy and avoid waste. This psychology must be built in through enlightened administrative practice. You might think physicians would not work this way. They are doing it now. It is traditional for residents and interns to work during their training for relatively low pay. It is traditional and an honor for practicing physicians to be invited to volunteer to teach. For three months a year, once a week, this is a refreshing change for many physicians. If we are to attract physicians to work in this fashion, some things are essential. All of them are advantageous to patients.

The physician organizational structure advocated here is familiar to practicing physicians, and many are now in such county hospital positions. Recruiting other physicians would not be difficult, once they were presented with the opportunity to practice high quality medicine, with a sound and fair plan, which they could leave at any time.

The scientific and medical care facilities must be kept truly top class. Working conditions must be good. There would be no need for frills or waste; but the physicians must have the best in patient care facilities. Commercial suppliers would be well served to provide their newest and best products to keep the physicians in the habit of knowing about their products. This use would serve another purpose. The physicians would quickly determine the best. This in the long run is cheaper.

Morale must be kept high, so should feelings of security. This is the currency! Physicians must be left alone to do their work, to create their professional world. This is currency! We must never, allow the quality of our medical care to deteriorate, even to stagnate. This is terribly false economy.

We must all be cognizant of the magnitude of the change. The very fabric of medical practice, indeed of the culture, is altered by changes in the economic context of medical care delivery. Even the type of student entering the medical schools will change. Students will enter the specialties, the areas of medical practice that best meet their emotional and intellectual needs, rather than their financial needs.

To a large extent, physicians have been pushed aside. Often political considerations, and the limits of the politician's knowledge of a problem have prevailed. There have been unnecessary complications imposed from afar. Administrative mistakes and administrative largess have proliferated. Now that some trial attorneys have been able to win enormously expensive lawsuits from County charitable hospitals, they are driving away more of the volunteer faculty. What better deep pocket than a County Treasury?

These things must be kept out of the Safety Net Hospital-Clinics. This is a big hurdle. The SNHC must be run from the bottom up by those with intimate practical understanding of the medical and associated problems involved. The nursing problems, the highly trained ancillary personnel, and the clerical and maintenance aspects are all important. How these are administered is crucial. The entire ambience, the atmosphere must be changed from what it has become.

Safety Net Hospital-Clinic Financing

One of the crucial questions of this Safety Net Concept is how it should be financed. How much money would this cost? How will the cost be met? We must know more about it. First, the plan is financially sound, and it uses much of what we already have, for much of the infrastructure and the psychological precedents are already in place, much is not in place. New facilities are necessary, and older structures need repair or replacement. All this may require bonded indebtedness. Today is an excellent time for that. Interest rates are low and the country is awash with capital blocked from venture investment by high capital gains taxes.*

The SNHCs should be financed by a surtax consisting of the same percentage of everyone's income tax *payments,* paid along with everyone's federal income tax. Everyone would pay the same percentage of their income tax payment. And everyone could avail themselves of the same exact care purchased by that funding.

Everyone would know that the amount of their funds provided them medical care, no questions asked, the rich

---

* Interested readers should consult "The Fortune Encyclopedia of Economics," published by Warner and available at many libraries.

no differently from the poor, most of whom would pay nothing. That money would buy the freedom from fear of inadequate medical care we should all be concerned about. Once arranged so we can all afford to have this care, we must all feel it is the quality of medical care we could—and would use. Indeed, we should settle for none less than the best quality of care available anywhere. This plan would buy security. It would encourage responsible use. The income tax payment-percentage rate would change as the SNHCs costs changed. These costs would be public knowledge, the costs made public every year. So the tax becomes highly visible, and it should be. It should become a project of the people, rather than one of the government.

This SNHC tax money should be immediately moved from the U.S. Treasury (on the basis of population and operating efficiency) to each state for distribution to the individual county or regional hospitals, once these are established. (This is discussed in detail later on).

Care must be taken to prevent the federal and state government from imposing unwise conditions on the distribution of these funds. This would require help from Congress.

The states would pass the money directly to the SNHC State Executive Committee for the operation of the Safety Net Hospital-Clinics. This committee should be appointed by the Governor in a manner to be detailed later, with more definitive organizational details. (See Fig. 2 on page 193 for an organizational details chart.)

The State Executive Committee elects a chairman who would function somewhat like the Federal Reserve Board Chairman functions, in that this person would act as the spokesman, executive and representative between meetings.

This committee would have available a financial report from each individual Safety Net Hospital-Clinic, similar to current reports to stockholders of publicly-owned corporations. Much of the current knowledge and existing law in this area could be used as a model.

The operating efficiency and eligibility for the next year's funds would be determined by a comparative analysis of these reports by the State Executive Committee. These reports would be prepared and audited according to accepted accounting procedures, and made public.

Medicaid can be dismissed. It should be eliminated with each state shifting these funds to their SNHCs. But not as insurance. Medicaid has helped many people, yet it has caused more problems than it has solved. Perhaps it could be continued as an option in some of the big city charity hospitals.

For the Safety Net Hospital-Clinics there is such a simple solution to the problem of accessibility. They will demand no money and no admission card from their patients who enter for care. It cannot be repeated too often: anyone appearing who is sick will receive care. The SNHC will compete with other local physicians on the basis of medical competence. Admission, TRIAGE and the appointment process would be the greeting effort. This is one place that will be a haven for patients and physicians alike, where money does not enter into the relationship among the patient and the physician or physician assistants. Neither does anything else. This is currency! Many physicians would be strongly attracted to such a situation.

Medicare is another matter. It might persist as a competitive option, or be engulfed by the Safety Net Hospital-Clinics. Some of those who have Medicare enjoy the illusion they are not paying their medical bills. And many rightly believe they have paid for this "insurance." They have the advantage of going to the physician of their choice. For this reason alone, Medicare should be allowed to persist as a competitive alternative, at least until it self destructs or survives on its merits. Those who do not want to worry about paying some differential to their physician might opt for the SNHC. Medicare needs a bit of competition too.

How are we to deal with persons who have paid their Medicare premium, and who come to the SNHC for care? They would be treated like everyone else. After all, they are paying their part of their income tax too.

Who would relinquish their Medicare? These might be people requiring expensive care, people not having enough Medigap insurance to cover their care, or those with some personal reason. Perhaps they want to get a second opinion. On the other hand, since patients with Medicare treated at the SNHC would owe no money, there would be no need for Medigap insurance or the fear of leftover bills to pay out of pocket. Nor would their be the expense and bother of voluminous paper work.

Most patients would be quick to drop the Medicare cost and bother, and to that extent, Medicare would be discontinued. The Medicare that did survive (among those electing to get their medical care from private physicians) would do so on its own merits, and so remain as a nice alternative option for those willing to pay the premium.

Gifts, memorials, and bequests would stay with the Safety Net Hospital-Clinic to which they were given. How they would be used at that site would be a matter for administrative decision. Each State SNHC Executive Council would establish a policy on this matter in advance. It is not uncommon for grateful patients or grieving survivors to want to give donations to a hospital. This should be encouraged. Tax-free bequests, if allowed, would most likely become popular, and in time would lower the percentage of surtax paid by the populace. Indeed, such a thing would assure the finest facilities for future generations.

Suggested Operational Details

It was suggested above that a certain percentage of our annual income tax *payment* would be taken for support of the Safety Net Hospital-Clinics as a top priority. It could not be mingled with any other aspect of the federal government's budget. Rather it would be sent directly to the respective states. There follows further details of one plausible way this would work.

The total sum collected for each year would be made public promptly, together with the amounts distributed to each state and to each SNHC. Money would be distributed according to the census of patients treated that previous year by each recipient SNHC, and a formula relating the operating efficiency of that institution. Again, not just census but efficiency would be the considerations. Such things as efficient use of hospital beds, cost of drugs dispensed, etc., would be considered. The amount of money going for patient care, for employee salaries and bonuses, for administrative and peer review costs would be published details of the accounting. At the state level this money must by law be distributed by that state's SNHC State Executive Council directly to the individual Safety Net Hospital-Clinics in a manner to be detailed in a moment.

By law, a report of the money received and spent the previous year by each hospital would be published. Again, this report would resemble the stockholders report of a publicly owned corporation, complete with a certified audit. The cost of the audit would be charged to each state's funds and paid by the Executive Council.

The ten most economical hospitals in the nation, judged by a complex formula (beyond the scope of this book) would be awarded an extra 10% of their total allocation. Their portion of this would be distributed to each employee of the winning hospital. The bonus would be divided equally, meaning every employee would get the same amount. The winners would be decided by a committee of ten: two Physicians and two accountants from each of five State Executive Councils drawn annually at random. In case of a tie, the five chiefs of the respective Executive Councils would decide the winner. A new committee of ten would be chosen each year. The bonus would be funded by an assessment from each of the non-winning facilities.

Patient Acceptance of the Safety Net Hospital Clinics

The basic premise is this. If one gives the populace the opportunity to choose from competitive alternatives, these alternatives will sort themselves out and will be most adaptive, (provided the options are not perverted). Patient, physician and third-party abuses can best be controlled by competition among the options. Orders from above, especially from the political or insurance arena, can never be so efficient.

Even if the care at the SNHC is free to all, and if they indeed practice top quality medicine, not everyone would go there. For one reason, most patients have no understanding of what constitutes top quality, scientific medical care. One must look at why a patient chooses a physician. Patients, when they become ill and must choose a physician, have very little factual information about the competence of physicians. Most patients see a new physician because of a friend's recommendation; less frequently by another physician's referral. The patient has very little basis for judgment. Hospital nurses, and sometimes physicians' assistants, *may* have pragmatic advice about which physicians are most competent in their area; but very few people have access to them.

Once in a physician's office, patients have input about the physician's personality, fees, office ambience, and staff. Once they have gone this far, very few patients will "backout," but some will not return, and roughly twenty-percent of patients will not get their prescriptions filled. There are perhaps many reasons for this.

The crucial thing for the physician, is to instill confidence, demonstrate caring and provide comfort. One way to do this is by getting results, and by exhibiting what we call a good bedside manner. Getting results without providing a good bedside manner may not be perceived by the patient as good medical care. It has been my experience that being rushed through a physician's office bothers patients a great deal, and it should, for it makes a statement.

For a Safety Net Hospital-Clinic to be effective, it must pay attention to these crucial determinants of patient acceptance and satisfaction. This is true even though the patient will have the enormous advantage of having their physician chosen for them by an expert TRIAGE agent. This person will not only be knowledgeable in a given specialty, but will know about the competence of his or her colleagues, and will strive to provide patients with continuity of care. Even referrals to private physicians outside the system will be made, if the patient requests this, or if it is in the patient's best interest.

Not everyone will go to these SNHCs by any means. Such facilities may not have as their concern much of what some patients consider important. Yet, even for them that safety net is always there. These Safety Net Hospital-Clinics will have little incentive to market themselves, as do the other competing systems of medical care. Even so, to be successful and competitive, they must provide the above essentials of confidence, caring and comforting that patients require. The statement that is so important here is the SNHC must remain competitive, both within the system and within their geographical area.

Chances are good there will be a heavy patient load; but there will be an innovative organization with a different goal than money. The SNHC will be a different system than has ever been tried. (Yet in most of its medical practice aspects it is well tried.) It is difficult to state this difference succinctly, there are so many complexities, so many subtle psychological aspects, as well as the obvious one of available top quality medical care for all. Emphasis should be placed on the inbuilt provision for continuous improvement in medical science and quality of care. Some of the socialized systems elsewhere in the world have suffered in this regard.

Patients may have incorrect expectations. They will soon find things entirely different than have military dependents, and those attending veterans' clinics, where only the bare pampering essentials are present. Yet physical surroundings similar to our better HMOs or cooperatives can be expected. Plush offices, and many of the other trappings may not be there; but the emphasis on each patient's feelings, along with honest competent care, concern, and instruction will surprise and delight many. Such an ambience can be produced and reproduced if sufficient administrative emphasis is placed there—and, most importantly if the staff is contentedly idealistic, being picked for such attributes.

Most importantly too, every effort must be made to accommodate patient choice of physician at every SNHC. Continuity of care is essential. Interestingly, such enforcement demands that physician employees be personable and honestly solicitous, for the simple reason patients will ask for those physicians who satisfy their needs. Such physicians will stand out, not only in the eyes of patients, but in the promotion standings of physicians. Patient satisfaction will be given high priority, and so will good scientific medical care. The two are by no means mutually exclusive.

Physician arrogance will simply not be tolerated, regardless how naive the patient or how specialized the physician. Arrogance often masks lack of social skills, feelings of weakness, insecurity or resentment, and this will be made clear to all staff physicians. It will not be tolerated. Better yet it will become unnecessary.

Even if patients, by and large, lack the information to wisely choose their physician, they value highly that prerogative, as they should. This is especially so if they have become accustomed to a certain physician who, over the course of time, has come to know them and their illnesses quite well. At the SNHC this will be understood and appreciated.

Those who truly need and cannot afford private care will welcome the chance to get quality care, frills or not. This does not mean the system will be devoid of gentle, caring, yet efficient medical care for them, still the care may be different than the expectations of the more affluent.

People who can afford what they consider good medical care will quickly opt for it. Of these people, many will be quick to note, but slow to admit, they do not relish being put together with poor people. This is especially true if it happens they are put in a large ward housing their hospital bed; or if the hospital were located in the slum section of a big city.

Few of those in power understand the poor, because they lack a first-hand knowledge of them. Most physicians have been trained ministering to the poor. Patients in our charity hospitals today develop strong bonds of loyalty to and faith in their physicians. Many of the poor (not all) exhibit a refreshing lack of cynicism, impatience, and skepticism so common in private practice patients.

Often the poor are not demanding. To the truly needy, such clinics become a haven. Even though such patients wait, they do so because they realize the physician is busy with others. This puts less stress on the physician, and permits more concentration on patient care. In private practice, some patients will fret and become angry if the physician is ten minutes late for their appointment, yet many of these same people will gladly take more than their allotted time with the physician once there.

Administration of a SNHC

This section is included for those who want a more detailed plan.They will find in this section a direction that will form a basis for criticism and productive change.

The administration of an individual SNHC would begin from the bottom up. All employees from the janitor to the head of a department would be represented. Each level would elect a supervisor. They would serve one-year terms. There would be a janitor's group, a housekeeper's group, a nurse's aid group etc. Volunteers would be able to join whatever group their skills indicated. An assistant supervisor would be chosen from each section by random choice. The assistant supervisor would be the supervisor-elect for the following year. Where this is practical, the names of all members (except new employees that year) and those who have served as supervisor for the previous two years, would be put in a receptacle and the name drawn. The person chosen could decline, and if so, another name would be chosen.

The department supervisors and assistant supervisors would form a study committee to meet once a month to adjudicate grievances. They would examine suggestions from the suggestion boxes. They would discuss recommendations and directives for the general operation of the hospital and clinics at their level. These would include censure for waste and for lack of caring, recommendations for expenditures, and savings of expenditures (including capital equipment). The most important aspect of their meeting would be an integration and cross-understanding of the problems and operations of each department and ways to improve efficiency overall. The most important thing would be lending to efficient patient care, a commitment to an aura of self-discipline and self-esteem.

Information about each month's agenda and actions on this agenda would be sent directly to the Department Chief and to the head professional administrator. (There would be an ancillary professional administrative staff, depending on the size of the facility.)

Each medical department head would run their department with the help of the Assistant Dept. Chief, and with attention to input from the supervisors on the line. The Medical Department Chief and Assistant Chief would work closely with the professional administrator, the administrative staff, and the nursing staff. The Medical Department Chief's responsibilities would include assignment and supervision of medical duties, patient care, scheduling etc. They would have the responsibility to keep the numbers of employees at all levels in their department to a minimum, and everyone operating at maximum efficiency. They would oversee the recruiting and training of medical volunteers, and of coordinating with the professional administration staff. They would be in direct charge of the overall teaching program, for which they might appoint a full time director, depending on the size of the facility.

In each Safety Net Hospital-Clinic there would be one Physician Chief heading the entire operation, who is chosen by random drawing from the department heads. This Physician Chief would serve a one-year term. An Assistant Chief would be the Medical Chief-elect. Those having served the past three years would be excluded from the drawing, if sufficient numbers exist. Any department head could decline if chosen. The executive department then would consist of a Chief, an Assistant Chief, and a full-time professional Hospital Administrator who would be subordinate to the Chief, except The Hospital Administrator would automatically hold a seat on the State Medical Advisory Council. The Hospital Administrator would be a career position.

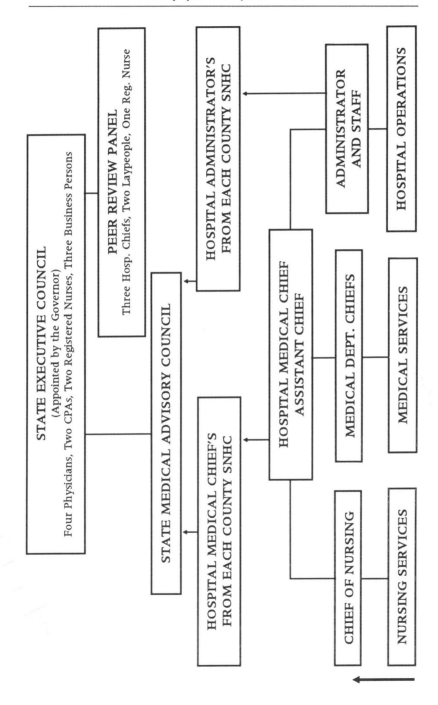

STATE EXECUTIVE COUNCIL
(Appointed by the Governor)
Four Physicians, Two CPAs, Two Registered Nurses, Three Business Persons

PEER REVIEW PANEL
Three Hosp. Chiefs, Two Laypeople, One Reg. Nurse

HOSPITAL ADMINISTRATOR'S
FROM EACH COUNTY SNHC

ADMINISTRATOR
AND STAFF

HOSPITAL OPERATIONS

STATE MEDICAL ADVISORY COUNCIL

HOSPITAL MEDICAL CHIEF
ASSISTANT CHIEF

MEDICAL DEPT. CHIEFS

MEDICAL SERVICES

HOSPITAL MEDICAL CHIEF'S
FROM EACH COUNTY SNHC

CHIEF OF NURSING

NURSING SERVICES

The State Medical Advisory Council

The State Medical Advisory Council would be comprised of two parts. One body would consist of the career Hospital Administrators from each member hospital of that state system. They as a group could pass recommendations up to the State Executive Council, or down to the individual hospitals. These recommendations could be about any subject within their area of expertise, including recommendations for referral of physicians or others to the State medical Licensing Boards for criminal or other disciplinary matters.

Each state's SNHC Medical Advisory Council will have a second part composed of the Physician Hospital Chiefs from all the state's SNHCs. These two groups, consisting of both the Chiefs and the Head Administrators (except for emergency meetings), will meet for a few days once a year. They will stay in close communication at all times. In time, remote video conferences will become commonplace. They will make recommendations about any aspect of the state hospital operations.

The Safety Net Hospital-Clinic Physician Chiefs are charged with physician discipline for technical incompetence, negligence, errors or omissions judged to be greater than chance. They would also adjudicate evidence of insufficient training, defects of character, habitual carelessness, ineptness, lack of caring when treating patients, laziness, alcoholism, improper drug use, or failure to perform in situations where judgment by their peers is considered necessary and just. Hospital Chiefs will be charged to put great effort into *prevention* of such problems. They will not be required to wait for a patient complaint to take action on these matters.

The State Medical Advisory Council could make recommendations to the State Executive Council, including hiring of Medical Department Chiefs or Assistant Chiefs when vacancies occur. They could check with the other Hospital Chiefs for redundancies in their staffs, making a transfer possible within the system. This group could pass recommendations down pertaining to all the state's SNHC. Examples might be: preventative medicine actions, coordinated screening clinics, information pertaining to the location and sharing of expensive capital equipment, locations with facilities specializing in esoteric or expensive tests, and information pertaining to cooperation in, or confirmation of research efforts being done by individual hospitals.

The Peer Review Panel

Patient complaints and charges of errors and omission will be brought before an arbitration group called the Peer Review Panel. This panel will review all charges and take the appropriate action depending on the charge. Every effort will be expended until satisfactory methods of assuring patient representation and requiring strict physician accountability can be developed. The Medical Department chiefs and the SNHC Chief will cooperate with the State Licensing Boards. They can request and arrange arbitration or court trials. See fig. 2.

The Peer Review Panel would be composed of three physicians, two lay persons, and one registered nurse. The actual persons composing any given panel, particularly the specialist physicians, will vary according to the expertise thought necessary for fair peer review and disposition of each case.

(These may be Department Chiefs if the hospital-clinic is large enough, or they may be physicians brought from other hospital-clinics if necessary or prudent.)

The members of this panel will be chosen by a committee of three from the State Executive Council. This committee of three will be appointed each year by the chairman of the State Executive Council. Four continuous one-year terms are the maximum permitted this committee of three.

Other duties of the Peer-review Panel will include recommendations and arrangements with the proper government bureau for monetary compensation for injuries arising out of the course of treatment, whether that treatment was considered negligent or not. This group would require the advice and consent of a panel of medical and psychological experts on disability and rehabilitation, consisting of at least one expert in each field.

The evaluation of human injury, and the determinants required for recovery and rehabilitation are the natural province of the medical profession. They belong here in the SNHCs, a province of the Peer Review Council.

The use of this facility to adjudicate industrial injury compensation cases and other accident cases would be most efficient. It would be economical for the entire society if this body were so empowered by the appropriate legislature. Judges and juries sitting in adversarial proceedings are not competent to perform this function, as time and experience have amply shown, and the legal expense is too high. If we are to reduce the expense of medical care we must cut where we find excess. In so many situations legal expense becomes medical expense. Certainly legal actions resulting from medical care are a part of medical costs.

The State Executive Council

It is not within the power of, nor is it the job of the State Executive Council to micromanage beneath the level of the SNHC Physician Chief, except the Council will have the power to require the discharge of any SNHC Physician Chief of Staff for due cause. This event, should it occur, may be overturned by a two-thirds majority vote of the Advisory Council. This must be done within thirty days of the Executive Council's notification of this action to the Advisory Council. This notification is required, and is to be done promptly and in writing.

The State Executive Council has the duty and the power to establish overall policy and direction with the advice and consent of the State Advisory Council. It has the duty to collect and distribute the funds due it from the federal, and in turn, the state governments. It has the duty to be and advocate for the financial interests of its state Safety Net Hospital-Clinic system through active liaison and interchange with the federal and state agencies collecting the tax. It will act as a general watchdog over all the financial (and other) aspects of the system, including setting salaries of the physicians, residents, interns, physician assistants and nurses.

It can call hearings and adjudicate matters it considers to be financial abuses or political opportunism within its state system, so long as it does not micromanage below the SNHC Medical Chiefs. It can issue general directives and suggestions to the local Chiefs of Staff. There will be active communication between the individual Hospital Chiefs and the State Executive Council.

The State Executive Council must approve by a majority vote all capital expenditures over ten thousand dollars-or some suitable sum. They may initiate or approve necessary new building construction or the creation of other needed infrastructure which may or may not require conjunctive action with other state or federal departments.

The State Executive Council has the duty to protect patient rights, and aid in the accountability of the physicians and others in the state system. The Peer Review panel may ask it for aid.

The State Executive Council shall be composed of four physicians familiar with the clinical practice of medicine. Two of these physicians are to be taken from the SNHC system and two from the state at large. Retired physicians would be given preference. Also on the council are two registered nurses, one of whom works within the SNHC system, two Certified Public Accountants, and three business leaders (not politicians, but real business persons) from the state.

The council, in this distribution, will be appointed by the governor of each state from a slate of candidates submitted by their representative societies. These societies would include the County Medical Societies, State Nursing Associations, etc. Once appointed, the group will meet according to accepted parliamentary procedure and elect a chairman who will not vote except to break a tie. Again, the chairman will act as executive and speaker for the group. This group shall meet at least twice a year, or such other times as the chairman or a majority of the members require it. The group will work on a volunteer basis, except for say $300.00 per day (plus cost of living increases) expenses when in session. They will serve four year terms, except no member may serve more than two consecutive terms.

One-half the Council, including two of the business persons will be replaced every four years. This council will be allowed a full-time secretary and one secretary's assistant, who will be hired by the council. The council will fund their salaries and operating expenses. These expenses will be included in the annual report to the public previously mentioned, and count against the general operating fiscal efficiency of that state. The State Executive Council Chairman's position may require a salary, although it might be wise to have it remain a volunteer position.

This body may, with experience, and by a two-thirds vote, change its number or distribution, so long as they were ever vigilant against infiltration by groups seeking domination.

In time all the State Executive Councils at their annual meeting may vote to form a coordinating body to deal with things thought to be for the common benefit of all the states. Improving the State Executive Councils by changing the number or distribution of the members would be one such subject. Pooling purchasing power would be another example. However, the autonomy of each state's control of its SNHC must be preserved.

Some counties may be too small in population to support or require a SNHC. In that event, they will be merged with another facility. Another function of the State Executive Council, working with the State Advisory Council, is to initiate, direct and oversee the distribution of contiguous County medical care facilities to produce satisfactory medical coverage of those areas. They are to oversee the location and construction of those facilities, and/or the abandonment and sale of unused facilities, should this occur. They are to direct the location and use allocation of expensive capital equipment.

The State Executive Council, working with the State Medical Advisory Council, may decide, initiate and direct the purchase of its own ambulance services, or negotiate economically feasible financial cooperation with local ambulance facilities. The State SNHC Executive Council, working with the State SNHC Advisory Council, has the task of procuring drugs, supplies, and equipment at the lowest possible cost. This may entail the cooperative efforts of all the states. For this and other purposes connected with integration and cross-fertilization, Physician Chiefs of all the state SNHC will meet in convention once a year.

The State SNHC Executive Council working with the State SNHC Advisory Council, has the task of overseeing the coordination, recruiting and organization of volunteer help for all levels of the operation.

Finally, for all their endeavors, it is the policy established herein for the SNHC Advisory and Executive Councils to eschew paid feasibility studies. Rather, they are (within the scope of their permitted functions) empowered to delegate one member to act to accomplish a specific task. This member, once appointed may appoint up to four assistants from the State Executive Council (or elsewhere). Both Councils are empowered to delegate a specific task, and a specific time to accomplish it. If the delegate is not successful within the appointed time, the group acting as a body may extend the time, or appoint another to do the job. Any member assigned such a specific duty may, without prejudice, return to the Council at any time to report, to obtain further guidance, or to resign from the assigned duty.

How Could Such a Plan be Sabotaged?

In the military, because of the vital nature of the mission, and the requisite facing of risk etc., arrangements are different from that of commercial employment or even civil service employment. The same applies to the technical personnel constituting the Safety Net Hospital-Clinics, whose mission, especially for the physician employees, is also vital and risky. For this plan to succeed, the physician employees must be given a special status. They might be treated, for example, as federal government employees, very similar to the military; without government or union interference.

Perhaps Congress could create such a status by law, carefully designed to be within both state and federal constitutions, perhaps limited to a certain time period, say a decade or two. What this service could do for the country would seem important enough to at least allow such a system a chance. **These professional SNHC employees must be immuned from malpractice litigation** as it exists today within the common meaning of that term.

Probably the most serious threat to the success of this solution to the medical cost crisis, will be some contingent fee attorneys, Congress or unions. Union problems apply particularly to civil service unions. Probably the most naive aspect of this entire proposal is the belief that these kinds of interference can be prevented. If the requisite dedication and idealism is to prevail, the system must be left alone to handle its own regulatory problems in its own way. This will give the populace a chance to see how a system, whose sole aim is to provide competent scientific medical care, can function when allowed to be free of today's federal and state governmental ways of operation.

If by their works the SNHC system proves itself unworthy, there will be ample time to institute outside involvement into scientific medical affairs. If the system indeed proves itself worthy to handle its own complex problems, this would provide a precedent for the entire scientific community and become a major step forward in jurisprudence. In a sense, it will give the public a chance to observe two competitive ways of managing the job of medical care delivery.

If we are to get competent physicians to work for less money in these situations, they must be protected from today's misguided courtroom hazards (these have been amply detailed herein). If not, then citizens must pay to indemnify physicians, both financially and psychologically, as they are doing now. This cost is enormous and growing. So is the threat, and it involves far more than just physicians. This menace will effect every aspect of the SNHC medical practice. It would put us back to where we are now. It is indeed one of the keys to the solution of the present medical cost crisis. That is one of the crucial nonmonetary compensations talked about throughout this book. It is a problem managed care as it now appears, cannot and will not solve, in my opinion.

To solve this problem have the SNHC system set to function from the beginning in a quasi-military fashion, or after the current models of congressional or judicial immunity. Even these are being harassed more and more. Except for criminal matters, in all matters pertaining to medical science, disability, the extent of disability and errors and omissions, this system would handle its own disciplinary and regulatory affairs through the system of administration detailed previously. The medical councils discussed above are uniquely suited for this job, all having active physicians on the council. (Instead of putting the fox in the hen house, such immunity from some trial attorneys would take the fox out of the hen house).

Concerning some unions and the non-medical employees of the SNHC, this book is advocating a unique structure that would go far toward solving the high cost of medical care. An attempt to provide such care as outlined herein should not, it would seem, violate the social goals of most unions. This is not an easy problem, this problem of providing competent medical care for all, regardless of ability to pay. One solution is to gather together, compensate and motivate both paid and volunteer workers, who too, are to be offered compensation other then money.

To be sure, adequate working conditions, safety, and compensation are essential; but overstaffing, featherbedding, fighting change, viewing a need for adaptability as a burden, and especially industrial insurance abuse cannot be tolerated. The SNHC system is uniquely organized and competent to care for all industrial injuries and compensation, as well as its own. Provision for workers compensation would be the same as provided for Congressional employees, or for U.S. Public Health Officers.

Workers, too, should be afforded great job security, pension rights etc., even though they best not become a part of the civil service system as I understand it. They should specifically remain as a competitive counterforce to the present civil service system. Job satisfaction and retirement security could be backed by the individual state governments. These should be organized under a new system, beyond the scope of this book to detail. The job of these workers is vital; its very nature requires the saving of life and the amelioration of suffering. This is more than a job at most any level. It is a calling.

We have now, for at least two generations through cultivation of deception, dependence and discontent, at many levels of society, encouraged expectations that are very wrong, and for which the society will pay heavily in time. In a small way, the SNHC, beside furnishing medical care, could, if allowed, begin to correct these self-damaging expectations.

The staff of these SNHCs are experts who should be called upon to furnish some of the technical information used by OSHA and aspects of the Environmental Protection Agency. The Safety Net Hospital-Clinics would be well situated to formulate their own practices in this regard.

In fact, personnel of these agencies should be required to come to an established branch of the SNHC to have their knowledge of chemistry, bacteriology, virology, basic principles of biology, contamination, technical aspects and judgments concerning safety and related skills and practices examined, approved, and licensed. This would help to fill a serious void in scientific knowledge, hampering so many of those charged with formulating regulations in these areas.

This knowledge void may well extend right up to the politically-appointed head of these agencies. Like the Food and Drug Administration, even though the head of the agency is a political appointee, the scientific, specialized knowledge required by that job must be appreciated, and sufficient scientific background must become a prerequisite. The SNHC should help to stamp out junk science in government. In reality, acceptance of these agencies by the scientific community would increase their power.

This entire endeavor is an experiment, an experiment involving many facets. How many of these will work? Will employees who have a voice in management be able to build an esprit, and develop for themselves their own kind of non-monetary compensation? Can they work alongside volunteers who work entirely for non-monetary compensation?

To repeat, this society must decide whether it wants to (or can) solve its medical cost problems, or keep its failing insurance and regulatory mistakes and tort law abuses. This book advocates that the two systems coexist, and thereby test which actually works best insofar as this can be determined. Also, whether the power can be marshalled to effect change once these changes are determined desirable.

Getting It Done

What follows is a project list for starting a Safety Net Hospital-Clinic:

1. Put in place the legislation necessary to collect and distribute the Safety Net Hospital-Clinic money via the income tax as discussed. Provision should be made to anticipate the collection and distribution of Medicaid, Medicare and other funds, if these programs become integrated into the SNHC system. Some of these funds could be used to pay for initial infrastructure. This transfer of funds would be temporary, as the expense of these programs is phased out over time and removed from the budget. This transfer of funds would be important, for the need would be greatest at the beginning. Converting selected, already functioning facilities would be a good way to minimize initial start-up costs.

2. Distribute the money to the states. The money is to be kept in a separate fund.

3. The respective state governors then appoint the initial State Executive Council. (The Council members are

appointed for four-year terms with a maximum of two consecutive terms. One-half of each occupation category (physician, Certified Public Accountant, nurse, and two business people) are changed or reappointed each term, There are four physicians, two CPA's, two nurses and three business people from that state on the Executive Council).

4. Each State Executive Council meets and elects a chairman.

5. Each state governor meets with the Executive Council of each state to decide on a sum of money necessary to seed the Council's initial operation. (We should anticipate a time, as more hospitals come on-line, where bonded indebtedness, grants and conversion of existing private facilities may need be sought for infrastructure.)

6. The Council elicits the help of volunteers and private seed grants. (It will initially find volunteers, during its organization process, and later at its initial site. The Council should recruit experienced, usually retired, self-sustaining volunteers both at the time of organization and at the initial site, and at other sites as they develop).

7. The Council surveys the County hospitals, or other hospital sites within the state, to find a site suitable for an initial Safety Net Hospital-Clinic complex.

8. The Council selects one site for an initial pilot start-up effort. (It is assumed this will be happening in each state; but by this time efforts will be progressing at different rates.)

9. The Council will find secondary choices for possible next-in-line start-up. It is crucial that all sites be well located in the area chosen, with an eye toward serving the middle class. These sites will be in that location for a long time. It will be difficult to move them. Transportation must be provided to bring the poor to these sites. Such

cross fertilization of experience is so important for our efforts to improve out growing culture of poverty.

10. Once a site is chosen, the State Executive Council should hire a Hospital Medical Chief and an Administrative Chief. (They would constitute the first State Medical Advisory Council. Initially they would work full-time, along with the State Executive Council and volunteers, to make ready an initial facility. The time this took would depend, of course, on the existing facilities of the initial site chosen.)

11. The Medical and Administrative Chiefs, together with the assistance they requested from the State Executive Council and volunteers, would form an initial crew to begin operations. (They would prioritize services going on-line. Actual medical operations should begin as soon as possible, even though they were conducted on a small scale.)

12. From this point forward, the facility would be allowed to grow, correcting and profiting from its mistakes, and acting as a pilot plant. Staff should be chosen with the presumption they, in time, would be teaching interns, residents, and student nurses.

13. The State Executive Councils and the Medical and Administrative Chiefs, should maintain close contact with each other, especially during this initial formative period, (This should occur both within and across state lines. Even though each state will retain its autonomy, in the beginning much could be gained by close contact and support across state lines.)

14. Once the initial facility is operating, soon a second facility should be started, and a third etc. One should counter the tendency to be too sure about the first one and move on.

15. Once a facility has reached sufficient size (and this should be anticipated because accreditation takes time), it should apply for and achieve approval to serve as a clinical teaching facility for interns, family practice residents, and student nurses. (Some facilities will soon grow to qualify for resident specialty training depending on their care in initial staff selection.)

Suggestions for Government Action

For the sake of completeness and a better view of the problems this innovation would pose, a list of suggestions for government action follows:

1. Congress passes legislation to add the requisite surtax to the federal income tax, and helps assure passage of these funds directly to each state's SNHC Executive Council. There might be a provision for impounding funds for a state until that state has setup a SNHC Executive Council.

2. Congress enables the states to operate their SNHC programs.

3. Congress might pass legislation setting forth guidelines for appointing the state SNHC Executive Council. This might be left to the states.

4. Congress passes legislation setting forth guidelines for conditions of employment for physicians including immunity from errors and omission liability, broad guidelines for the structure of the peer review process, pension funds, etc.

5. Congress passes legislation enabling the physicians on the SNHC staffs to be responsible only for technical medical matters including the operation of the nursing staffs. The professional administrators would handle the

other problems. (The nursing staffs would be allowed their autonomy, yet they would also need protection from the "malpractice problem.") This act alone will assure a plentiful supply of both physicians and nurses.

6. Congress passes legislation exempting all employees of the SNHC system from the worker's compensation laws, and requires the SNHC to care for their own workers. Workers would agree to this as a condition of employment. Methods for monetary compensation would be determined by the states through a panel of medical experts.

7. Congress would pass enabling legislation such that the states could use the SNHC system for treating the state's worker's compensation problems, and for deciding compensation cases without an expensive legal process in the loop.

CHAPTER ELEVEN

More About the Safety Net Hospital-Clinic

The Safety Net Hospital-Clinics and their outreach facilities could become excellent instruments of preventative medicine and community medicine for all, regardless of ability to pay. Like going to vote, everyone would be encouraged to stop by for their flu shots, for example. Preventive medical care of all types can reduce costs and morbidity and relieve the emergency medical staff. For example, if a patient were recognized to have high blood pressure, proper treatment would lessen the chances of that person being brought into the emergency clinic with a stroke or a coronary occlusion.

It would be simple to appoint a time for mass blood pressure checks. There could be designated times for breast checks, prostate checks, pap smears. Age ranges could be specified to increase the utility of such effort. Routine general screening has been economically impractical for asymptomatic people—especially those in the younger age groups. Specific screening of high risk situations is feasible.

The health care of our poor is now much more expensive because proper preventative care is not available to them, or they do not avail themselves of such care when it is available. Perhaps we could all learn from each other, once we were brought together. Once care were available, attention could then be given to education and motivation for prevention. There would be heretofore unheard of capacity to deliver prevention, and ensure better public health practices. The possibility for ethical, statistical, genetic, and longitudinal research studies would be great. There are many possibilities.

Unprecedented opportunity would exist to teach groups of sexually active teenage girls and boys in a medical setting rather than a school setting. There are subtle but potent differences. Prenatal clinics for young pregnant mothers could be staffed by professionals, and helped by case finding to reach out to those who need it most.

Group psychotherapy and simple group instruction develops strength of will, serves as an outlet for hostility, and develops new and different attitudes to the responsibilities of bringing a baby into the world (whether the pregnant female intends to keep the baby or not).

Babies in the nurseries could be visited and the awful results of cocaine babies could be actually shown. Students could be shown patients dying of AIDS, instead of condoms. Violent gang members might be asked to watch an autopsy, and visit the morgue where death is real and permanent instead of exciting, as on television. Such experiences (especially the smells) impart deep gut level conditioning to nearly all intellectual levels.

This confrontation would make more real the reasons for responsible action. It would enhance the validity of the teaching. Many networks could be formed at little cost using volunteers, some of whom have been helped, and now want to reciprocate. Thus the culture of poverty, the ethnic intolerance, and class envy so rapidly becoming entrenched, could at least be given a chance to change for the common good. Why have we put the lid on the melting pot? How have we put the lid on the melting pot?

There is novelty but also a purity, an idealism, and stark biologic reality about a hospital clinic setting. This is different from many of our schools, where attempts to impose discipline and teach self-discipline are fraught with danger and carry an atmosphere of hatred and rebellion, rather than awe and positive motivation. Self-discipline and responsibility are in the air in a hospital. There is hope here. There is death. There is often a despair that puts teenage boredom in perspective—for teenagers.

Not all aspects of the hospital and clinics need be what is strictly considered medical, or preventative medicine. Ancillary services can branch out where need and social worker or therapist motivation exist. Suicide, homicide and accident prevention counseling and attempts to treat and to understand addiction and obsession in its various forms could be studied and integrated with other social work programs.

Much of this could be done at sites away from the busy hospital and clinic facilities, and integrated with programs already in place. Many of these things are even now being done.

Hostility and hatred could be tackled as a form of illness prevention, thus reducing the number of victims that must be handled by ambulance and emergency care. Many are not aware of the group of battered aggressive drunks that are hauled into the emergency room (shortly after the bars close) nearly every night in a big city. These are but an example of the injuries and homicides so much a part of the contemporary urban scene.

It is critical that these Safety Net Hospital-Clinics earn and keep a proper image within the community. This makes volunteer help more easily forthcoming. A given SNHC would most likely start with an image similar to a charity County hospital. Then by its good works, cleanliness, and freedom from political exploitation and commercialism, it could develop in its own unique way to serve its own particular community. Each could act as an example for the others, and all the various SNHCs could learn from each other.

Acute Care

Special care and attention should be devoted to hospice care and intensive care for two levels of terminal patients. There need be one area where the hopeless are prepared for death, their suffering minimized. This must take into account, with delicacy, the denial of patients, the family and others. It is important that their suffering be minimized, and no cruel or painful fruitless gestures indulged in. Nursing care here, together with ancillary personnel trained in hospice work, including grief recovery, are most important. The requirements of this facility and its very ambience set it apart.

Facilities must be specialized for terminal care of those who have a fighting chance to live. This facility can be integrated with the intensive and critical care units. This can be the most technical and demanding part of the hospital. Everything science has to offer should be used and developed here, as it should in the neonatal pediatric intensive care units. Nursing expertise, again, is of the utmost importance, and although emphasizing scientific medicine these facilities should be developed with this important nursing function in mind.

Many facilities might well be located in one area and shared. It may be possible for the more technical aspects of these units to be shared by several counties. Some examples of the more expensive technologies that could be shared are invasive cardiac procedures, nuclear medical facilities, CAT scans, magnetic resonance imaging, positron emission tomography, and esoteric laboratory procedures. Kidney dialysis is already set apart. An emerging need is specialty care facilities for immunocompromised patients.

What the SNHC Should Not Do

None of these facilities can afford to be used as domiciles for hopeless non-terminal cases. This function, however necessary and laudable, should be left entirely to other facilities. Neither should the SNHC be used for the care of the chronically demented. It should never degenerate into a dumping ground for addicts or the seriously retarded, as much as such facilities are needed. It is not a nursing home for care of the frail old. It is for necessary care of the sick.

This SNHC system should keep its fundamental purpose in mind, which is the care of the sickness of every citizen with emphasis on both the middle class and the poor. If the facilities are dumped on, this will drive the middle class away. The cultivation of a clean, inviting, optimistic, and lively ambience is crucial.

An Important Original Contribution of the SNHC

On the other end of the illness scale, is the first contact with the slightly ill patient. The utmost expertise and ingenuity is important here. The SNHC cannot afford to spend much physician time with the mildly ill. The innovations here are in the areas of reduced cost, greater efficiency and, as always, risk reduction. Among the hundreds of out-patients, there will be a few with the beginnings of severe illness. These must be sorted out as accurately as possible, and tested further or kept under observation; taking whatever time is necessary for that patient's care.

Much thought must be given to new ways to deal with this mass of patients who come for accurate diagnosis, proper delegation, reassurance, simple treatment and release. This will enable quality time to be taken with the more severely ill patient, and correct one of the problems common in today's HMOs, where patients must be equally rushed through, to some extent, to preserve client satisfaction.

We Must Question and Experiment to Learn

The subject of research has been mentioned more than once. Some will be quick to see patients of these hospitals as human guinea pigs. This old demagoguery is wrong. Good research is, if anything, ethical, and ideally it is opportunistic. It will appear where there is a question that can be answered by experiment. Consider these questions concerning outcomes research.

We have alluded to the difficult question of how one is to choose the best physician for one's particular needs. What can be measured? Why is the mortality from a certain heart surgery much higher in one hospital that another? How does it differ between one operating team and another? The difference in skill with the use of a certain procedure, or the choice of a given procedure may depend on a certain teacher. Sometimes the students of that teacher can be traced. Where does the problem lie? With the malpractice menace these things are unlikely to be brought into the open.

Why is the cost of a procedure twice in one area what it is in another? Why is the percentage of throat cultures of children more common in one region, even in one office, than in another? How do the outcomes differ? Why are patients presenting with an upper respiratory infection much more likely to get antibiotic therapy from one physician than another? Why does giving an antibiotic two hours before surgery reduce subsequent wound infection more than other methods? What are the outcomes from these differing approaches to therapy? Can it be determined that one is best, or can one determine the circumstances around which one is the better method?.*

With a nationwide system of Safety Net Hospital-Clinics, many of these questions could be answered among the different SNHC themselves; and between themselves and the private practice physicians of the region. Integrated training and constant efforts to improve medical care could be carried on much more effectively than at

* Blumenthal, D. Total quality management and physicians clinical decisions. JAMA. 1993, 269: 2775-2778.

present. Regional differences in disease patterns might emerge. The overuse of a certain procedure or drug might be corrected. This overuse may have originated as an honest belief, or perhaps avarice was involved. The SNHC system would be in a good position to ferret out such things. The results could be published in scientific publications for the benefit of all. Perhaps the SNHC system, in time, would have its own medical journal.

The art and science of domicilary care of the old, the helpless, the demented and the frail, while separated, must integrate with the SNHC too. This type of care must be studied and improved. Some of these people are in and out of the hospital frequently, especially during their terminal period. Much needs to be learned there too.

Physician Numbers

If one were to staff these SNHC in part with resident physicians (young physicians in specialty training) and interns; and if, once a student had been accepted to medical school, the government would pay the educational expense for the four years of medical school, would we not have too many physicians? Would we not have too many specialists? No; the problem may not be too many specialty trained physicians overall. The problem may be improper distribution of these physicians. To be sure, overcrowding of physicians in a desirable area will drive some out to less favorable locations. Sometimes these are the less competent at some aspect of patient care or even at the business side of medical practice.

Note again, this notion of too many specialists is an economic matter. If our sole concern was the growth and development of medical science and the quality of medical care, the matter of too many physicians would be viewed in an entirely different manner. It approaches the question, can this culture become too learned? We must remove the money from medicine insofar as is prudent. Insurance, and managed competition emphasizes and increases cost.

What if the graduates from the government supported schools were required to spend a period of service in the SNHC system? This is now common practice in other situations where the government has furnished the education of medical students. Even so, would there be enough young physicians to go around to all these SNHC locations? These are problems that are difficult to foresee. It is not difficult to forsee excellent medical care for everyone who comes for it, however.

One aspect of government paid tuition would be the emphasis on avoiding government control of the teaching institutions. There is real advantage for each school to retain its autonomy, its individuality. This seems like a slippery slope. Preservation of school autonomy may be a fond hope fraught with problems; yet this was effectively done in World War Two by means of the Army Specialized Training Program and the V12 Navy program.

At this time, most of our private hospitals do not have residents and interns. These young physicians are a definite advantage to every patient. They do not make patients into "guinea pigs" They are indeed a luxury that must be purchased by good teaching, which in turn requires excellent staff and facilities. Systems of rotation through the bigger and the smaller facilities would achieve a balance of learning experience for these young physicians.

If several counties together maintained one facility, there would still be a large number of SNHC facilities. The smaller facilities could train interns and family practitioners, and the bigger facilities could train the specialists as well.

This country now has excellent transportation facilities. To reduce the number of facilities, it might be more sensible, from study of geographical and demographic data, to arrange Safety Net Hospital-Clinics in varied locations in each state, not necessarily within each county. There could be branch clinics in the less populated areas, triaging and transporting selected cases to the bigger, better-equipped hospitals in the more central areas. The bigger HMOs are doing this.

It would be sensible to utilize, wherever possible, the existing facilities, provided the political systems entrenched there could be integrated into the operating principles of the SNHC. There might also be an integration with the medical school teaching hospitals. A nation-wide integrated and economical distribution of facilities would have many advantages, so long as the equally great advantages of individual autonomy were preserved as well.

Now consider what constitutes an unfavorable location for the average physician. This may be very different than one would think. Isolated or rural areas do not bother a physician so much as being an isolated physician. Isolation from intellectual stimulation and advancing medical science is the biggest deterrent. Even lack of cultural stimulation is not as important as lack of professional stimulation and lack of facilities for a community of scholars, for a community of specialists.

If these Safety Net Hospital-Clinics were (1) well distributed and well staffed; (2) were there other specialists so the physician would have the benefit of this invaluable range of skill; (3) if the physician had others with which to share night calls; and especially (4) if that physician had trained for three to five years in that location; the chances are good that the family would become rooted, and that physician would stay.

What Could Go Wrong

Government has the easiest way to sabotage the system. Would Congress let such sums out of their control without a myriad of suffocating restrictions? Would governors? Could medicine, which has so weakened its power, be allowed now to be left free of third party meddling? These are big hurdles. Who would, who could, champion this cause? Can we get the type of help from government we need? Or is there little hope for this kind of change? This much diversion of money and power could easily be sabotaged. Any number of antagonists might emerge, including those third parties who foresee their income and power being reduced. Private hospitals and the for profit private hospital corporations could have their interests compromised or they could be skillfully brought into the system.

Considerable capital expenditure will be required at first, and this initial funding could be presented as a major obstacle. The issuance of bonded indebtedness would need to be voted in some instances. This would require advocacy and willingness of the political system to get this on the ballot and to get the necessary votes. The state of the economy, and the fears about the state of the economy might be in the wrong phase. Interest on debt is usually low during a recession. The best time to enter into

bonded indebtedness is then the worst time psychologically.

Any system for change in medical care requires the
requisite political talents and energy to push it through.
Few physicians have this. Those who do and who leave
medicine for political or editorial careers soon lose touch
with medical practice, for medical practice skills move
ahead very rapidly. Such a change as espoused here requires the close association of powerful people with very
different values. Many physicians, and possibly organized
medicine, might be expected to oppose the Safety Net
Hospital-Clinics. On the other hand, they might embrace
it as the lesser of many potential evils. I hope this book
will interest people with the necessary diverse talents; and
perhaps spark a few to act.

Many people will not comprehend the power, the
simplicity, of free service at the door. A hospital-clinic
complex without a fee collection business office is unheard
of.

There will of course be complex business affairs,
salaries, purchases of supplies etc. Even though this will be
handled by the professional administrative division, integration and cooperation will be required. Strict accounting procedures will be necessary. Types of sutures, drugs,
medical equipment etc. will need medical input. There
would be two lines of input. One would flow up through
the administrative side and the other would originate and
be coordinated by the medical professional side. There is
much precedent and skill already functioning in private
and military hospital administration that can provide relatively easy answers in this area.

Some voters might see this as just another bureaucratic
scheme to create soft jobs for political favors; as is now so
common in some County hospital systems. How will this

be avoided? One possible way around these problems is to start small. Some politically astute person could get this started by advocating beginning in just a few areas. But how would the ability to include a surtax on the income tax be accomplished? This would take an act of Congress.

Can enough power in Congress be marshalled? In just this one instance can we throw out this slogan called "fairness," and have everyone pay the exact same percentage of their income tax *payment?* This would be really fair, "progressive" enough, and might well meet with little resistance. Would the temptation to make political capital by distorting this fairness be too great. For once a highly visible equal tax should be tried. This would be especially true if taxpayers could actually see what they were getting for their money in quite tangible terms.

Both physician and patient are free to avail themselves of whatever is, for them, the more desirable alternative. This should reduce discontent. Physicians as a rule will adapt to competitive pressures, where they would be demoralized by directives. The system advocated here is free of directives imposed from above, by bureaucrats bowing to other directives; or to the winds of political pressure. Such people may know little about the technical aspects of what they are doing.

Medicine is always technical. So often people with the best of intentions have no idea how naive they appear to a physician when they attempt to free associate with their innovations in some technical medical area. Such statements as these are not pleasant to read, but they are important to realize, lest the rift between patient and physician widen, and more important lest unnecessary deaths, illness, even discomfort occur. It is so important that this not happen.

The system advocated herein is simply what it is called. It is a safety net and it is a refuge. Once it is in place, no one ever need fear being unable to get good medical care. This is a tremendous freedom. This safety net also permits, even enhances, freedom of choice. It gives every patient the freedom of competitive advantage. That will sort things out. There will develop a market. Trust markets, they will guide one through complexity of this kind.

An SNHC Open Door Policy

Once they are in operation, every person should at least visit their Safety Net Hospital-Clinic. Every person would do well to volunteer even for a short time at their SNHC facility. Many would want to attend the disciplinary hearings, or some of the administrative meetings. Citizens should make the SNHC a part of their community. Even though one belonged to an HMO, the safety net emergency facilities might be required sometime. It would be comforting to know what to expect.

One problem would be the dumping of a patient onto an SNHC for whom long-term expensive care had become necessary. In a sense, that is one reason for the existence of the Safety Net Hospital. Where an HMO had a prepaid obligation to a patient, then dumping would be unfair. The patient, however, would have the right to either care and so could not be included in any tussle that ensued. Employers who continued to provide HMO membership as a feature of compensation could structure many combinations of HMO and SNHC care.

Patient Organized and Operated HMOS

To me, patient organized and operated Health Maintenence Organizations are especially interesting. They are important for they could become a viable alternative to the Safety Net Hospital-Clinics. More important they could be a viable alternative to a massive interposed third party insurance bureaucracy. Who needs that? Better we do our own.

This is the way a patient cooperative could begin. A group of determined and dedicated people can gather together a group of willing physicians and start their own health maintenance organization. Then, when enough patients are accumulated, they hire more physicians, and in time become a full fledged HMO. Yes indeed, HMOs can be started and operated by patients as well as by physicians or large corporations. I have been told this is a Pollyanna scheme by no less than a *Journal of the American Medical Association* (JAMA) peer reviewer. But consider the following example.

Write to the Group Health Cooperative of Puget sound, Administration and Conference Center, 521 Wall Street, Seattle Washington. Ask them to send you, as they did me, an illustrated booklet describing how they started. Their Historical Archivist sent me a booklet complete with pictures of the founders, and stories of their trials and tribulations getting started.

A small group of intrepid, determined individuals gathered two hundred patients. Each paid a fixed annual fee to their one physician. That is how it began.

The cooperative also sent a paper about their present condition called Group Health Facts. It shows they started in 1947. (The year I graduated from medical school). They now have 474,485 member patients. They employ 897 physicians and other medical staff members, and 1,498 registered nurses. They have 2,100 additional non-staff physicians employed to provide service in locations where there is no appropriate Group Health staff. They are their state's seventh largest employer. They are the nation's fifth largest group practice. Eighty-eight percent of the staff is Specialty Board Certified. They have twenty nine family medical centers, two hospitals, an inpatient center, a skilled nursing facility, and five specialty centers in Washington and Idaho. It is gratifying to see what can be done by patients and physicians working together.

CHAPTER TWELVE

Physicians and Their Patients

The purpose here is to give the reader a glimpse at medical student and physician attitudes, and the economics of a physician's private practice. It is as important for patients to have an understanding of physician's problems as it is for physicians to understand patient's problems. This would seem a prerequisite to a durable solution, and the first step toward a united resistance to damaging third-party intrusion.

Even the most avid proponent of third-party involvement must realize not only that third parties seek gain and perhaps control for themselves; but that this gain must come from physicians and/or patients, and both will be impacted. It is always easier to create antagonism if the parties to be separated are not familiar with the human aspects of the other. Furthermore, third parties' ideological interests often interpose between patient-physician satisfaction. A better understanding of physicians as people helps to put this into perspective. Ultimately, no one else can solve this medical cost crisis for us—we physicians and patients must solve our problems, and they are our problems. Even if we rely on hoped for third-party help for our medical cost problem, better knowledge about physicians can only be helpful. Many third parties who do not have the foresight to realize they will become patients, too, could profit from avoiding false propaganda concerning physicians—or patients. In no way will these vital life and death medical cost and medical care issues remain merely intellectual ones. They are loaded with myriads of strong emotions, so it is important to at least peek at some emotional aspects involving physicians. Finally, it is hoped the discussion to follow will help dispel the illusion of free medical care. Canadian and British authors cite this illusion of free care created by their socialized medical programs as the very undoing of these programs. This has certainly been the case with health insurance in this country.

In many aspects it is difficult to describe physicians apart from their patients. Hospitals and drug suppliers are also a part of a physician's life and physician attitudes. It is difficult to convey to patients some of the stresses these very human people called physicians undergo. The average physician works harder, under more stress, for longer and more irregular hours than most people would tolerate.

If more patients realized this perhaps they would be more tolerant. The patient who suddenly becomes very, very ill needs tolerance and explanation from a busy overworked physician, even though, to that physician, the patient has only a common, self limited illness.

Medical students have been steeped in the ethics and idealism of the profession. People who would tinker with these values should be careful to preserve those of importance to everyone, and so they must ask themselves these questions about values. Who are the keepers of the values of this present system? Physicians are, and patients should not brush aside this aspect of medical tradition. What are these values? Have they served us well? Which of them would we want to preserve regardless of how radical we change the present system?

This chapter will strive to help derive answers to such questions, and to illuminate these values even though some are subtle and difficult to communicate by written word. Cynicism is so difficult to avoid. It is so easy to trod over that which is tender, yet of ultimate value and usefulness. It is easy to ignore this emerging change by acting as if it did not apply to us. Also the ethics of physician-patient relationships must be ever held before us. This too is facilitated by a greater awareness of the personal aspects of physicians and patients each by the other.

Medical Students

The day students enter medical school after four years of college, they enter a different world; a world of cadavers to dissect and of brilliant, hard driving, no-mistakes-allowed teachers. Medical students at once encounter a new ethos, a different reality. They are never the same. They develop an instilled sense of urgency and competitiveness. Time for them is indeed of the essence. They have fear: fear of failure, fear of harming someone. Early on they begin to realize the awesome responsibility they are to assume.

The business side of medical practice is not taught to medical students. Perhaps for the same reason dishwashing is not emphasized to the prospective bride. If you ask the teachers, they say there is not enough time. In fact, medical school professors are continually bickering over how much teaching time and emphasis their particular specialty gets. Many professors feel too much has been cut from the curriculum already.

Most students begin their patient contacts with compassion. There is a strong need to help. They have all been taught the physician's creed: "To cure sometimes, to help often, to comfort always." Yet, after many hours on their feet without sleep, it is a rare student who has not said under their breath, (referring to some hapless patient) "Why don't you straighten up?"

Teachers of medical students must use care not to damage the student's compassion, while still requiring self-discipline and objectivity. Medical students are very critical of their teachers, yet teachers are often emulated, both consciously and unconsciously. Medical students, having all been steeped in hard work and self-discipline, still must harden their compassion somewhat to stand the strain. They are human. Some become arrogant, some become bitter, some become depressed. Suicides happen. Many would not be happy doing anything else. Some maintain a soft touch and compassion through it all. Such students are very precious to society.

Many students have financial difficulties including children and spouses to support. It is virtually impossible to work elsewhere for money while in medical school. It is a unique situation where even the smartest cannot absorb all the knowledge that is thrown at them. This is a very difficult adjustment for some, who were smart honor students when in undergraduate school. They were accustomed to school work being easy. Medical school is not easy for anyone. Yet it is so wonderful to be privy to this knowledge, and to have been prepared for it "from the ground up."

In addition to tuition and expenses, medical students have another dilemma. Can the students, or their parents or their credit, support five more years of residency after internship? Four years of undergraduate school, four years of medical school, a year of internship and five years of residency add up to fourteen years of training after high school. These fourteen years are not just fourteen years of putting in time. These fourteen years are brutal. On completing this rigorous course, students naturally have some expectations; so do their spouses, their children, their parents, their in-laws, and their creditors.

It is a disgrace that money should be a delimiting factor in who goes to medical school. Every citizen who earns an acceptance to medical school should have his or her entire expenses paid (for the four years of medical school) by government. The grade requirements should be rigorous, and anyone who does not make these grades should be dropped. In time, we could fill our Safety Net Hospital-Clinics with well-trained specialists and do this quite efficiently. We must strive always to upgrade the quality of medical care, and not allow the quality of the science and the training to slip in the name of economy.

Eventually in their internships and residencies, many young physicians will experience what it is like to virtually live in a big city hospital, (more about these later). There, among other things, they encounter hapless victims, death, violence, and tragedy. Students will experience humanity at its worst—and sometimes at its best.

In the big city hospitals of my experience, it was the intern's job to care for alcoholics, and vagrants in from off the street. Usually they were brought in by ambulance in extremis (unable to walk or unconscious). They merited a careful examination, for they were veritable storehouses of disease. They would be treated, the nurses would delouse them, give them a bath, they would be fed, their pneumonia or whatever treated along with their delirium tremens from alcohol withdrawal (if this became necessary). In a few days they would be back out on the street. Many were readmitted so often we knew their names and faces. It was virtually impossible to get them to come to the outpatient clinics before they became so ill.

Interns also experience deep gratitude from treated patients and become a party to miraculous cures, such as a nearly dead, dehydrated baby coming to life in hours, after intravenous fluid administration.

They will learn that all people are not created equal under anything. They will learn that many people can (or will) never change. They will learn that most things about people they can never change. They will learn that some of the poor prefer to stay poor. Some of the material poor lead very happy lives. They will see people who are kept in poverty by the slightest thing, which they adamantly refuse to change. They will see second-generation welfare patients, young mothers with babies perhaps, who have never known anything but welfare. These young physicians become first-hand observers of the culture of poverty, the culture of government dependence.

The Young Physician Begins Private Practice

As they begin practice, young physicians discover they have become different from most people. They suddenly find themselves on the paying side of the wealth distribution system. There are social security, employee withholding, employee medical plans, employee lawsuits, unions, and the IRS to contend with. No one has taught them about business.

Although the young medical doctors have been taught humanitarianism from the beginning, they have been shielded from this impossible mixture of humanitarianism, socialism and capitalism that is now reality for them. They never quite recover from the sharp inconsistencies. They have never been taught to charge. It seems embarrassing. They never dreamed they would be hated for making too much money, for having too much power, for being too successful.

Consider the perhaps subtle, yet unreasonable revulsion at being required to pay a physician who presides over the death of a loved one. It is natural to feel there was something more that physician could have done in any event. This and similar human tendencies add to the young physician's experience.

This is the day of complex third-party billing. Today an innocent mistake submitting a bill can get one faced with fraud. Medical school teachers have left their students rabbits in a jungle of regulation. The important thing to note here is the striving, risk and insecurity all the way. This along with the requisite enterprise, intelligence and long training, is building a demand on the part of the young physicians and their families for recompense. But in some, more than others, it is building a demand for tranquility and security. Many just want to be left unhampered to practice medicine.

There is chronic indebtedness—past, present and future. An office lease must be signed and the liability assumed. Liable, liable, liable. Much responsibility bedevils the physician from the beginning. It is a rare young physician today who does not become cynical, covertly hostile, more uncharitable. So this building of fear, hostility and insecurity seriously dampen the idealistic, humanistic traits inculcated in medical training. This should not be. Such feelings escalate the desire for recompense, even revenge. It harms both patient and physician.

The young physician is confronted with a host of seemingly unnecessary regulations and payments that consume every small business owner. It is the present injustice and insecurity they perceive that is so devastating to them. They buy liability insurance, malpractice insurance, industrial accident insurance, fire insurance, auto insurance, life insurance, disability insurance, and theft insurance. Being uninsured or underinsured is a constant problem with most physicians. The patient and the physician each buy insurance to protect one from the other!

Patient and Physician

It is essential to consider physicians and their patients together. We must avoid bringing anything between the patient and the physician. We must avoid creating a feeling of helplessness or hopelessness in either the physician or the patient. We must avoid coercion of either patient or physician in any form. We must stop the fear of patients that they might find themselves someday unable to afford needed medical care. We must stop the fear of physicians that they will be exploited or conscripted.

The patient and their physician are the key players. It is crucial to remove everyone else from the area of consideration. Then one begins by considering only the needs of physicians and patients. Give the physicians back their power and status and allow and encourage them to wallow in their idealism. Believe that this idealism is there, in spite of the many things that would destroy it.

Give the patient a basic Safety Net providing medical care regardless of ability to pay. Free the patient and physician from coercion and fear. Give both the patient and physician the freedom of various options, competitive alternatives, and an underlying Safety Net.

Many physicians initially wanting money come to the realization they have no time to spend it; or they cannot keep the money because they have no time to invest it. Many, as they go on in life, come to value non-monetary rewards more and more. Today they are getting less and less of these.

Physicians acquire value to their patients through their knowledge, experience and good works. Many others, of course, contribute much to the knowledge base. Without a patient to treat, that knowledge loses utility. It is our patients that give us security. It is to them we must go to regain it and so furnish them medical security.

The physician and patient are coupled. Anything that harms one harms the other. Remember they are both human; prone to unrealistic expectations, fears, external pressures, greed, lapses of attention, and need for approval.

To lower medical costs overall, patients must become willing to accept the physician's judgment that some aspect of wanted care is unnecessary. That sometimes carefully arrived at judgment calls turn out to be wrong. That it is necessary for patients to abandon the fallacy of indemnifying all risk and hence be more tolerant, or less opportunistic in this regard. (It would seem elementary economic common sense that overlaying insurance or government bureaucracies could never simplify or reduce medical costs.)

Those of us who love medicine still remain idealistic about human caring, yet we grieve over medicine's decline in public esteem at a time when medicine is at a pinnacle of technical achievement. We want to find and teach a redirection before valid knowledge and practice are cast aside (by a well-meaning public) as worthless, or too expensive. Growing numbers of the public, including powerful politicians, now seem to advocate throwing out this baby with the bath water amid a torrent of complexity, to the detriment of us all. Whether due to malice or ignorance does not matter, the loss will be the same.

Those of us who love the traditions of medicine, and who value the place of physicians in society, want to teach them to stop killing themselves. We want to get them to stop treating their patients as adversaries, and to stop rushing mindlessly and unhealthfully after something, rather than getting value and enjoyment from patient contact. Physicians should be emanating a subjective personal health. We want physicians to make their lives an expression of being, rather than a struggle toward something.

The Big City Hospitals Then and Now

The financial aspects of getting through medical school were a miracle for me, thanks to the Army Specialized Training Program, and a General of the Sixth Army Service Command whose name I never knew, and Mr. Moon of the University of Illinois Medical school, who accepted me.

After medical school, I became intimately acquainted with a number of charity teaching county hospitals and their out-patient clinics. I also served periods of training in two big city private hospitals, a veteran's hospital and a military hospital. This was as a medical student, an intern, a resident and later as a teacher. To be sure, there were aspects of the entire hospital operation of which I was unaware; but to me then, the system worked well. Never in my whole career have I seen a patient refused care by a physician because of inability to pay. Often the wait was long, the place was packed, and many of the poor needed a bath. This I understood in part. As a child there were times when we were dirty not because we wanted to be, but because we had no way to bathe. It is the same today. In many ways it is worse.

Perhaps I was not in a position to see it; but the county charity hospitals with their associated outpatient clinics did not seem to be wasting time and effort striving for money then. They did their job well. At least there was not this need to sign every progress note, list every procedure done, keep careful account of your time and sign piles of forms of all kinds, as it is now. Sign so the insurance may be collected from one hand and passed to the other, and always be sure the medical charts would stand up in court.

In most of those hospitals and clinics, first the medical students would examine the patient, and so on up the line. In the end, it was the attending men, our teachers, physicians picked for their excellence, who made the difficult medical decisions.* In famous clinics, in top university teaching hospitals, the same system was in effect as it is today. The university teaching hospitals of that day took

* The term resident refers to physicians in specialty training. The term attending physician refers to voluntary teaching physicians. If a resident has a problem, day or night the attending physician is called.

rich and poor alike, as they do today. The main concern was, and is, the complexity of the patient's problem.

The hospitals of my early experience ran well with far fewer employees, and they had much more esprit. They were run by physicians or career administrators with the help and cooperation of the nursing staff and other ancillary personnel for the care of patients. Each worker was recognized by all as a necessary and important part of the team. The members of this team had a common purpose, a dedication to patient care. It was common for the team members to work overtime if conditions warranted. This was not done out of sacrifice, but from interest in the patients. These workers were having fun until someone convinced them they were being exploited.

The county hospitals were like a home for the staff. Food and coffee were available night and day for the interns, residents, nurses, and attending physicians. Even the occasional ambulance driver was welcome to a piece of pie and a cup of coffee.

In the big private hospitals it was the same. When the staff dining room was closed at night, food and beverages were set out for the late night staff. Professionals of all types, answering emergency calls to the hospital, would pause at night for refreshments. There would be discussions about problem cases among those gathered there. Some busy obstetricians spent nearly as many nights sleeping in the hospital as at home. Patient care is a round-the-clock job. The hospital was a warm, hospitable place for the staff. We interns did not realize this was a way of training us in many aspects of being a physician, not the least of which was going without sleep.

I was a resident in one such county hospital for the first year after my internship. Later I taught in a smaller one that trained family practitioners, and later still taught young specialists in a large charity hospital associated with a medical school. In those early fifties and into the sixties, such hospitals and their clinics did an excellent job for those who had no other means of medical care. There was a friendlier atmosphere all around.

Then, as I remember, even back in the early sixties, things began to change. It was as if someone tried to fix the system and broke it.

Some of the county hospitals were closed for lack of funds. Patients became more difficult to satisfy. Few brought gifts of pie or cookies anymore. That word "entitlements" was heard. Patients became more demanding, less cooperative, more irresponsible. This began subtly at first. There was a bit of paranoia in the air. There was more red tape. Nurses and others who once were too subservient, now seemed to go to the opposite extreme. There were unions that had not seemed necessary before. These were good for some; yet there seemed a bit of tension in the air. Employees and supplies we thought made no sense at all appeared.

We soon learned that politicians and distant regulations were in charge; no longer were the physicians and professional administrators really in charge. As time went on, many of the physicians who had donated their time for years, did not come around anymore. Instead of having a long list of applicants to volunteer for the prestigious clinical teaching jobs, many areas were quietly begging for physicians to fill their positions. This was happening in big city charity hospitals. They were associated with medical schools, and depended on the medical school staff for their medical service.

Now these hospitals seem bloated with employees, some barely literate, each demanding their rights. Much of the professional's morale is gone. Physicians volunteering their services must often pay for their parking spaces. Hospital cafeterias are contracted out and food is furnished at the proper hours only to those presenting the proper ticket.

The constant threat of offending a different profession, a different sex, a different race hangs in the air. Patients become possible threats. Nurses must spend ever more of their valuable time keeping records. Everything must be carefully recorded because the charity hospital now operates under the guise that it is financed by insurance and policed by some lawyers.

Threats are everywhere. We are told it is necessary for teachers to sign all surgical procedure sheets, because that is the only way the hospital can get its insurance payment. Many teachers rebelled. We are at risk of being accused of insurance fraud, some fear, because many of the procedures had been supervised by the physician, but had been performed by the advanced residents with the teachers assisting. What had once seemed like little issues became important. Such fears are proliferating. There are concerns about malpractice exposures.

All this is not the fault of the hospital, we are told; it is just a sign of the times. Physicians on boards of directors or peer review boards became frightened over tales of lawsuits. It has become difficult to staff these. Attending physicians are hounded to turn in a complete record of their time spent to the administrators. This is so the insurance can be billed. That, we are told, is how this county charity hospital gets paid.

The humanness has been squeezed out of the system. The social workers are busy handling bureaucratically inspired procedures and paperwork. Whoever had set out to help the poor, did not understand the poor, it seemed. The problems of the poor did not go away by throwing money or demagoguery at those problems. More than anything, the poor needed honest, individual attention, training, understanding and respect for their individuality. There were so many of them. Hordes of immigrants—documented and undocumented—appeared from most everywhere requiring medical care. We treated all who appeared. One cannot stop treating people by government decree. What should physicians do, let them give birth in the streets?

And so those accustomed to caring for charity patients in an atmosphere of free giving must now pay careful attention to clocking in and many other demands. One becomes accustomed to these things, but the atmosphere is different. We have lost much.

With the Safety Net Hospital-Clinics we should re-establish the idealism of county hospital charitable institutions of the past, with the extra-government social covenants that provided care for the poor before programs such as Medicaid existed. Physicians and patients will suffer a great loss if they ever lose this tradition. It must remain and be transferred to every physician regardless of how well society provides safety net refuges. Through such methods, we will promote moral fitness and strong emotional humanistic ties to our teachers and to our patients, as well as intellectual scientific fitness. Medical practice will never be a science alone. There will always be the art. A great part of this art is the heart—caring. The art and the science are linked. We must also avoid a further loss of patient or physician individual responsibility and freedom of choice. These are the foundations of moral virtue and good health.*

---

* See F. Andrew Morfesis, Letters to the Editor, JAMA, Sept. 25,1991, v.266, no.12, pp.1647.

The Contemporary Physician

If work is to become a tiresome duty rather than a passion, and fear is made to take the place of idealism, then of course, more payment is required, and compassion is reduced to a minimum. One can reduce the cost of physician services to the extent it is realized physicians, more than most, work for idealistic reasons, for status, for the opportunity to pursue study and research, for the freedom from fear and the freedom from the many harassments piled on a private-practice-small business. Complete relief of the business duties inherent in private practice today would please most physicians. It should please patients as well, for they would profit handsomely.

Physicians must be given financial security, otherwise they will strive to provide it for themselves through investment of excess earned income. This takes time away from patient care and demoralizes many physicians, for so often they are poor at investing. To the extent these things are provided, physicians will work for less.

Give physicians who are providers for the Safety Net generous pay, and give them financial security. Keep away those jealous of physician power and prerogatives. This book describes ways to do this.

Leave these Safety Net physicians free to do what they are trained to do that no one else can do. That is, *patient care* and *advancement of the art and science of medicine.*

Let someone else manage the ancillary personnel, pay their withholding, their Social Security, their pension plans. When an employee feels they have been wrongly hired or fired, injured on the job, subjected to harassment, or unjustly treated, let some responsible administrator go to court, or handle the situation within the SNHC system. Such administrative duties waste physician's time. (It is absolute folly to expect insurance companies to do this. Insurance bureaucracy will only take away physician time from patient care and spiral costs upward unnecessarily.)

Multiply the inefficiency of having physicians do this administrative work by thousands of physicians, and a picture of considerable economic waste emerges.

In addition to this costly inefficiency, one should consider what portion of the cost of a physician visit is really what a patient pays to the legal, insurance and government industries. Actual spendable physician income averages about 20% of what you pay a private practice physician.

Were we to reduce the pay of physicians, how much would this really lower the cost of this vast commercial enterprise we call medical care delivery? This system is the source of high-paying jobs for a host of trained ancillary personnel. It is the recent source of outrageously expensive hospitals and drugs. Some of these drugs sell for a fraction of that cost just over the border in Mexico. Medical enterprise is the source of some of the highest price/earnings ratios in the stock market, and a rash of initial public offerings of biotechnical firm's stock. Many employees complaining about the cost of medical care hold such stock in their pension plans, if not personally. Are we sure we want to curb these costs; or will we continue with the deception that someone else will pay our costs for us?

The Business of Medicine

If the physician is to run a small business, then the patient should expect to be confronted with a for-profit business. One should also appreciate the folly of cost control strategies that eschew market incentives in favor of governmental regulation. One distortion begets another.*†

Medicine is certainly good business. It is recession-proof. It gives employment to a surprising large number of our populace and many are highly trained. We must decide if we really want to put physicians, and medical care in general, in such a business context to the almost certain exclusion of other values. Even worse would be to put physicians into constant confrontation with the large wealthy corporate insurance, hospital, or health maintenance industries. The patient is certain to get lost in the struggle.

To give the reader some idea of the extent and cost of our medical industry, there follows a partial list of trained ancillary medical personnel to be paid somehow: such as nurses, licensed vocational nurses, practical nurses, pharmacists, pharmacist's helpers, physician office helpers involved in patient care, physician office help involved in the business and administrative aspects, physician office helpers involved in insurance billing. There are physiotherapists who hire medically experienced clerical personnel in their front offices and trained professionals for their back office help. There are nursing home staffs, there are dieticians, X-ray technicians, and a host of other technicians, some of whom many people have never heard about. There are occupational therapists, music therapists, clinical psychologists, clinical social workers. The list goes on and on. New technicians are added almost

---

* See Medical Economics Dec, 18, 1989, the entire issue.
† See also: New Eng. Medical J. v.321, No.9, 607-612 and Mueller, J. The cost of Social Spending-Joblessness, The Wall Street Journal, July 13, 1993, Op-ed page.

daily. We now need specially trained technicians for magnetic resonance imaging, and for positron emission tomography. There are a variety of specialized personnel involved in kidney dialysis, cardiac invasive procedures, CAT scans, and others. Medical care requires more than physicians. Medical costs must provide for more than physicians—much more. Medical care is one of our major industries.

The above lists only some of those ancillary personnel directly involved. It does not mention the drug industry, the instrumentation and equipment industry, the biotechnical industries, the nursing home and hospitals, etc. About 17% of our work force, by one estimate, work directly in the medical care enterprise.

Drugs and Medical Supplies and Devices

Have you ever stopped to think what a miracle a simple pill or capsule is? Produced by the thousands, in exact dosage, in perfect preservation and cleanliness, carefully marked to an appearance standard so each can be identified at once? We are enormously talented in this area.

Rampant increases in drug costs, which occur in part because there is an awareness that insurance companies will pay them, drive up insurance costs, and higher insurance costs lead to more use and to an increased demand for more costly drugs. Drug companies are quick to meet this demand—at a cost. Duplicative drug products with slightly different chemical formulas or slight differences in action, enable different patents and different advertising claims. These new drugs are hawked, advertised at great expense, the product to users, and the stock to investors.

Look at the drug and insurance corporations by means of the stock market. Two of the top money producers are the insurance stocks and the pharmaceutical stocks. Millions of shares are in the hands or in the pension funds of millions of people. Many of these people are clamoring for reduction of their medical costs. Many of these are mouthing the plight of the underinsured and the uninsured, and the high cost of medical care. Many are calling for the government to solve the problem of the high cost of medical care while profiting from shares of these stocks.

But the reasons for high drug costs are more complex than manufacturer, distributor and stockholder greed. Making expensive promotion efforts unnecessary or untenable is a good way to reduce drug costs. Prescription drugs are unique. Price purchasing decisions and quality purchasing decisions are removed from the consumer. These are made by the prescribing physician or the dispensing pharmacist.

Were more of these drugs taken off prescription, the consumer could responsibly make more of these decisions than is presently allowed in this country. They could still be bought at the direction of the physician. Many physicians now recommend non-prescription (over the counter drugs) when they can, because these are in general cheaper, (prescription pharmacists must do a lot of expensive stocking and bookkeeping chores). Many drugs could be taken off prescription. This would probably increase the legal menace, but it would tend to lower drug prices for many reasons with very little increase of risk.

While the cost of prescription drugs is indeed outrageous, so is the cost of FDA regulation. The fact this function is important and necessary does not mean that it could not be done more efficiently and cheaply, with far less political posturing and bureaucratic inefficiency. This cost, of course, is passed along to the consumer (each handler adding a percentage), as are the outrageous costs of litigation expense. At any given time, at least one drug company is fighting an expensive court battle.

Through employers, insurance and government, drug costs are shifted to the taxpayer and the consumer. The drug consumer, once again, has little say in these purchasing decisions either. Forcing employers to pay does not help the unemployed, or the self-employed. It harms the small employer directly. It harms everyone indirectly. Forcing employers to pay certainly increases the numbers of unemployed.

Medicare does not cover drug costs. Pressure from the older Medicare class of consumer may someday be helpful in lowering drug costs. This still does not leave the consumer with sufficient decision prerogative.

Drugs tend to be over-prescribed by some physicians as a way to more quickly dispose of that patient visit. Some physicians tend to prescribe the newer fashionable drugs. These are usually more costly. This may equally well occur in HMOs where the presence of a formulary is no complete barrier.*

For example, consider a patient with a nervous stomach. It is easy for a hurried physician to prescribe a fashionable and expensive new drug (on the formulary) instead of remembering the older, more effective, much

---

* A formulary is a list of drugs to be used, more or less exclusively, where possible, by some group of prescribers. For example, an HMO's physicians, by agreement together, develop a list of commonly used drugs (for which many variants would work) for a given purpose and decide to stock only one or two of them. The formulary drugs are then purchased in large quantities with some considerable price leverage.

less expensive small dose barbiturate and belladonna tablets. In this case probably also on the formulary. Again, the consumer-patient plays no part in this decision.

So market forces are distorted, and in this instance are apt to remain so. There are solutions, and they are discussed in the sections on the Safety Net Hospital-Clinics. These refer to purchasing decisions delegated to expert purchasers buying in large amounts for well considered formularies. They apply as well to some HMOs. Again, they are not total solutions because physician time and training are important factors.

Most importantly, at the SNHC things are turned around. The specialist watches and instructs the generalist when it comes to the quality of medical practice. Instead of a monetary (economics) gatekeeping, we would have a medical knowledge gatekeeping, a crucially important difference.

A formulary is another form of gatekeeping. The clinic pharmacist's computer data bases contain this formulary, enabling them to check quickly each prescription and query the physician who has written an off formulary prescription.

In this way, the institution can buy a select group of drugs in large quantities and press for a discount. If the drug company is unwilling to meet the cost constraints, the institution can put a similar drug in its formulary. This, plus the use of generic drugs (cheaper copies of drugs whose patents have expired) are ways price pressure is put on drug companies. The drug companies, however, can increase the price of drugs the private physician has ordered for patients on some kinds of medical insurance to counter the cost of the formulary discounts.

There are many ways the Safety Net Hospital-Clinics and the drug, medical device and equipment companies can work together that would be mutually beneficial to us all. The loss in profit from lowering the drug cost to the SNHCs would be offset by the great reduction of drug company expense for advertising, even for packaging. Again, drug companies would not need to *sell* their products to individual physicians. The SNHC's purchasing agents would buy them from a knowledge of the scientific literature. And, of course buy them in huge amounts.

Summary

The traditional concept of medical care wherein the patient and physician are directly accountable to each other in all ways is the only concept that is workable in the long run. As physicians, it is our duty to provide medical care to all regardless of their ability to pay. This has been a sacred concept since Hippocrates. Cynics may say it will not work. Anyone who knows physicians knows that it will. The method espoused in this book shows how it can be encouraged.

Many believe the acquisition of medical knowledge is a matter of paying the money for the schooling, passing the required courses and getting the required license. However, students are given only the knowledge their teachers will pass on to them. As a condition to passing on this knowledge, the teacher requires adherence to a certain code of ethics. This concept is instilled in medical students from the beginning. It does not follow that a hospital, a government agency or an insurance company is similarly bound.

A ninety-year old lady from a small Midwestern village with cancer of the mouth was brought into a major medical clinic for treatment. Somehow she did not have Medicare. She said to the physician (who was to begin a long expensive course of fractional doses of X-ray therapy), "I do not have any means to pay you." The physician I observed was touched. I heard him tell her, while holding her hand, that she need not worry about money, their concern was to cure her. There would be no charge. Most of us are fiercely proud of this aspect of ourselves. Naturally this could not be extended to all patients. The point is to illustrate an emotion, a strong idealism, a tradition that is still carried on by most physicians. The existence of SNHCs would ensure it's survival.

When patients are ill, often they are frightened. They expect the best of scientific medicine, regardless of their ability to pay. They want to be cared for, and above all they want someone to spend quality time with them. They want compassion. They want understanding and they want information. They want results.

Patients deserve competence. It is difficult for patients to judge this. Patients want explanations. They want to know what is wrong, and what they can expect. It matters not whether that information is precisely correct scientifically, so long as it is simple, believable and easily grasped. There is always something the patient can be instructed to do, there is some hope, some place where reassurance is plausible.

A good physician should know his technical material, and know it well. This is especially true of the specialist. A good physician should keep up with the current medical knowledge. The clinic or office should be immaculately clean, with an atmosphere of friendly dignity. The staff should be pleasant and never curt or surly. A good physician would never tolerate this. Above all, a good physician inspires trust and confidence.

This thing we call continuity of care is indeed valuable technically as well as psychologically. It is easily disparaged. Do not sell this short for yourself. For most of us, when we find a physician who seems to be just right for us, it is a real comfort. Even though one is ill and perhaps afraid, this kind of relationship—also a friendship—is invaluable.

Even if that physician refers you to another, there is still that feeling almost as if "your doctor" were there too. You know you could go back and confide your feelings; and get that person's honest opinion, criticism, blessing or interpretation of what that other doctor said. All this is more a matter of doctor personality than doctor specialty or general practice. Such a personality should be stressed at every SNHC.

If you have such a relationship, and you had doubts about an initial visit to a Safety Net Hospital-Clinic, why not use them both? Your private doctor would be there for you until you became confident and had established a satisfying relationship with the physician or physicians at the specialist's office, or at the specialty clinic at the Safety Net Hospital-Clinic. You could as well keep your private physician and decide which to see as you went along.

We have lost much. We have lost much that is honest, that is tender. Don't let more be taken away from you. Do not stand by and let it slip through your fingers. Patients saying, "My doctor," with trust and affection, is so precious. It is priceless. So is "My patient." They are in danger of being trodden under. We, both of us, must preserve this. We need not give up quality care. We need not forego good medical care for all, regardless of ability to pay, nor should we be stampeded by opportunists.

Some distant official or employee, administrative system, or some other third-party once interposed, does not, cannot care. This prostitutes something very precious. That something is a feeling, a comfort, reassurance, a personal touch that third parties may not value for you. Is this a luxury or a necessary part of competent medical care?

If you and your doctor have this kind of relationship, private practice may be for you, with the knowledge that you can pay your doctor yourself, and if sometimes you could not pay, your doctor would take care of you nevertheless. It would be better with the Safety Net Hospital-Clinic as a backup. That way you can bet the odds and probably beat the cost of insurance. As more people did this without insurance, the cost of private medicine would decrease.

The responsibility would once again become more direct between doctor and patient. The quality of care would increase, and the aspects of the present system that are spiraling medical costs upward will slowly reverse. The SNHC will not only furnish you with a catastrophic care backup, it should, if allowed to develop, begin to correct some of the costly abuses in industrial accident, auto accident, and malpractice situations. These can be solved without the emphasis on money, and so lower costs for all.

Some may question this emphasis on the doctor-patient relationship. Does this only occur in private practice? There are large private clinics of fee-for-service physicians that can resemble HMOs in the way patients are handled. It is equally true that some HMOs try, insofar as possible, to encourage this doctor-patient relationship. Some people do not want or need such personal support, even as they face death. Yet we must be ever vigilant or we will lose this important aspect of medical care. Medical science is improving the efficacy, the power, and the price. With scientific emphasis comes a tendency to be more objective, more impersonal. We need not forego one to get the other.

There is seemingly no understanding of the social repercussions that are almost certain to follow if things continue along as they are now. To wit: patients will become ever more dependent on insurance companies and for deeper pockets to pay the ever greater insurance premiums. What will be accomplished by economically enslaving most of us to insurance companies? Is this not favoring only the rich and the powerful with freedom of choice? All this insurance medicine may seem tolerable since it appears free—until you or your very loved one becomes desperately ill. Then you may well want the best, along with some tender loving care.

Government involvement will stimulate, once again, bureaucratic interference from government types and activists and radicals on both sides, who are well meaning, but innocent of, and far removed from these narrow medical specialities. They are inept. They are presumptuous. They are out of their field. This may well result in another round of central government tinkering for the politician's and their powerful supporters advantage.

We must remove the uncertainty and high cost attached to health care, but not because it is not worth it. The public demands it. They demand it because today's sophisticated medical care is absolutely necessary. The better it gets, the more necessary it will become, and the more expensive. Yet who would forgo this care? Medicine and biology are becoming two of our most sophisticated sciences.

There is another problem that can best be solved once recognized for what it is. This problem is the diminution of responsibility of the individual patient, and the relationship between patients and their physicians. One can deny it, but there is a cost and this cost must be paid one way or another. All these costs must be paid by each of us, even though we think we have shirked our share. We can strive to reduce these costs much more effectively if only we face up to them, and together cast out all unnecessary expenses, especially unnecessary layers of administrative or insurance bureaucratic expense that only hide us from ourselves.

How a physician is paid should have no effect on the development of such a meaningful interpersonal relationship as is being here discussed. Perhaps patients do need help. It will help to give patients more options, putting them in a better bargaining position to deal directly with the physician.

An important aspect of this book is the advocacy of gradual change (evolving through the use of various options) to the present system called here "competitive alternatives." Third-party interference must go the same way. There are too many well entrenched obstacles for change to come about other than through the gradual evolution implicit in a competitive market. If one has a barrel of explosives to detonate, it is better to divide it into small piles and explode them one at a time.

What will managed care do to the doctor-patient relationship? This is best explained succinctly by changing this term to read **Third Party Managed For Profit Care**. Concerning the term managed competition consider this. Today's cottage industry called private medical practice is in danger of being swallowed by big corporation industry. Where will the patient's place be then? For what and with whom are these behemoths to compete? Will it not be for the patient dollar, anyone's dollar? Once again competition among physicians for patients will be diverted away. With whom will the physicians be competing? Will patients profit as physicians become subervient? To whom will physicians answer? Not really to the patients directly. Who will profit here?

That these big corporations compete does not change the fact every medical dollar that can be will be diverted from medical care to corporate administrative cost, to marketing and to profit.* Although these big corporations compete, it does not mean a form of competition that would benefit patients.

---

* See Jellinek MS, & Nurcombe, Barry. Two wrongs don't make a right. JAMA. 1993;270:1737-1739.
See also Branch Wm. et al. Becoming a doctor. N. Engl J. Med. 1993;329:1130-1132. These articles are easy to read and you will enjoy the contrast. This contrast says much.

The Conclusion

This book attempts to bring the reader closer to the mind and practices of physicians and their contemporary world, including their patients, for a better understanding of the forces that affect physicians and patients. Perhaps each will get to know the other better, and from this understanding forge a solution to our medical cost problems. One very possible solution is developed; the essence of which is the preservation of patient and physician choice, the use of non-monetary remuneration to reduce physician need for more money, and the restatement of higher medical standards through the use of what are called Safety Net Hospital-Clinics, free to all.

The pitfalls of our present medical insurance system were stressed. The flaws of monetary redress to achieve physician accountability were discussed.

The Safety Net Hospital-Clinics were viewed as a refuge for patients *and* for physicians, while preserving the present methods of medical care delivery as alternative options. This combination is seen as a way to begin the long road to lower medical costs. This can only come about through satisfied patients and satisfied physicians. Neither can be surfeited, all must give a little. This refuge, this absolute insurance would be paid for by an additional percentage of everyone's income tax *payment.*

If work is to become a tiresome duty rather than a passion, if disgust is made to take the place of idealism, then of course, more payment is required, and compassion is reduced to fit expediency. One can get the money out of medicine to the extent it is realized physicians, more than most, work for idealistic reasons and for status, for the opportunity to pursue study and research, for freedom from fear, and for freedom from the many harassments now piled on small business.

Physicians should be allowed financial security, otherwise they will strive to provide it for themselves through diversion into investments, and increased income. This takes time and attention away from patient care, and demoralizes many physicians, for they are so poor at it. Again, such things are called here non-monetary compensation.

We must stop the fear of patients they will someday be unable to afford necessary medical care; and we must stop the fear of physicians they will be someday conscripted or exploited.

This book describes a way.

Dr. Donald G. Lindsay, M.D.
P.O. Box 3233
Ventura CA 93003

Afterword

There follows a personal message. What are we handing to future generations? Toward what are we leading—or drifting?

Expectations

Creating dependence is always, at least in part, the setting of false expectations. Anyone deceptively promising expectations that cannot be met is a menace. This manipulation of expectations, this deception invariably leads to disorder. Physicians know they should never create expectations they cannot fulfill. This is the common reason patients become disgruntled and seek out attorneys.

Careful examination of one's expectations concerning medical care should be a sequel to reading this book. Neither medical costs nor physicians, apparently, satisfy the expectations of this society. Nor can the politicians help in this regard. They are a part of our discontent.

When expectations exceed ability, dissatisfaction, hostility and sometimes violence result. Illness of many kinds emerge. Masked depression is common. When power exceeds and perverts ethical, idealistic values a whole series of problems occur. Ignorance on one end, and callousness toward ethical fealty on the other seem to be the two poles. Consider more specifically these two ends of the social scale: the professions—namely the medical, the educators and especially the legal-jurisprudence professions on one and the under educated, underprivileged urban youth on the other.

We have raised unfairly the expectations of some who must be satisfied with a low wage because that is all they are worth, not because they have lacked opportunity. There are those who could be worth more, yet they have never known or refused self-discipline and determined effort. Often, this has been replaced, poisoned with empty promises, with misplaced sympathy, with welfare checks, with dependence. The effect of that poison is hate, violence—or some other social burden. Nor does this mean that everyone should go to school. Some with great potential are simply not suited for this. We must explore other ways.

Our culture seems to excel at producing criminals and destructive gangs,*even though we have many ethical self disciplined individuals with pride in their work, what ever that work may be. Why is this so? Generations of sociologists, criminologists, psychotherapists, and those with compassion have apparently not been successful despite much pedantry, and little understanding of the facts of our biological existence.

Running to the suburbs is only a temporary solution. The most irresponsible solution is to put the problems onto future generations. Our media must be more socially responsible, and so must some attorneys. They must real-

---

* Skolnick AA, NMA Seeks Prescription to End Violence. J.A.M.A. 1993;270:1283-1284.

ize that while starting fires attracts attention, so desirable for their enterprise, putting out those fires is necessary for their own survival. Nor are our judges blameless.

We must face the reality that many of our non-producers we can never change. Government can help this little. (It could help most by simply keeping order). Government will fail at this welfare business just as it has in the past. It is trying to alter a basic biological verity. People are not born equal. We must face-up to another reality.

In this country we have a diminishing need for the unskilled low-wage earner. There are a billion of them in Asia eager to work for a fraction of our expectations. Many of them are already here (and more are coming) eagerly working away, happy with their lower expectations and productive with their greater incentives. Somehow we notice more their products that are only a few days away. They are cheaper. We want and need them. They raise our standard of living. To try to shut out these products simply will not work. How often must we rediscover this. Neither will encouraging them to stop their reproductive limitations. Demagoguery will not help. Raising the worlds standard of living will help.

Self-hatred, low esteem often projects out as hatred, violence, an unwillingness to be part of the culture, and feelings of being exploited. Why do some fan these smoldering resentments? For some, their survival is not a primary issue. Part of their problem is their fantasy of invulnerability. The reality is death comes easily, and it is permanent. It is not simply a dramatic event. Are there those so complacent, so blind to these realities, they would aid and abet this violence?

This has become a medical problem. Idleness of our youth and our poor leaves them demoralized, bored, morose and prone to violence. One of the few low skilled, high paying jobs we leave them is selling drugs, a business we make lucrative by making drugs illegal. We thereby force them to enforce their own laws. What do our laws mean to these poor people? Many would rather go to jail for their education than to college, and we as a culture oblige.

While our drug laws have given the jurisprudence and enforcement business a boost, they have in reality only criminalized vice. We confuse vice and crime. History is replete with instances of failure to criminalize vice. We must return to the sharp distinction between crime and vice. Crime directly harms others and is the proper province of law enforcement. Vice takes its own victims, it directly impacts the user. If anything, vice is increased by making it illegal, since it is a basically masochistic act which then progresses to detrimental physiological changes to the individual.

Vice requires treatment, medical treatment, and it requires extensive research. Perhaps someday if "the law" will let us openly attack it, we in science will understand the physiological and genetic basis of addiction as we are now just beginning to understand the physiological and genetic connections between violence and alcohol, which point the way to treatment.

This does not mean that crime and vice do not overlap and in these instances (as with drunken driving) strict law enforcement is effective and essential; but there is a world of difference between this and prohibition. We must be clear that we are here dealing with the criminal effects of vice and be careful not by our laws to increase this.

All this is indeed part of the medical cost problem, very much so. Violence is a fatal disease, as most every intern and emergency room physician knows. Paradoxically, an effective way to control violence is through fear of death. But not just any fear will do. It must be "deep body" fear. This is a primordial fear the body responds to, and it overrides the cerebral. This may seem stern to many. In fact, it may be instilled in benign ways.

How are we to get more of what we want? We must assess our strengths and our weaknesses realistically.

We must behave more competitively on a global basis. If we as a nation want high wages and working standards, then we must value facile adaptive ability. As populations increase it becomes ever more necessary to adapt, to change, to educate ourselves, and develop needed skills in areas where this country has natural advantages.

One of our present advantages as a nation is medical ability, our medical care advances and inventions. We produce superior medical equipment, medicines and similar products. But we are driving them to countries like Singapore, Switzerland and Germany by excessive litigation, restrictions and regulations. This we can not afford. We can lead in medical care delivery innovation as well. Perhaps this can include providing very high quality medical care to all.

We as a nation have been known, trusted and looked-up to for our method of government. Is this slipping through our fingers? Are we deadlocked in deadlock? Sometimes our hard working Congress seems to exemplify resistance to change.

Our weakness is enhanced by our failure to appreciate we are closely tied to the world. We are also closely bound to reality. That world is catching up, as is reality. We cannot close off either. In some areas many other countries are already ahead. It is not just that they are ahead. Some areas are ahead at our expense, simply because they are better.

Furthermore, we must provide for everyone regardless of their ability to pay, if we are to indulge in the tremendous biological luxury of succoring the violent, the morose, the criminal, the non-productive, and worse, the powerful socially irresponsible.

At the same time, increased individual productive efficiency through the use of complex machines is becoming a necessity. This demands skilled labor, and input from well-educated people. We know this, yet allow selfish, short-sighted, organized power groups to retard our progress. As a culture, as a democracy we must learn to throw-off the yoke of such self-interests. Sometimes the difference between demagoguery and leadership is difficult to discern.

Lack of foresight regarding these complex ongoing dynamisms, and an unwillingness to learn from the mistakes of other countries are but two examples of our folly. As we are learning from Russia, once people "progress" to dependence on government, incentive to produce disappears or becomes perverted, to be replaced by vying for positions of power and control. Worse, once a people have become accustomed to such values, it becomes very difficult to change. Their adaptive and survival capacities are often permanently hampered. No biological system can tolerate this for long.

Productive capacity among nations or individuals is rarely equal. Should a productive person owe society a debt, or should society owe the highly productive a debt. Who do I owe? Who owes me, if things are to be fair? If nothing else, such questions, such perversions are biologically unsound, and we are all biological entities. The concept of taking is implicit in this thing we now call "fairness;" not giving, but taking. Such notions, like dependence, lead straight to violence, and to anarchy. When it becomes necessary to invent euphemistic terms for our actions, to couch in deception our very government's pronouncements, danger is upon us.

If more than 20% of the fruits of their labor is taken from most people, incentive to work diminishes. Individual energy is perverted to protecting themselves from this government taking.

Those who receive are harmed too. Their Ability weakens and eventually is forgotten. Lack of toughness, of self reliance, lack of adaptability in the realm of enterprise follow, duplicity and struggle for control take their place. Cynicism moves in. Welfare does not produce gratitude or a more civil order, it produces crippling dependence and media incited envious hostility. How then are we to help the poor help themselves? How are we to prevent our underprivileged youth from killing as a pastime? Why do we forget the plight of the murdered so quickly? This denial is indeed a symptom of decline.

Our pool of capital is diminishing, the dependency and expectation level is increasing, and our national debt is increasing, even as we go about offering our services, our expensive military protection, and our borrowed money to the world.

We buy into this notion of the justice of redistribution of wealth, while clinging to the pride and security of ownership. For this inconsistency (or shall we call it ambivalence), we are paying and will continue to pay in ways that most of us, perhaps none of us understand completely. Look around you.

Consider merely evidence concerning medical costs. When you see a large fancy medical insurance building, note that there we have thrown away a part of your medical dollar. Realize this is happening because many of us view the illness that sent us to the physician as a misfortune, making a subterfuge necessary for payment. We have been conditioned to seek another (a victim) to pay for our misfortunes. Many of us would rather pay more than admit that we must pay at all. Of course illness is a misfortune; but not in the sense that you must see a physician. What if there were no physicians to see? What if they were poorly trained, even just perfunctory?

When an attorney takes 40% of one's winnings, or when the insurance company takes its hidden portion, perhaps it does not seem the same as if one paid this out of pocket. The denial extends further. As we receive these payments, then with the other hand we pay for the winnings of everyone else. On balance we are all becoming poorer. Whether we receive these payments or not, we all pay indirectly for the largess afforded the "winners." Even though some were receiving their just due.

Much of what this society demands is taken from us slyly. If the IRS did not use the clever tactic of withholding, if we all had to dig down in our pocket each quarter and pay that income tax, many more people would be resisting government spending, which they now view as government giving.

Have you noticed that it takes both spouses working to make ends meet, even with all the things your employer must do for you? Have you noticed that it is all you can do to pay the rent? In many areas of the country there is no way one can afford a house. Remember we must now compete against the world. Wake up USA and look around at reality.

Do the poor need help? Do the sick, the old, the infirm, the handicapped? Of course they do. Who must help them? All of us. This is as it has always been. The problems, the needs of the needy are escalating. Perhaps we should concern ourselves with why this is so, rather than through some deception, such as throwing taxpayer money at the problem, feel that we are solving it.

Why not stick the rich? (Whatever that means). Because we, all of us in this country, need their capital. If we through "progressive" taxation take from the "rich" their capital, we are in a sense really taking *our* capital. We are taking capital necessary for all of us to produce wealth. Capital can be thought of as recoverable, concentrated, crystallized effort. Such effort required effective incentive. As a rule its owner must have a surplus to risk it, as well as sufficient incentive. Growth, jobs, increasing standard of living require risked capital. Yes they do, they really do. It is essential to comprehend this totally and that is difficult.

The question here is not which socio-economic group will miss the loss of capital the most, the better question is which loss will society miss the most. Bluntly, what will happen to the standard of living of us all if that capital is transferred to the non-producers? If it is transferred or remains with our top producers? How much can we afford to transfer to the non-productive? How will we know when enough is enough? Can we rely on political opportunism for such information?

We cannot rely on government to make productive use of capital, it tends to harm as much as help. Those of us not blinded by dependent needs or envy, surely know this by now. To make productive use of capital, not only takes risk and singleness of purpose, it demands diversity and the real possibility of failure.

Failure in the private sector wipes-out that enterprise as a rule. In government, failure often brings more money to keep some ideology afloat. Of course a society can have a direction, what we might call a gross national purpose. Yet this cannot be too narrowly defined or too inflexible.

The ultimate measure is simply successful survival. **Our immediate task is survival of our middle class.**

Once again, to be willing to risk capital, most people must have a surplus of it, plus drive and enterprise. This takes incentive. To prevent failure, it takes more incentive and work to educate oneself, to train oneself, then enterprise, more hard work and tenacity. Many of our poor stay that way because they simply refuse to undergo the tedium of work or tenacious self-discipline. Should we aid and abet this to keep ourselves unbothered?

We as a culture have debased the dignity of menial work, even the dignity of a servant culture, and replaced it with a culture of poverty.*

So many of us envy wealth. The truth is once a viable middle class is developed and maintained, in such a society, beyond a certain point, most of what wealth purchases is illusory. Perhaps wealth enhances status, itself illusory; yet the wealth purchases not much for a lot. This will hold true so long as we maintain a large middle class with a high standard of living, and so long as we do not destroy the viability of the producer. There becomes less and less need for class envy.

This is not to imply that there would be a diminution of upper social mobility. In such a society there is strong incentive to risk wealth, to invest it. The producer must have capital. Without both capital and incentive we will have no middle class. Incentive and capital are the most easily destroyed aspects of producer viability.

Object lessons of these facts abound today all over Eastern Europe. Socialism does not produce a classless society. It produces a controlling class and a controlled

---

* See Oscar Lewis, CHILDREN OF SANCHEZ, Random House, NY,; 1961 and LA VIDA, Random House, 1966.

class. We are seeing this develop here, now. We seem to be abetting rather than reducing discontent, increasing sharp class distinctions. Those who would help the plight of others should shoulder some social and cultural awareness and develop a mature responsible approach.

The politically expedient envious distinction of rich and poor, now so popular, is ruining the society in many ways, some overt and some subtle. How can the emerging deception-dependent socialist cancer be replaced by social pressure, by the thrust to find things to do for all? How will we correct why the non-producers are not producers on an individual by individual basis? Perhaps there are many we cannot train for a skill or a profession? What are they to do?

Government can help most by correcting its past mistakes, by lifting regulations that prevent individuals from employing our less skilled, and thus enable many small employers to favor, train and then stay with such people. These laborers in turn must become more adaptive, more accustomed to the insecurity of job change. It is their self-reliance we have destroyed and perhaps we have harmed our own. This no biologic system can permit.

So we have regulations, well-intentioned and short-sighted, that prevent many of us from employing a low wage earner or two. The risk of financial ruin and especially the bother to learn all the complex regulations are too great, and many of these jobless feel they do better on welfare. More specifically, many who would furnish jobs are stopped by the necessity of expensive industrial insurance, social security, and the risk of being ruined financially by some accident, some lawsuit, or enforcement of some complex regulation.

There follows portions of a written communication from a contractor seeking to win a construction job bid.

This person was under the impression that he was dealing with a naive home owner subject to confusion over the regulations alluded to above. The intimidation went something like this: "There are a number of workers in your area that are not state licensed contractors as required by law. I have included this to alert you to the hazards you could face. The law is very strict in this matter. All must be state licensed contractors, except jobs totalling under two hundred dollars, and employees working for wages. You as a home owner cannot legally hire a non-licensed carpenter unless he is your employee, and then only to work on your own property. You would then be his employer and must provide worker's compensation insurance, unemployment insurance etc. If you do not provide worker's compensation, you could be fined, jailed or both. If an employee were injured, he could secure an award from the Division of Industrial Accidents and obtain a judgment on your assets to secure payment. The state will make a demand on you to pay within ten days. Failure to pay within the time limit requires a mandatory fine of three hundred dollars and ten days in jail. The employee is allowed to sue on top of the award. According to the IRS guidelines, a worker without a contractor's license doing work for someone that requires a license is their employee. If you falsely classify the employee as a contractor, you have committed a felony." There was much more.

How can we get the threatening, out of touch zealots to stoop to reality?* Also, can we help develop more trade unions that teach, conduct apprenticeships for high school graduates, and give these workers the pride and dignity they deserve? Can we turn our labor union politicians

---

* See Mc Govern, op. cit.

from enemies of management, at any cost, as a career goal, to more interest in worker training, and can we turn management from viewing as adversaries the labor union members who follow these leaders? Mutual exploitation has not worked.

Can we turn management, yes and labor union politicians, to friends of those coming into the labor market; real friends, not friendly exploiters? Can we get workers to be less cynical about their work? Will world competition force management to listen to those workers on the line who want to point the way to more efficient productivity? Most likely workers, management, and labor politicians all are partially to blame. This is common in most situations of animosity.

We all project our own problems into our opinions. Examination of one's own feelings of compassion for the non-producer may well uncover feelings of inadequacy, or perhaps uncover the hidden notion that work is never enjoyable. We can train a generation or so in this belief, and in the belief they deserve care; or we can train a generation to believe in achievement, and confidence in their ability and pride in their self-reliance and adaptability.

Instead of the thrust to label people as unfortunate, the thrust to get something for nothing, to buy a vote by such a stance, the atmosphere could change from one of deception and dependence to one of energy, self-discipline, and therefore pride. Pride in one's job, pride in oneself, and above all an atmosphere of adaptability and industry. Unfortunately this may require first a show of discipline. In a governmental system where unanimity behind such a show of strength is politically infeasible, a show of discipline may not be tolerated, outside the military services.

Those whose occupation it is to help the physically handicapped, know full well that an atmosphere of self pity engendered often by misplaced compassion, or promises of money for continued disability can slow, even prevent, the striving and change so necessary for the handicapped to recover a happy and useful life. Is a non-producer handicapped? To what extent? On what personal, social and cultural conditions does this depend?

And so to medical care, the dilemma is simple. Are we to remove medicine from the realm of commerce or not? Is there some partial solution, some half way between socialism and capitalism? Chances are good we will get what we pay for; but in what currency? What has escalated our expectations? What will these new physicians now in school want?

How can you or I bring about changes? First each must fight our own complacency. Even now the restlessness, the thirst for answers to this medical cost dilemma and the greater problems beneath, are blowing in the wind. "Socialized medicine," forcing employers to carry medical insurance on all employees, cleaning house and senate, term limits, presidential line item veto, local voter initiatives are being considered.

People in a similar manner could rally around the Safety Net Hospital-Clinic system and bring it about. The remainder would take care of itself, so long as the basic principles outlined in this book were understood and followed. Freedom from coercion for every patient and physician; their working together, shoulder to shoulder, each ever considering the other is the best way to begin.* And so with our government, while we may disparage it,

* Beach SG. Letters to the Editor. N. Engl. J. Med. 1993;329:808-808.

we are a people who get in there, again and again, striving, arguing together to make it work. For medicine, especially for patients, and physicians, the time is now.

I could not dig: I dare not rob:
Therefore I lied to please the mob.
Now all my lies are proved untrue
And I must face the men I slew,
What tale shall serve me here among
My angry and defrauded young?
                    From "A Dead Statesman"
                    by Rudyard Kipling

Suggested Readings

Overview

JOURNAL OF THE AMERICAN MEDICAL ASSOCIATION:

1.Kritchevsky SB, Simmons BP. Continuous quality improvement concepts and applications for physician care. JAMA 1991;1266:1817-1823

2.Lundberg GD. National health care reform. JAMA. 1992;267:2521-2524.

3.Todd, JS. Problems with incentives. JAMA. 1990; 264: 1294-1295

4.Rosenblatt RA. Specialists or Generalists. JAMA. 1992; 267:1665-1666.

5.Kravitz RL, et al. Differences in the mix of patients among medical specialties and systems of care. JAMA. 1991; 267: 1617-1623.

6.Greenfield S, et al. Variations in resource utilization among medical specialities and systems of care. JAMA. 1992;267:1624-1630.

7.Ransohoff DG, Lang CA. Sigmoidoscopic Screening in the 1990s. JAMA. 1993;269:1278-1281.

8.Reiser SJ, The era of the patient. JAMA. 1993;269:1012-16.

THE NEW ENGLAND JOURNAL OF MEDICINE:

9.Inglehart JK. The American health care system. N Engl J Med. 1992;326:962-967.

10. Ginzberg E. The monetarization of medical care. N Engl J Med. 1984;310:1162-1165.

11. Relman AS. Reforming the health care system. N Engl J Med. 1990;323:991-992.

12. Colwill JM. Where have all the primary care applicants gone? N Engl J Med. 1992;326:387-391.

13. Petersdorf RG. Primary care applicants—they get no respect. N Engl J Med. 1992;326:408-409.

14. Lister J. (Letters to the Editor about Canadian System). The American health care system. N Engl J Med. 1992,327:436.

15. Fuchs VR, Hahn JS. How does Canada do it? N Engl J Med. 1990;323:884-890.

16. Relman AS. Controlling costs by "managed competition"-would it work? N Engl J Med. 1993,328:133-135.

17. Kronick R., Goodman DC, Wennberg, The marketplace in health care reform. N Engl J Med. 1993,328:148-152.

THE WALL STREET JOURNAL:

18. Rector, R. Americas Poverty Myth, Sept. 3, 1992.

Cherish Your Choice

19. Lindorff Dave, MARKETPLACE MEDICINE: THE RISE OF THE FOR-PROFIT HOSPITAL CHAINS. 316 PP. ISBN 0553-07552-7 New York, N.Y., Bantam Books, 1992.

THE JOURNAL OF THE
AMERICAN MEDICAL ASSOCIATION:

20. Chassin MR, Quality of care. JAMA. 1991.266:3472-3473.

21. Fuchs VR, The best health care system in the world? JAMA. 1992;268:915-916.

22. Nash DB, Is the quality cart before the horse? JAMA. 1992;268:917-918.

23. Brown RE, A national health program for the United States. JAMA. 1992;267:552-558. (42 references).

24. Bronow R. A National Health Program. JAMA. 1990; 263:2488-2489.
25. McDougall JD. (Calgary, Canada) et al. A national health program. (In letters to the editor, re Bronow.). JAMA. 1990; 263:2445-2447.
26. Albert A, Bennett C, Rand corp.,& Bojar M. Health Care in the Czech Republic (Letter from Prague). JAMA. 1992;267:2461-2466
27. Emanuel JE, Emanuel LL. Four models of the physician-patient relationship. JAMA. 1992;267:2221-2226.
28. JAMA. Guilt by association (book re collective association and antitrust) JAMA. 1992;267:2020.

THE NEW ENGLAND JOURNAL OF MEDICINE:

29. Welch GH, Fisher SH. Let's make a deal—Negotiating a settlement between physicians and society. N Engl J Med. 1992;.327:1312-1315.
30. Simmons HE, Rhodes MM, Comprehensive health care reform and managed competition. N Engl J Med. 1992;327:1525-15272.

THE WALL STREET JOURNAL:

31. Health-Care Primer, in Review and Outlook, Jan. 5,1992.
32. Enthoven AC, How employers boost health costs. Jan 24,1992.
33. Reinhardt UE, You pay when business bankrolls health care. Dec. 2, 1992.
34. Beck DP, Transplants: hope and despair. In letters to the editor, March 24, 1992.
35. Grayson CJ Jr. Experience talks: shun price controls. March 29, 1993

THE WASHINGTON POST NATIONAL WEEKLY EDITION:

36. Ornstein N, Health care reform: the politics. Apr. 5-11,1993.
37. Samuelson RJ, And the practicalities. Apr. 5-11,1993.

THE SANTA PAULA CHRONICLE, Santa Paula CA. Apr. 15, 1992.

38. How much fat is there in health care? pp.3B.
39. Condition critical: the American health care forum 1B.

MISCELLANEOUS:

40. Osgood JW, Smith MD, Putnam JM. Health care reform (Its impact on the stocks of various companies) Alex Brown and Sons, Inc., Baltimore, MD. Oct. 13, 1992. All ten pages.

Medical Insurance

THE JOURNAL OF THE
AMERICAN MEDICAL ASSOCIATION:

41. Todd JS, Problems with incentives. JAMA. 1990;264:1294-95
42. Shulkin DJ et al. Impact of the Medicare fee schedule on an academic department of medicine. JAMA. 1991;266:3000-3003.
43. Harrington C. A national long-term care program for the United States. JAMA. 1991;266:3023-3029.
44. Jesilow P,Geis G,Pontell H. Fraud by physicians against Medicaid. JAMA. 1991;266:3318-3322.
45. Casalino PL. Balancing incentives: how should physicians be reimbursed? JAMA. 1992;267:403-405.
46. Berenson R,Holahan J. Sources of the growth in Medicare physician expenditures. JAMA.1992;267:687-691.
47. Tancredi,LR. Book review of Peter Huber's Galileo's Revenge: Junk Science in the Court Room. JAMA.1992;267:1136-1137.
48. Kravitz RL et al. Differences in the mix of patients among medical specialties and systems of care—results from the medical outcomes study. JAMA.1992;267:1617-1623.
49. Greenfield S et al. Variations in resource utilization among medical specialties and systems of care-Results from the medical outcomes study. JAMA.1992;267:1624-1630.
50. Rosenblatt RA. Specialists or Generalists-On whom should we base the American health care system? JAMA.1992;267:1665-1666.

51. Flanagin A, Sullivan-Fowler M (editors). JAMA 100 years ago: Fees and fees. JAMA.1992;267:front page.
52. Lundberg GD. National health care reform. JAMA. 1992;267:2521-2524.
53. Cotton P. Basic benefits have many variations, tend to become political issues. JAMA.1992;268:2139-2141.
54. Marwick C. Using high quality providers to cope with today's rising health care costs. JAMA.1992;268:2142-2145.
55. Bindman AB,Grumbach K. America's safety net-The wrong place at the wrong time? JAMA.1992;268:2426-2427.
56. Evidence Based Medicine working Group-Gordan guyatt(chair). Evidenced based medicine. JAMA.1992;268:-2425. (excellent bibliography).
57. Reiser JS. The era of the patient. JAMA.1993;2691012-17.
58. AMA council on scientific affairs. Physicians and family caregivers-A model for partnership. JAMA.1993;269:1282-
59. Kibelstis JA. The right road for medicine. JAMA.1992,267:2034.(A most important letter page in letters to the editor)
60. Maloney JV. A critical analysis of the resource-based relative value scale. JAMA. 1991;266:3453-3458.
61. Maloney JV. The resource-based relative value scale. JAMA.1992;268:3363-3365.
62. Blendon RJ,Edwards JN,Hyams AL. Making the critical choices. JAMA.1992;267:2509-2520.
63. Johnson WG et.al. The economic consequences of medical injuries—Implications for a no-fault insurance plan. JAMA.1992,267:2487-2492.

THE NEW ENGLAND MEDICAL JOURNAL

64. Relman AS. The trouble with rationing. N Engl J Med. 1990;323:911-913.
65. Relman AS. Reforming the health care system. N Engl J Med.1990;323:991-992.
66. Sullivan LW. Healthy people 2000. N Engl J Med. 1990;323:1065-1067.
67. Inglehart JK. The American health care system. N Engl J Med.1992;326:962-967.

68. Inglehart JK. The American health care system: Medicare. N Engl J Med.1992;327:1467-1472.
69. Lister JL. The American health care system-introduction. N Engl J Med.1992;327:438.
70. Relman AS. Controlling costs by "managed competition"-would it work?. N Engl J MED.1993;328:133-135.
71. Kronick R,Goodman DC,Wennberg J. The marketplace in health care reform:The demographic limitations of managed competition. N Engl J Med.1992;328:148-152.

SURGERY

72. Maloney JV jr. A report on the role of economic motivation in the performance of medical school faculty. Surgery. 1970;68:1-19.

THE WALL STREET JOURNAL:

73. Rector R. America's poverty myth. Sept. 3, 1992. Editorial page.
74. O'Neil G. Working the kinks out of worker's comp. Managers Journal. Mon. April 19, 1993.

Risk

75. Kaplan S.et.al. Expert systems for diagnosis and decision under substantial uncertainty—A Classical (Bayesian) approach. Presented to Forum On Artifical Intelligence and Management. Sponsored by the U.S. Dept. of Defense, 1990, 27 pages.

THE JOURNAL OF THE
AMERICAL MEDICAL ASSOCIATION:

76. Light DW. The practice and ethics of risk-rated health insurance. JAMA.1992;267:2503-2508. (54 references).
77. Jencks SF,Wilensky GR. The health care quality improvement iniative-A new approach to quality assurance in Medicare. JAMA.1992;268:900-903. (A most important article).

78. Ramsey PG,et.al. Use of peer ratings to evaluate physician performance. JAMA.1993;269:1655-1660.

THE NEW ENGLAND JOURNAL OF MEDICINE:

79. Blumenthal D,Epstein AM. Physician payment reform—unfinished business. N Engl J Med.1992;326:1330-1334.
80. Blendon JR et al. Physician's perspectives on caring for patients in the United States, Canada, and West Germany. N Engl J Med.1993;328:1011-10166.

Malpractice, Doctors and Lawyers

THE JOURNAL OF THE AMERICAL MEDICAL ASSOCIATION:

81. Garnick DW,Hendricks AM,Brennan TA. Can malpractice guidelines reduce the number and costs of malpractice claims? JAMA.1991;266:2856-2860.(42 references).
82. Thorpe KE, etal. Reducing the number of uninsured by subsidizing employment-based health insurance. JAMA.1992;267:945-948.
83. Weiler PC,Newhouse JP,Hiatt HH. Proposal for medical liability reform. JAMA.1992;267:2355-2357.
84. Medical News and Perspectives. Image of perfection once the goal—now some women just seek damages. JAMA.1992;267:2439-2442.
85. Medical news and perspectives. The uninsured and the debate over the repeal of the Massachusetts universal health care law. JAMA.1992;267:1113-1117.
86. Goldschmidt PG, Can practice guidelines reduce malpractice claims? JAMA.1992;267:2602-2603.

87. Parmet WE. The impact of health insurance reform on the law governing the physician-patient relationship. JAMA.1992;268:3468-3472.

88. Localio AR. Relationship between malpractice claims and cesarean delivery.JAMA.1993;269:366-373. (76 references).

MISCELLANEOUS:

89. Localio AR, et al. Relation between malpractice claims and adverse events due to negligence—results of the Harvard medical practice study III. N Engl J Med.1991;325:245-251.

90. George AJ. Using genes to define motherhood—the California solution. N Engl J Med.1992;326:417-420.

91. Moseley W. The medical injury compensation reform act of 1975 (MICRA). The Ventura County Medical Society Times, June 1992, pp7

92. Koshland DE jr. Science and Society. Science. 1993;260:143.

93. Koshland DE jr. Get-rich-quick science. Science. 1993;259:1103.

94. Hayward S, Peterson E. The Medicare monster—a cautionary tale. Reason. January 1993, pp19-25.

95. Los Angeles Daily Journal. California verdicts and settlements, Sept.18,1992 p9, also on page 15 "Look Before You Litigate": Information on 1870 active and retired judges in the Daily Journal's new judicial profile service, a six-volume set.

THE WALL STREET JOURNAL:

96. Crovitz LG. The more lawsuits the better, and other American notions. Rule of law section Apr. 17, 1991.

97. Bailey GW. Litigation abuse is destroying my company. (Sixteen of our co-defendants have been bankrupted. Under the "joint and several responsibility" rule, the last asbestos supplier standing will be liable for all the judgments against all asbestos defendants). Rule of law section. July 15,1992.

98. Review and Outlook. The American disease. Jan. 20, 1992 p.A12.

99. Green,Sharon. A woman's right to choose breast implants. Jan 20, 1992. P.A12.

100. Bernstein DE. Junk science in the court room. March 24,1993. pp. A15.
101. Edmond, John. Phoenix Arizona. In letters to the editor. Tort law reaches fairy-tale levels.

Things You Should Know About the Solution

102. Articles about being nurses by Jeanne Chaisson, and by Suzanne Gordon. Technology Review, October 1992 pp.44-51.
103. Wasson J et al. Telephone care as a substitute for routine clinic follow-up. JAMA.1992;267:1788-1793.
104. Rubin RH et al. Watching the doctor watchers: How well do peer review organization methods detect hospital care quality problems? JAMA.1992;267:2349-2354.
105. Loritz J. What residents can do to help the uninsured and underinsured. In Resident Forum, JAMA.1992;267,no.18, May 13.

THE WALL STREET JOURNAL:

106. Friedman M. Gammon's Law points to health-care solution. On editorial page, Nov.12,1991.
107. Wessel D,bogdanich W. Closed market: It might pay to comparison shop for health care, but few patients or insurers do.
Front page, January 22,1992.
108. Lescaze L. Book review of Vaclav Havel's book "Summer Meditations" entitled Czech writer's Presidential wit and wisdom. July 31, 1992, PP.A9. (delightful).

Things You Should Know About Physicians

109. Cassell, EJ. The nature of suffering and the goals of medicine, 254pp. Oxford univ. Press, 1991.

110.Hafferty FW. Into the valley: Death and the socialization of medical students. 234pp. Yale Univ. Press, New Haven, Conn. 1991.

111.Kogan BS (editor). A time to be born and a time to die: The ethics of choice. 267pp. Aldine de Gruyter, Hawthorne, N.Y. 1991.

112.Gardell-Cutter MA,Shep EE (editors). Competency: A study of informal competency determinations in primary care. Philosophy of Medicine Vol.39, 289pp. Kluwer Academic, 1991.

113.Gleick J. Chaos. Penguin Books, N.Y.,N.Y.1987.

114.Ferris T. Comming of age in the milky way.pp381-388.

THE JOURNAL OF THE
AMERICAN MEDICAL ASSOCIATION:

115.Bergman SS. The debt and the cash flow of residents: In letters JAMA. 1990;264:1247-1249.

116.Reidenberg MM. A plea for prices in physician prescribing. JAMA.1991;266:3285.

117.Bloom BS, Wierz DJ,Pauly MV. Cost and price of comparable branded and generic pharmaceuticals. JAMA.1986;256:2523-2530.

118.Frazer LM, et al. Can physician education lower the price of prescription drugs? Ann Intern Med. 1991;115:116-121.

119.Reiser S. Consumer competence and the reform of American health care. JAMA.1992;267:1511-1515.

120.Eddy DM. Cost effective analysis. JAMA. 1992; 267: 1669-75.

121.Sackett DL. A primer on the precision and accuracy of the clinical examination. JAMA.1992;267:2638-2643.

122.Branstetter T. Blue Moon. JAMA.1992;267:2453.

123.Medical News. Vaccine information pamphlets here, but some physicians react strongly. JAMA.1992;267:2005-2006.

124.The 1991 JAMA Peer Reviewers list. JAMA. 1992;267:2089-95

THE NEW ENGLAND JOURNAL OF MEDICINE:

125.Taylor CR. The reading habits of year II medical students. N Engl J Med. 1992;326:1436-1440.
126.Oryshkevich BA. Are we mortgaging the medical profession? N Eng J Med. 1992;326:274-276.
127.Bromberg MD. Letter to the editor in reply to "The health care industry: where is it taking us?. N Eng J Med. 1992;326:205. (A most provocative short letter).
128.Blumenthal D. Administrative issues in health care reform. N Eng J Med. 1993;329:428-429.
129.Emanuel EJ & Brett AS. Managed competition and the patient-physician relationship. N ENG J Med. 1993; 329:879-882.

THE WALL STREET JOURNAL: (EDITORIAL PAGE)

130.Healey WV. Put more clinicians into government, April 20, 1993, pp A18.
131.Kirkpatrick M. The misery of our cities, book review of "The Dream and the Nightmare", by Myron Magnet apr. 22, 1993, pp. A12.

Miscellaneous

THE WALL STREET JOURNAL: (Editorial page)

132.Gigot, PA. Dems step up to well-stocked bar, Sept. 4, 1992
133.Leatherman, S. Americans don't want a health-care revolution, June 17, 1993.
134.Muller, J. The cost of social spending—joblessness, July 13, 1993.
135.Blast, J. Dead on arrival—Clinton health plan, June 10, 1993.
136.Pulliam, Mark, The need for tort reform, a report for the Golden Eagle Club of San Diego in Notable and Quotable, June 1, 1993.
137.Bonilla, C. The price of a health care mandate, Aug. 20, 1993.

138. Gammon, Max. Among Britian's Ills a Health Care Crisis. Wall Street Journal, Sept. 8, 1993, page A14.
139. Editorial. Health Care Contraption. Wall Street Journal, Sept.14, 1993, Page A20.
140. O'Rourke, P.J. Health Reform: License to Kill. Wall Street Journal, Sept. 23, 1993, Page A14.

LATE ADDITIONS

141. Fuchs VR. No pain, no gain. JAMA.1993;269:631-633.
142. Abilson, PH, Pathological growth of regulations. Science; Vol 260, 25 June 1993.

Index

A

Access, 122, 124
Accountability
    perversions of, 57, 120
Acute care, 127
Administration costs, 121
Adversarial skills, 3
Adversarial approach, 91
Adversary proceedings, 71
AIDS, 211
Alternative options, 4, 171
AMA, 30, 40, 43
Ambulance service, 127, 200
Ancillary medical personal
    list of, 243
Assurance, 45
Attitudes
    medical student, 226
Attorneys
    procedure based fee schedule,
    113

B

Basic plan, 123
Basic premise, 186
Bayes theorem, 69
Biopsy

defined, 38
Branch clinics, 219

C

Cancer, 5
    colon, 6
Capital requirements, 14
Care, 28
Catastrophic care, 145
Catastrophic coverage, 31
Central planning, 4
Certainty, 77
Change
    effects of, 140
Chaos theory, 107
Charity practices, 33
Chicanery, 5
Choices, 27
Choosing a physician, 187
Class envy, 212
Clinical professors, 11
Cocain babies, 211
Cocercive advantage, 105
coercion, 2
Community medicine, 210
Competition, 2
Competitive advantage

for patients, 135
Competitive alternatives, 8, 75
Competitive options, 123
Complexity
    biologic systems, 107
Computer interfacing, 146
Conditional probability
    definition, 69
Contingent fees, 17, 85
Continuity of care, 133, 160
    definition, 7
Cost shifting, 15, 43
Costs
    drug promotion, 141
    physician employee, 42
County charity teaching
hospitals
    a tradition, 176
Courtroom power, 84
Courtroom venture capitalists,
    18
Courts
    as problem solvers, 102
Creative paying, 49
Culture of poverty, 207, 212,
231

D

Day surgery, 38
Deception, 34, 40
Deception & dependence, 204
Deep pocket, 14, 70, 116
Delegation
    point of, 128
Dependence, 34
Dependence and deception, 15
Diagnostic decision point, 4, 158
Disputes
    non-punitive solutions, 91
Doctor-patient relationships, 21

Double triage, 154
Drug company stocks
    pension funds, 40
Drugs, 242
    cost of, 141, 244
    prescription, 245

E

Emergency clinic, 101
Emergency units, 139
Employer's insurance costs, 41
Enfavor
    definition, 84
Entitlement, 5
Entitlements, 238
Esculating costs, 47
Ethnic intolerance, 212
Expectations, 204
Experimental verification, 97

F

Faculty
    volunteer clinical, 174
Family physician, 8
    definition, 164
Family physicians, 138
Feasibility studies, 200
Fee codes, 48
Fee schedule, 37, 39
Fees, 142
Float, 40, 116
    definition, 35
Fractals, 107
Free care, 2, 10, 126
Free market, 4

G

Gastroenterologist, 6
Gastroscope
    definition, 6
Gate keeper
    a definition, 128
Gatekeeper, 154, 167
General physician
    definition, 8
Generalists, 164
Global budgeting, 23
Goal,the, 149
Governing bodies, 1
Grim Reaper, 4
Group Health Cooperative of
Puget Sound, 174, 224
Group psychotherapy, 211
Guiding principles, 130

H

Half vast concepts, 13
Health care and drug stocks,
242
Health care reform, 23
    plans for, 119
Health insurance, 120
Health Maintenance
Organization (HMO), 25
Heavy users, 124
Hospice care, 213
Hospital
    costs, 53
Hospitals, 235
Human injury
    evaluation, 196
Hypochondriac
    definition, 7

I

Industrial insurance, 58
Inclusive fees, 39
Income tax payment, 10
Incremental control, 121
Initial assessment, 169
Initial contact decision, 157
Injury compensation, 196
Insurance, 233
    billing bureaucracy, 56
    creative billing, 49, 57
    fire, 45
    over utilization, 55
    teaching of insurance billing
    personnel, 57
Insurance company, 31
Intensive care, 213
Internal Revenue Service, 33
Interns, 230
internship, 9
Intestinal polyps
    a definition, 6
Itemized billing, 37

J

Junk science, 4, 73, 108, 204

K

Knowledge base
    medical, 5

L

Legal cost crisis, 83
Legal opportunism, 162
Legal reform, 115

M

Malpractice, 16, 33, 73, 82, 87
  costs, 38
  Los Angeles County
    Hospital, 101
Malpractice Insurance Costs, 18
Malpractice lawsuits
  charity hospitals, 98
Malpractice myths, 18, 111
Malpractice threat costs, 18
Managed competition, 120, 123
Mass purchasing, 141
Means test
  a definition, 161
Medicaid, 13, 36, 123, 183
Medical care, 1
  costs, 122
  definition, 3
  experience, 2
Medical care bargain, 179
Medical care delivery system, 14
Medical cost crisis, 47
  solution, 11
Medical costs, 1
Medical insurance
  catastrophic, 46
  co-payment, 46
  essential, 44
  is not insurance, 45
  overuse, 47
  patients, 41
  See also Health insurance, 30
Medical insurance billing codes,
  37
Medical procedures, 37
Medical profession, 33
Medical quality control
  practices, 71
Medical school autonomy, 218
Medical students, 228

  training, 175
Medicare, 13, 36, 48, 54, 183
Medigap insurance, 48, 54
Micro-managing, 13
Millionaires, 10
Mixing humanitarianism,
  socialism and capitalism, 15
Monetary exchange
  not the only solution, 98
Monetary liability for medical
  negligence, 18
Monetary punishments, 74
Money, 15
Money as redress, 17
Moral fitness, 240
Must be required to, 122

N

National Health Board, 23
Negligence, 17, 72, 87
  definition, 96
Neonatal care, 214
New patients
  definition, 157
Non-adversarial inquiry, 108
Non-monetary remuneration,
  174
Nonmonetary values, 9
Nurses, 134
Nursing
  training programs, 175

O

Options, 8
  adding, 126
  empower patients, 29
OSHA, 63

Outcomes research, 17, 91,
 129, 216
 definition, 74
 explaination, 92
Over-utilization, 29
Overpopulation, 115
Overuse, 139
Overview, 9

P

Padding the bill, 39
Patient care, 237
Patient education, 160
Patient forcefulness, 104
Patient freedom, 11
Patient overuse, 162
Patient power, 12
Patient telephone calls, 160
Patients and physicians
 together, 233
Peer review, 91
Peer review journals, 106
Performance profiles, 71
Permanent staff, 137
Personal comfort, 134
Physician
 financial security, 241
 volunteers, 137
Physician accountability, 18, 97
Physician arrogance, 189
Physician morale, 13
Physician oversupply, 217
Physician's problems, 226
Physicians with SNHC
 location requirements, 219
 volunteers, 100
Physicians creed, 229
Placebos
 definition, 107
Point of delegation, 167

Polemic
 definition, 69
Political control
 of medical problems, 100
Poor people, 190
Prepaid health plans
 definition, 29
Prescription drugs, 40
Preserve the essentials, 19
Preventive medicine, 131, 210
Prevention, 17
Primary care
 a definition, 164
Primary care physician, 12
 definition, 7
Proctoscopic exam
 definition, 7
Profession
 meaning of, 17
Protection of SNHC physicians,
 201
Providers, 4

Q

Quality, 124

R

Reasons medical care is
 expensive, 14
Reassurance, 3
Refuge
 patient, 126
Regions too small to support a
 SNHC, 199
Regulatory agencies, 42
Relative value fee schedule
 (RVS), 36

Research, 215
Residency
    definition, 8
Residents, 9, 174
Risk, 2, 17
    definition, 68
    exposure, 89
    for doctors, 74
    office surgery, 38
    outcome set, 71
    set of prior conditions, 71
    SNHC, 75
    state variables, 71
Risk assessment, 17, 70
Risk factor profiles
    physician, 129
Risk limits, 79
Risk reduction, 69, 72
Risk zones, 72, 79
RVS code, 49

S

Safety Net Hospital-Clinic
(SNHC), 9, 62, 205
    a description, 136
    a refuge, 163
    accessibility, 183
    accountability, 143
    administrative details, 190
    ambience, 138
    and competing physicians,
        147
    and other physicians, 153
    and patient power, 151
    and small business
        employers, 146
    and social service, 150
    and supplemental care, 145
    as a teaching facility, 175
    as part of the community, 223

as patient's advocate, 151
autonomy, 138
care of the mildly ill, 215
competitive pressure, 140
EPA, 204
financing, 181
for testing physician, 205
for testing regulators, 130
functions, 127
fundamental purpose, 214
gatekeeping, 247
gifts, memorials and bequests,
    184
how medical care would differ,
    143
impediments, 131
integration, 127
isolated areas, 171
mission, 171
operational details, 185
organizational details, 182
OSHA, 204
peer review, 132
Peer Review Panel, 195
physician chief, 192
physician immunity, 201
physician incompetence, 194
professional hospital
    administrator, 192
protecting them, 149
purchases, 247
risk assessment, 140
Safety net legal service, 88
second opinion, free, 12
security for everyone, 148
shared services, 214
single item billing, 39
slogans, 94
small business, 233
social work programs, 212
State Executive Council, 197

solution, 12
State Medical Advisory
  Council, 194
suggestions for government
  action, 208
workers compensation, 203
Socialized medicine, 12, 55
Socialized systems, 2
Solution, 2, 9, 12
  contemporary medical, 3
  in brief, 11
  two parts, 126
  oversimplified,
  opportunistic, 3
  political, 2
Specialists, 5, 7, 12, 109, 138,
  164
Specialty screening clinics, 157
Staff salaries, 138
Standard Health Plan, 23
State autonomy, 207
State Medical Licensing Boards,
  104, 194
Student nurses, 137
Supplemental insurance, 14
Surtax, 10
Survival of the fittest, 4

T

Teaching hospital-clinics, 11
The Game Of Court, 83
The problems, 118
Third parties
  definition, 3
  proponents of, 226
  zero risk, 68

Third party
  care, 29
  control, 66
  interference, 3
Tort truth, 109
Triage, 150
  definition, 11, 154

U

Uncertainty, 68, 119
Uninsured and underinsured,
  the, 16, 120
Unintended consequences, 13
Unit value, 37
Unnecessary surgery, 12

V

Venture capitalists
  courtroom, 85
Voluntary clinical teaching
  staff, 11

W

Working together, 16

Y

Young physicians, 231

Z

Zero risk
  damage, 80

Order Information

MEDICAL COST CRISIS is so important you may want to order extra copies for those you know are interested in change.

If the book is not yet available in your local book store it can be ordered through PUBLISHERS DISTRIBUTION SERVICE by calling 1-800-345-0096.

A single copy is $15.95 plus shipping and handling.

For a free information packet, or to be put on the mailing list for future updates, send requests to: TONAL CO. PRESS, P.O. Box 3233-1, Ventura, CA 93006 or Fax: 805-642-5156.

(Please Print)

Company name: _____

Name: _____

Address: _____

City: _____ State: _____ Zip: _____

Dr. Lindsay is also available for consulting, speaking, radio or TV appearances.